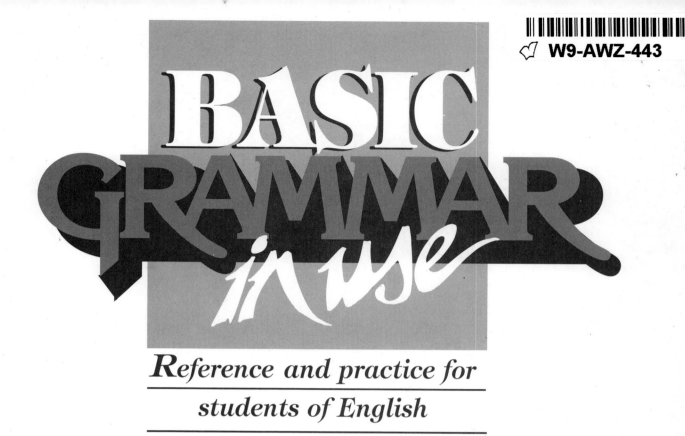

BASIC GRAMMAR in use

Reference and practice for students of English

Raymond Murphy

Basic Grammar in Use is based on the British Text *Essential Grammar in Use* by Raymond Murphy, first published in 1990.

Published by the Press Syndicate of the University of Cambridge
The Pitt Building, Trumpington Street, Cambridge CB2 1RP
40 West 20th Street, New York, NY 10011-4211, USA
10 Stamford Road, Oakleigh, Melbourne 3166, Australia

First published 1993
Third Printing 1995

Printed in the United States of America

Library of Congress Cataloging-in-Publication Data
Murphy, Raymond.
Basic grammar in use : reference and practice for students of English / Raymond Murphy.
p. cm.
"Based on the British text Essential grammar in use ... published in 1990."
Includes index.
ISBN 0-521-42606-5 (student's book : pb) - ISBN 0-521-42607-3 (answer key)
1. English language – Textbooks for foreign speakers. 2. English language – Grammar – 1950 – I. Murphy, Raymond. Essential grammar in use. II. Title.
PE1128.M774 1993 92-15429
428.2′4 – dc20 CIP

A catalog record for this book is available from the British Library

ISBN 0-521-42606-5 Student's Book
ISBN 0-521-42607-3 Answer Key

Layout and text composition: M E Aslett Corporation
Illustrators: Brian Battles, Daisy de Puthod, Chris Evans, Randy Jones, Leslie Marshall, Ed McKenry, Wally Neibart, Shaun Williams
Other illustrations by M 'N O Production Services and Moffitt Cecil

CONTENTS

Contents

Contents

Articles

Determiners and pronouns

Adjectives and adverbs

Word order

Prepositions

Contents

To the student

This is a basic grammar book for beginning to low-intermediate level students of English. There are 106 units in the book and each unit is about a different point of English grammar. There is a list of units at the beginning of the book *(Contents)*.

Do not study all the units in order from beginning to end. It is better to choose the units that you need to do. For example, if you have a problem with the present perfect ("have done" / "have been," etc.), use the *Index* (at the back of the book) to find the unit(s) you need to study (Units 14–18).

Each unit is two pages. The explanation is on the left-hand page and the exercises on the right.

Explanation

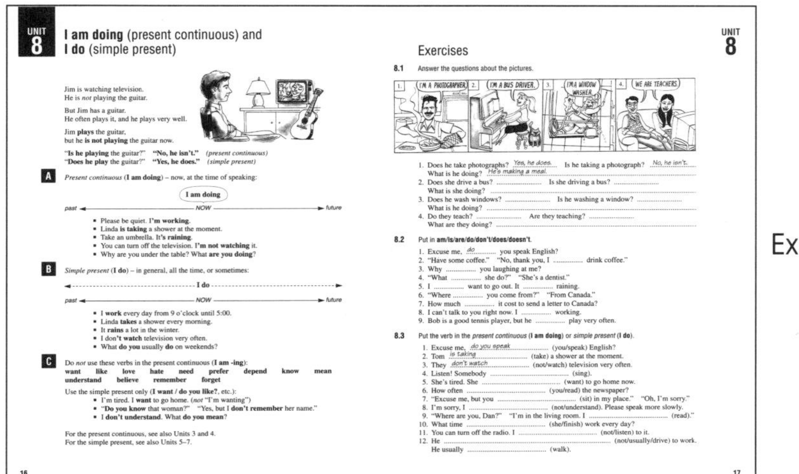

UNIT 8

I am doing (present continuous) and
I do (simple present)

Jim is watching television.
He is *not* playing the guitar.

But Jim has a guitar.
He often plays it, and he plays very well.

Jim **plays** the guitar,
but he **is not playing** the guitar now.

"**Is he playing** the guitar?" "**No, he isn't.**" *(present continuous)*
"**Does he play** the guitar?" "**Yes, he does.**" *(simple present)*

A *Present continuous* (**I am doing**) – now, at the time of speaking:

I am doing

past ← NOW → future

- Please be quiet. **I'm working**.
- Linda **is taking** a shower at the moment.
- Take an umbrella. It**'s raining**.
- You can turn off the television. **I'm not watching** it.
- Why are you under the table? What **are you doing**?

B *Simple present* (**I do**) – in general, all the time, or sometimes:

← I do →

past ← NOW → future

- I **work** every day from 9 o'clock until 5:00.
- Linda **takes** a shower every morning.
- It **rains** a lot in the winter.
- I don**'t watch** television very often.
- What **do you** usually **do** on weekends?

C Do *not* use these verbs in the present continuous (**I am -ing**):
want like love hate need prefer depend know mean understand believe remember forget

Use the simple present only (**I want / do you like?**, etc.):
- I'm tired. I **want** to go home. (*not* "I'm wanting")
- "**Do you know** that woman?" "Yes, but I **don't remember** her name."
- I **don't understand**. What **do you mean**?

For the present continuous, see also Units 3 and 4.
For the simple present, see also Units 5–7.

16

Exercises

UNIT 8

8.1 Answer the questions about the pictures.

1. I'M A PHOTOGRAPHER.
2. I'M A BUS DRIVER.
3. I'M A WINDOW WASHER.
4. WE ARE TEACHERS.

1. Does he take photographs? *Yes, he does.* Is he taking a photograph? *No, he isn't.*
   What is he doing? *He's making a meal.*
2. Does she drive a bus? .... Is she driving a bus? ....
   What is she doing? ....
3. Does he wash windows? .... Is he washing a window? ....
   What is he doing? ....
4. Do they teach? .... Are they teaching? ....
   What are they doing? ....

8.2 Put in **am/is/are/do/don't/does/doesn't**.

1. Excuse me, *do* you speak English?
2. "Have some coffee." "No, thank you, I .... drink coffee."
3. Why .... you laughing at me?
4. "What .... she do?" "She's a dentist."
5. I .... want to go out. It .... raining.
6. "Where .... you come from?" "From Canada."
7. How much .... it cost to send a letter to Canada?
8. I can't talk to you right now. I .... working.
9. Bob is a good tennis player, but he .... play very often.

8.3 Put the verb in the *present continuous* (**I am doing**) or *simple present* (**I do**).

1. Excuse me, *do you speak* (you/speak) English?
2. Tom *is taking* (take) a shower at the moment.
3. They *don't watch* (not/watch) television very often.
4. Listen! Somebody .... (sing).
5. She's tired. She .... (want) to go home now.
6. How often .... (you/read) the newspaper?
7. "Excuse me, but you .... (sit) in my place." "Oh, I'm sorry."
8. I'm sorry, I .... (not/understand). Please speak more slowly.
9. "Where are you, Dan?" "I'm in the living room. I .... (read)."
10. What time .... (she/finish) work every day?
11. You can turn off the radio. I .... (not/listen) to it.
12. He .... (not/usually/drive) to work.
    He usually .... (walk).

17

Exercises

Use the book in this way:

1. Look in the *Contents* and/or *Index* to find the unit(s) you need.
2. Study the left-hand page (explanation and information).
3. Do the exercises on the right-hand page.
4. Ask your teacher to check your answers (or refer to the Answer Key).
5. Study the left-hand page again if necessary.

Don't forget the six *Appendixes* at the back of the book (pages 214–221). These will give you information about irregular verbs, short forms, spelling, and phrasal verbs.

To the teacher

Basic Grammar in Use is a textbook for beginning to low-intermediate level students of English. It combines reference and exercises in one volume and can be used as a classroom text or for self-study.

Level

The book is intended for beginners and false beginners (students who have some familiarity with English). It could also be used by low-intermediate students who still have particular problems with some basic grammar points, or who still make grammatical mistakes and need a book for reference and practice.

The explanations are addressed to the student and, therefore, are as simple and as short as possible. The vocabulary used in the examples and exercises has also been restricted so that the book can be used at a beginning level.

How the book is organized

There are 106 units in the book, each focusing on a particular area of grammar. The material is organized in grammatical categories (refer to the *Contents*). Units are *not* ordered according to difficulty and, therefore, should be selected and used in the order appropriate for the student.

Grammar points can be located either in the *Contents* or in the comprehensive *Index* at the end of the book.

Each unit has the same two-page format. The grammar point is explained on the left-hand page, and the corresponding exercises appear on the right. There are also six *Appendixes* at the back of the book that deal with irregular verbs, contractions, spelling, and phrasal verbs. You might want to draw students' attention to these.

Using the book

It is not intended that anyone should work through the book from beginning to end. Rather, it is for you to decide what to teach and in what order to teach it, depending on the needs of your students.

The book can be used with the whole class or with individual students.When used with the class, you can present the grammar point in whatever way you prefer. The explanation on the left-hand page is used not actively but as a record of what has been taught. Students can refer to the explanation later. The exercises can be done in class or as homework.

The book can also be used by individual students who need additional practice, review work, or who have problems not shared by other students in the class.

A separate Answer Key is available for teachers and self-study users.

Acknowledgments

Illustrators

Brian Battles: 5, 9 *(bottom)*, 15 *(bottom)*, 23 *(bottom)*, 31, 37, 47, 51, 53, 61 *(bottom)*, 74 *(bottom)*, 75, 77, 81, 83, 85, 87, 91, 147, 153, 157 *(bottom)*, 163, 167, 173 *(top)*, 177, 178, 179 *(middle, bottom)*, 183, 199 *(bottom)*

Daisy de Puthod: 118 *(bottom)*, 121, 123 *(top)*, 179 *(top)*

Chris Evans: 65, 118 *(top)*, 162 *(bottom)*, 192

Randy Jones: 8, 9 *(top)*, 10, 11, 12, 13, 14, 15 *(top)*, 17, 22, 23 *(top)*, 24, 25, 38, 42 *(top)*, 43, 44, 50, 52, 54, 64, 88, 90, 92, 94, 96, 102, 103, 104, 106, 107, 108 *(top)*, 109, 114, 115, 116, 117, 123 *(middle)*, 136, 138, 140, 142, 156, 157 *(middle)*, 158, 159, 161, 165, 172, 173 *(bottom)*, 184, 186, 187, 188, 194, 195, 198, 199 *(top)*, 206 *(bottom)*, 208, 210, 212, 220, 221

Leslie Marshall: 108 *(bottom)*

Ed McKenry: 42 *(bottom)*, 164

Wally Neibart: 2, 4, 6, 7, 16, 18, 26, 27, 28, 29, 30, 32, 33, 40, 41, 46, 48, 49, 56, 57, 58, 59, 60, 61 *(top)*, 62, 63, 65, 66, 74 *(top, middle)*, 76, 82, 84, 98, 99, 100, 110, 111, 112, 120, 124, 128, 129, 130, 134, 135, 144, 146, 150, 151, 152, 154, 160, 162 *(top)*, 168, 169, 170, 171, 174, 190, 191, 193, 196, 197, 200, 201, 202

Shaun Williams: 206 *(top)*

UNIT 1

am/is/are

She'**s** a doctor.	It'**s** hot.	They'**re** rich.
She **isn't** a nurse.	It **isn't** cold.	They **aren't** poor.

Positive		
I	**am**	(I'**m**)
he	**is**	(he'**s**)
she	**is**	(she'**s**)
it	**is**	(it'**s**)
we	**are**	(we'**re**)
you	**are**	(you'**re**)
they	**are**	(they'**re**)

Negative					
I	**am**	**not**	(I'**m not**)		
he	**is**	**not**	(he'**s not**	*or*	he **isn't**)
she	**is**	**not**	(she'**s not**	*or*	she **isn't**)
it	**is**	**not**	(it'**s not**	*or*	it **isn't**)
we	**are**	**not**	(we'**re not**	*or*	we **aren't**)
you	**are**	**not**	(you'**re not**	*or*	you **aren't**)
they	**are**	**not**	(they'**re not**	*or*	they **aren't**)

- Can you close the window, please? I'**m** cold.
- I'**m** 32 years old. My sister **is** 29.
- My brother **is** a police officer. He'**s** very tall.
- John **is** afraid of dogs.
- It'**s** 10 o'clock. You'**re** late again.
- Ann and I **are** very good friends.
- My shoes **are** dirty.

- I'**m** tired but I'**m not** hungry.
- Tom **isn't** interested in politics.
- Jane **isn't** home right now. She'**s** at work.

- Those people **aren't** Canadian. They'**re** Australian.

You can say:

- It **isn't** cold. *or* It'**s not** cold.
- They **aren't** home. *or* They'**re not** home.

that'**s** = that **is** there'**s** = there **is** here'**s** = here **is**

- Thank you. **That's** very kind of you.
- Look! **There's** Bob.

For **am/is/are** (questions), see Unit 2.

Exercises

1.1 Write the contraction (she'**s** / we **aren't**, etc.).

1. he is *he's*
2. they are they're
3. she is not ....
4. it is ....
5. I am not ....
6. you are not ....

Write the full form (she **is** / we **are not**, etc.)

7. we aren't *we are not*
8. I'm ....
9. you're ....
10. they aren't ....
11. it isn't ....
12. she's ....

1.2 Put in **am**, **is**, or **are**.

1. The weather *is* very nice today.
2. I .... not tired.
3. This suitcase .... very heavy.
4. These suitcases .... very heavy.
5. The dog .... asleep.
6. Look! There .... Carol.
7. I .... hot. Can you open the window, please?
8. This bridge .... one hundred years old.
9. My brother and I .... good tennis players.
10. Ann .... home but her children .... at school.
11. I .... a student. My sister .... an architect.

1.3 Write full sentences. Use **am/is/are** each time.

1. (my shoes very dirty) *My shoes are very dirty.*
2. (my bed very comfortable) My ....
3. (your pencils in your bag) ....
4. (I not very happy today) ....
5. (this restaurant very expensive) ....
6. (the stores not open today) ....
7. (Mr. Kelly's daughter six years old) ....
8. (the houses on this street very old) ....
9. (the exam not difficult) ....
10. (those flowers very beautiful) ....

1.4 Write positive or negative sentences. Use **am** / **am not** / **is** / **isn't** / **are** / **aren't**.

1. (Paris / the capital of France) *Paris is the capital of France.*
2. (I / interested in sports) *I'm not interested in sports.*
3. (I / hungry) I ....
4. (it / warm today) It ....
5. (Rome / in Spain) Rome ....
6. (I / afraid of dogs) I ....
7. (my hands / cold) My ....
8. (Canada / a very big country) ....
9. (Brazil / in Africa) ....
10. (diamonds / cheap) ....
11. (boxing / a dangerous sport) ....
12. (cats / big animals) ....

UNIT 2

am/is/are (questions)

Positive		*Question*	
I	**am**	**am**	I?
he / she / it	**is**	**is**	he? / she? / it?
we / you / they	**are**	**are**	we? / you? / they?

- "**Is your mother** home?" "No, **she's** out."
- "**Is it** cold in your room?" "Yes, a little."
- **Those shoes are** nice. **Are they** new?
- **Are books** expensive in your country?

- "How old **is** Joe?" "**He's** 24."
- "What color **is your car**?" "**It's** blue."
- "Where **are you** from?" "Canada."
- "How much **are these postcards**?" "They're 40 cents each."

what**'s** = what **is** who's = who **is** how**'s** = how **is** where**'s** = where **is**:

- **What's** the temperature?
- **Where's** Pat?
- **Who's** that man?
- **How's** your father?

Short answers	
Yes, I **am**.	No, I**'m not**.
Yes, he / she / it **is**.	No, he**'s** / she**'s** / it**'s** **not**. *or* No, he / she / it **isn't**.
Yes, we / you / they **are**.	No, we**'re** / you**'re** / they**'re** **not**. *or* No, we / you / they **aren't**.

- "**Are you** tired?" **"Yes, I am."**
- "**Are you** hungry?" "**No, I'm not**, but **I'm** thirsty."
- "**Is he** Japanese?" **"Yes, he is."**
- "**Is Ann** at work today?" **"No, she isn't."**
- "**Is this seat** free?" **"Yes, it is."**
- "**Are these** your shoes?" **"Yes, they are."**
- "**Am I** late?" **"No, you aren't."**

For **am/is/are**, see Unit 1.

UNIT **2**

Exercises

2.1 Write questions from these words. Use **am/is/are**.

1. (your mother home?) *Is your mother home* ?
2. (your parents home? .... home ?
3. (this hotel expensive?) .... ?
4. (you interested in art?) .... ?
5. (the stores open today?) .... ?
6. (the zoo open today?) .... ?

2.2 Write questions with **What/Who/How/Where/Why . . . ?** Use **am/is/are**.

1. (what color your car?) *What color is your car* ?
2. (where my key?) Where .... ?
3. (where my socks?) .... ?
4. (how old your father?) How .... ?
5. (what color his eyes?) .... ?
6. (why John angry with me?) .... ?
7. (how much these shoes?) .... ?
8. (who your favorite actor?) .... ?
9. (why you always late?) .... ?

2.3 Ask the questions. (Read the answers to the questions first.)

	You		Paul
1.	(your name?)	*What's your name* ?	Paul.
2.	(married or single?)	*Are you married or single* ?	I'm married.
3.	(Canadian?)	.... ?	No, I'm not.
4.	(where / from?)	.... ?	From the U.S.
5.	(how old?)	.... ?	I'm 25.
6.	(a student?)	.... ?	No, I'm a teacher.
7.	(your wife a teacher?)	.... ?	No, she's a lawyer.
8.	(where / from?)	.... ?	She's from Brazil.
9.	(her name?)	.... ?	Anna.
10.	(how old?)	.... ?	She's 25 too.

2.4 Write positive or negative short answers (**Yes, I am** / **No, he isn't**, etc.).

1. Are you married? *No, I'm not.*
2. Are you tall? *Yes, I am.*
3. Is it cold today? ....
4. Are you a teacher? ....
5. Are you tired? ....
6. Is it dark now? ....
7. Are your hands cold? ....
8. Are you hungry? ....
9. Is your father tall? ....
10. Is it sunny? ....

UNIT 3 I am doing (present continuous)

She**'s eating**.
She **isn't reading**.

It**'s raining**.
The sun **isn't shining**

They**'re running**.
They **aren't walking**.

A

The present continuous tense is:
am/is/are -ing (do**ing**/eat**ing**/rain**ing**/runn**ing**/writ**ing**, etc.).

I	**am** (not) **-ing**	I**'m** work**ing**.
he / she / it	**is** (not) **-ing**	Tom **is** writ**ing** a letter. She **isn't** eat**ing**. The telephone **is** ring**ing**.
we / you / they	**are** (not) **-ing**	We**'re** hav**ing** dinner. You**'re not** listen**ing** to me. The children **are** do**ing** their homework.

For the contractions **'m/'s/'re/isn't/aren't**, see Unit 1.

B

am/is/are -ing = something is happening *now*:

I**'m** work**ing**.
She**'s** wear**ing** a hat.
They**'re** play**ing** soccer.
I**'m not** watch**ing** television.

past ← NOW → *future*

- Please be quiet. I**'m** work**ing**. (= I'm working now)
- Look! Sue **is** wear**ing** her new hat. (= she's wearing it now)
- Don't go out now. It**'s** rain**ing**.
- "Where are the children?" "They**'re** play**ing** in the park."
- *(on the telephone)* We**'re** hav**ing** dinner now. Can you call back later?
- You can turn the television off. I**'m not** watch**ing** it.

Spelling:

com**e** → com**ing**	ru**n** → ru**nn**ing	l**ie** → l**y**ing
smok**e** → smok**ing**	si**t** → si**tt**ing	d**ie** → d**y**ing
writ**e** → writ**ing**	swi**m** → swi**mm**ing	

See also Appendix 4 (4.3 and 4.4).
For the present continuous, see also Units 4 and 8.

Exercises

3.1 Complete the sentences. Use **am/is/are** + one of these verbs:

building **coming** **cooking** ~~**playing**~~ **standing** **studying** **swimming**

1. Listen! Pat *is playing* the piano.
2. They .... a new hotel downtown.
3. Look! Somebody .... in the river.
4. "You .... on my foot." "Oh. I'm sorry."
5. Hurry up! The bus ....
6. "Where are you, Sam?" "In the kitchen. I .... dinner."
7. *(on the telephone)* "Hello. Can I speak to Ann, please?" "She .... for an exam right now. Can she call you back later?"

3.2 What's happening right now? Write *true* sentences.

1. (I / wash / my hair) *I'm not washing my hair.*
2. (it / snow) *It is snowing.*
3. (I / sit / on a chair) ....
4. (I / eat) ....
5. (it / rain) ....
6. (I / do / this exercise) ....
7. (I / listen / to the radio) ....
8. (the sun / shine) ....
9. (I / wear / shoes) ....
10. (I / take / an exam) ....
11. (I / read / a newspaper) ....

3.3 What is the difference between picture A and picture B? Write two sentences each time. Use **is/are (not) -ing**.

1. *In A the man is listening to the radio. In B he is playing the guitar.*
2. In A the woman .... In B she ....
3. In A .... In B ....
4. ....
5. ....
6. ....

UNIT 4

Are you -ing? (present continuous questions)

Positive		
I	**am**	**-ing**
he / she / it	**is**	**-ing**
we / you / they	**are**	**-ing**

Question		
am	I	**-ing . . . ?**
is	he / she / it	**-ing . . . ?**
are	we / you / they	**-ing . . . ?**

- "**Are you** feel**ing** all right?" "Yes, I'm feeling fine."
- "**Is it** rain**ing**?" "Yes, take an umbrella."
- Why **are you** wear**ing** a coat? It's not cold today.
- "What**'s Tim** do**ing**?" "He's making dinner."
- "What **are the children** do**ing**?" "They're playing outdoors."
- Look! There's Sue. Where**'s she** go**ing**?

The word order in these questions is:

	is/are	+ *subject*	+ **-ing**
	Is	she	working today?
	Is	Ms. Smith	working today?
Where	are	they	going?
Where	are	those people	going? (*not* "Where are going those people?")

Short answers	
Yes, I **am**.	No, I**'m not**.
Yes, he / she / it **is**.	No, he**'s** / she**'s** / it**'s** **not**. *or* No, he / she / it **isn't**.
Yes, we / you / they **are**.	No, we**'re** / you**'re** / they**'re** **not**. *or* No, we / you / they **aren't**.

- "**Are you** listen**ing** to the radio?" **"Yes, I am."**
- "**Is Rosa** work**ing** today?" **"Yes, she is."**
- "**Is it** rain**ing**?" **"No, it isn't."** *or* **"No, it's not."**
- "**Are your friends** stay**ing** at a hotel?" **"No, they aren't."** *or* **"No, they're not."**

For the present continuous, see Unit 3.

Exercises

4.1 Look at the pictures and ask a question. Choose one of these verbs.

crying **eating** **going** **laughing** **looking at** ~~**reading**~~

1. What *is she reading* ?
2. Where ?
3. Why ?
4. What ?
5. What ?
6. Why ?

4.2 Write the question **"What . . . doing?"** with different subjects.

1. (he) *What is he doing* ?
2. (they) What .... doing?
3. (I) ?
4. (your wife) ?

Now write the question **"Where . . . going?"** with these subjects.

5. (we) *Where are we going* ?
6. (those children) ?
7. (the girl with long hair) ?
8. (the boy on the bicycle) ?

4.3 Ask the questions. (Read the answers to the questions first.)

1. (you / watch / TV?) *Are you watching TV* ? — No, you can turn it off.
2. (the children / play?) ? — No, they're asleep.
3. (what / you / do?) ? — I'm making my dinner.
4. (what / Jim / do?) ? — He's taking a nap.
5. (it / rain?) ? — No, not right now.
6. (that clock / work?) ? — No, it's broken.
7. (you / write / a letter?) ? — Yes, to my sister.
8. (why / you / run?) ? — Because I'm late.

4.4 Write positive or negative short answers (**Yes, I am / No, it isn't**, etc.).

1. Are you watching TV? *No, I'm not.*
2. Are you wearing shoes?
3. Are you wearing a hat?
4. Is it raining?
5. Are you eating something?
6. Are you feeling all right?
7. Is the sun shining?
8. Is your teacher watching you?

UNIT 5

I do/work/have, etc. (simple present)

They **have** a lot of books.
They **read** a lot.

She's eating an ice cream cone.
She **likes** ice cream cones.

A

They read / **I like** / **she likes**, etc. = the *simple present*:

I/we/you/they	**do**	**read**	**like**	**work**	**play**	**watch**	**have**
he/she/it	do**es**	read**s**	like**s**	work**s**	play**s**	watch**es**	ha**s**

Remember:
he/she/ it -s: **he** likes (*not* "he like") **my sister** plays **it** rains

- **I live** in Los Angeles, but **my brother lives** in New York.

have → **has**: I have → she/he/it **has**

Spelling:
-es after **-s/-ch/-sh**: pass → pass**es** wat**ch** → wat**ches** fini**sh** → fini**shes**
also: do → do**es** go → go**es**
stud**y** → stud**ies** carr**y** → carr**ies**

See Appendix 4 (4.1 and 4.2).

B

We use the simple present for things that are true in general, or for things that happen sometimes or all the time:

- I **like** animals. I **have** three dogs and six cats.
- The stores **open** at 9:00 a.m. and **close** at 5:30 p.m.
- He **works** very hard. He **starts** at 7:30 a.m. and **finishes** at 8 o'clock in the evening.
- The Earth **goes** around the sun.
- We **do** a lot of different things in our free time.
- She's very smart. She **speaks** four languages.
- It **costs** a lot of money to stay at luxury hotels.

C

We use the simple present with **always/never/often/sometimes/usually**:

- She **always gets** up at 7 o'clock.
- I **usually drive** to work, but **sometimes** I **walk**.
- Jack **never has** breakfast in the morning.
- The weather here isn't very good. It **often rains**.

For the simple present, see also Units 6–8.
See Unit 88 for word order (**always/never/often**, etc.) with the simple present.

Exercises

5.1 Write the **he/she/it** form of these verbs.

1. read *reads*
2. repair ....
3. watch ....
4. listen ....
5. love ....
6. have ....
7. push ....
8. do ....
9. think ....
10. kiss ....
11. buy ....
12. go ....

5.2 Complete the sentences. Use the correct form of these verbs:

boil close cost cost drink go have have like meet open ~~speak~~ teach wash

1. She's very smart. She *speaks* four languages.
2. Steve .... four cups of coffee a day.
3. We usually .... dinner at 7 o'clock.
4. I .... movies. I often .... to the movies with friends.
5. Water .... at 100 degrees Celsius.
6. In my hometown the banks .... at 9:00 in the morning.
7. The City Museum .... at 5 o'clock on Saturdays.
8. Food is expensive. It .... a lot of money.
9. Shoes are expensive. They .... a lot of money.
10. Sue is a teacher. She .... math to young children.
11. Your job is very interesting. You .... a lot of people.
12. Peter .... his hair every day.
13. An insect .... six legs.

5.3 Study this information:

		Bob and Ann	*Tom*	*you*
1.	drink juice in the morning?	never	usually	?
2.	read the newspaper?	often	never	?
3.	get up before 7 o'clock?	sometimes	always	?

Now write sentences about Bob and Ann, Tom, and yourself. Use **always/usually/often/sometimes/never**.

1. *Bob and Ann never drink juice in the morning.*
   Tom .... in the morning.
   I ....
2. Bob and Ann .... newspaper.
   Tom ....
   I ....
3. ....
   ....
   ....

UNIT 6

I don't . . . (negative simple present)

A

The negative simple present is **don't/doesn't** + *verb*:

She doesn't like apples.

He doesn't drive.

<table>
<tr><th colspan="2">Positive</th></tr>
<tr><td>I
we
you
they</td><td>work
like
do
have</td></tr>
<tr><td>he
she
it</td><td>works
likes
does
has</td></tr>
</table>

<table>
<tr><th colspan="3">Negative</th></tr>
<tr><td>I
we
you
they</td><td>do not
(don't)</td><td rowspan="2">work
like
do
have</td></tr>
<tr><td>he
she
it</td><td>does not
(doesn't)</td></tr>
</table>

- I **drink** coffee, but I **don't drink** tea.
- Sue **drinks** tea, but she **doesn't drink** coffee.
- They **don't have** any children.
- Rice **doesn't grow** in cold countries.
- We **don't know** many people in this town.

B

We use **don't/doesn't** + the *base form* (**like/do/speak/work**, etc.):

- I don't **like** washing the car. I don't **do** it very often.
- She speaks Spanish, but she doesn't **speak** Portuguese. (*not* "she doesn't speaks")
- It's a nice house, but it doesn't **have** a garage. (*not* "it doesn't has")

C

Remember:

I/we/you/they	**don't**	▪ **I don't** like golf.
he/she/it	**doesn't**	▪ **He doesn't** like golf.

- **I don't** like Fred and **Fred doesn't** like me. (*not* "Fred don't like")
- **My car doesn't** use much gas. (*not* "my car don't use")
- Sometimes she is late, but **it doesn't** happen very often.

For the simple present, see also Units 5 and 7.

Exercises

6.1 Write the negative.

1. I play the piano very well. *I don't play the piano very well.*
2. Jack plays tennis very well. Jack .... very well.
3. You know the answer. ....
4. She works very hard. ....
5. They do the same thing every day. ....
6. Ann has a car. ....

6.2 Write the opposite (positive or negative).

1. I understand. *I don't understand.*
2. She doesn't drive. *She drives.*
3. They know. They ....
4. He loves her. ....
5. They speak English. ....
6. I don't want it. ....
7. She doesn't want them. ....
8. He lives in Taiwan. ....

6.3 Study the information and write sentences with **like**.

	DO YOU LIKE...?	*Bill and Rosa*	*Ann*	*you*
1.	classical music?	yes	no	?
2.	golf?	no	yes	?
3.	horror movies?	no	yes	?
4.	dogs?	yes	no	?

1. *Bill and Rosa like classical music.*
   Ann ....
   I .... classical music.
2. Bill and Rosa .... golf.
   Ann ....
   I ....
3. Bill and Rosa ....
   ....
   ....
4. .... dogs.
   ....
   ....

6.4 Complete the sentences. All of them are negative. Use **don't/doesn't** + one of these verbs.

cost drive go have know play see sell smoke wash wear

1. "Have a cigarette." "No, thanks. I *don't smoke.*"
2. They .... newspapers in that store.
3. She has a car, but she .... very often.
4. I like plays, but I .... to the theater very often.
5. My car is usually dirty because I .... it very often.
6. It's a cheap hotel. It .... much to stay there.
7. He likes soccer, but he .... very often.
8. I .... much about politics.
9. She's married, but she .... a ring.
10. He lives next door, but we .... him very often.
11. "Can you lend me five dollars?" "Sorry, I .... any money."

UNIT 7

Do you . . . ? (simple present questions)

A

We use **do/does** in simple present questions:

Positive	
I we you they	**work** **like** **do** **have**
he she it	work**s** like**s** do**es** ha**s**

Question		
do	I we you they	**work . . .?** **like . . .?** **do . . .?** **have . . .?**
does	he she it	

B

The word order in these questions is:

	do/does	+ *subject*	+ *base form*	
	Do	**you**	**work**	on Saturdays?
Where	**do**	**your parents**	**live?**	
	Do	**they**	**have**	a car?
How often	**do**	**you**	**wash**	your hair?
What	**do**	**you** usually	**do**	on weekends?
	Does	**Chris**	**play**	tennis often?
How much	**does**	**it**	**cost**	to fly to Hawaii?
What	**does**	**this word**	**mean?**	

What do you do? = What's your job?:

- **"What do you do?"** "I work in a bank."

C

Remember:

do I/we/you/they
does she/he/it

- **Do they** like music?
- **Does she** like music?

D

Short answers	
Yes, { I/we/you/they **do**. / he/she/it **does**.	No, { I/we/you/they **don't**. / he/she/it **doesn't**.

- "**Do you** have the time?" **"No, I don't."**
- "**Do they** speak English?" **"Yes, they do."**
- "**Does he** work hard?" **"Yes, he does."**
- "**Does your sister** live in Toronto?" **"No, she doesn't."**

For the simple present, see also Units 5, 6, and 8.

Exercises

7.1 You are asking somebody questions. Write questions with **Do/Does . . . ?**

I WORK HARD. HOW ABOUT YOU? DO YOU WORK HARD?

1. I work hard. How about you? *Do you work hard* ?
2. I play tennis. How about you? .... you .... ?
3. I play tennis. How about Ann? .... Ann .... ?
4. I know the answer. How about you? .... the answer?
5. I like hot weather. How about you? .... ?
6. My father drinks coffee. How about your father? .... ?
7. I exercise every morning. How about you? .... ?
8. I speak English. How about your friends? .... ?
9. I want to be famous. How about you? .... ?

These questions begin with **Where/What/How . . . ?**

10. I wash my hair every day. (how often / you?) *How often do you wash your hair* ?
11. I live in Mexico City. (where / you?) Where .... ?
12. I watch TV every day. (how often / you?) How .... ?
13. I have lunch at home. (where / you?) .... ?
14. I get up at 7:30. (what time / you?) .... ?
15. I go to the movies a lot. (how often / you?) .... ?
16. I go to work by bus. (how / you?) .... ?
17. I always have eggs for breakfast. (what / you?) .... ?

7.2 Use the verbs in the list to make questions. Use the word(s) in parentheses ( ).

cost do do drink go have like play rain ~~speak~~

1. (you) Excuse me, *do you speak* .... English? — Yes, a little.
2. (you) What .... ? — I'm a secretary.
3. (your sister) What .... ? — She works in a bank.
4. (she) .... coffee? — Yes, two cups a day.
5. (your brother) .... volleyball often? — Yes, He's a very good player.
6. (it) How often .... here in the summer? — Not often. It's usually dry.
7. (you) .... music? — Yes, I love it.
8. (they) What time .... usually .... to bed? — 10 o'clock.
9. (you) What .... usually .... for lunch? — A sandwich and some fruit.
10. (it) How much .... to stay at this hotel? — Sixty dollars a night.

7.3 Write positive or negative short answers (**Yes, he does** / **No, I don't**, etc.).

1. Do you drive a car? *No, I don't.*
2. Do you live in a big city? ....
3. Do you have a cold? ....
4. Does your sister speak English? ....
5. Do you play a musical instrument? ....
6. Does it rain a lot where you live? ....

UNIT 8

I am doing (present continuous) and **I do** (simple present)

Jim is watching television.
He is *not* playing the guitar.

But Jim has a guitar.
He often plays it, and he plays very well.

Jim **plays** the guitar,
but he **is not playing** the guitar now.

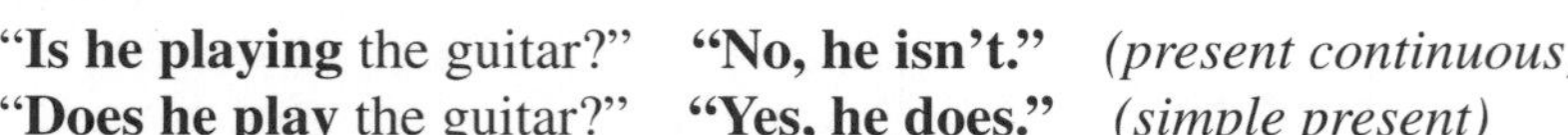

"**Is he playing** the guitar?" "**No, he isn't.**" *(present continuous)*
"**Does he play** the guitar?" "**Yes, he does.**" *(simple present)*

A *Present continuous* (**I am doing**) – now, at the time of speaking:

I am doing

past ◄—— *NOW* ——► *future*

- Please be quiet. **I'm working**.
- Linda **is taking** a shower at the moment.
- Take an umbrella. It**'s raining**.
- You can turn off the television. **I'm not watching** it.
- Why are you under the table? What **are you doing**?

B *Simple present* (**I do**) – in general, all the time, or sometimes:

◄- - - - - **I do** - - - - -►

past ◄—— *NOW* ——► *future*

- I **work** every day from 9 o'clock until 5:00.
- Linda **takes** a shower every morning.
- It **rains** a lot in the winter.
- I **don't watch** television very often.
- What **do you** usually **do** on weekends?

C Do *not* use these verbs in the present continuous (**I am -ing**):
want like love hate need prefer depend know mean understand believe remember forget

Use the simple present only (**I want / do you like?**, etc.):

- I'm tired. I **want** to go home. (*not* "I'm wanting")
- "**Do you know** that woman?" "Yes, but I **don't remember** her name."
- I **don't understand**. What **do you mean**?

For the present continuous, see also Units 3 and 4.
For the simple present, see also Units 5–7.

Exercises

8.1 Answer the questions about the pictures.

1. Does he take photographs? *Yes, he does.* Is he taking a photograph? *No, he isn't.*
   What is he doing? *He's making a meal.*
2. Does she drive a bus? .... Is she driving a bus? ....
   What is she doing? ....
3. Does he wash windows? .... Is he washing a window? ....
   What is he doing? ....
4. Do they teach? .... Are they teaching? ....
   What are they doing? ....

8.2 Put in **am/is/are/do/don't/does/doesn't**.

1. Excuse me, *do* you speak English?
2. "Have some coffee." "No, thank you, I .... drink coffee."
3. Why .... you laughing at me?
4. "What .... she do?" "She's a dentist."
5. I .... want to go out. It .... raining.
6. "Where .... you come from?" "From Canada."
7. How much .... it cost to send a letter to Canada?
8. I can't talk to you right now. I .... working.
9. Bob is a good tennis player, but he .... play very often.

8.3 Put the verb in the *present continuous* (**I am doing**) or *simple present* (**I do**).

1. Excuse me, *do you speak* (you/speak) English?
2. Tom *is taking* (take) a shower at the moment.
3. They *don't watch* (not/watch) television very often.
4. Listen! Somebody .... (sing).
5. She's tired. She .... (want) to go home now.
6. How often .... (you/read) the newspaper?
7. "Excuse me, but you .... (sit) in my place." "Oh, I'm sorry."
8. I'm sorry, I .... (not/understand). Please speak more slowly.
9. "Where are you, Dan?" "I'm in the living room. I .... (read)."
10. What time .... (she/finish) work every day?
11. You can turn off the radio. I .... (not/listen) to it.
12. He .... (not/usually/drive) to work.
    He usually .... (walk).

UNIT 9

I watched/cleaned/went, etc. (simple past)

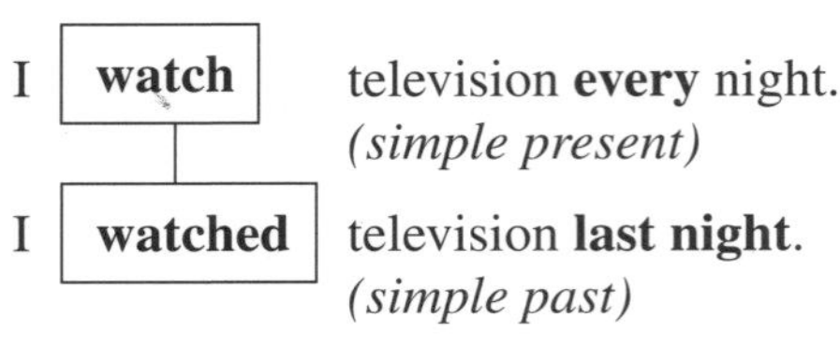

I **watch** television **every** night.
(simple present)

I **watched** television **last night**.
(simple past)

watched is the *simple past*:

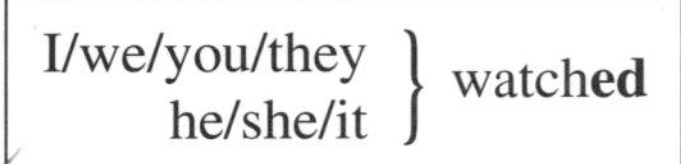

I/we/you/they, he/she/it } watch**ed**

A

The simple past is often **-ed**. For example:

work → work**ed** brush → brush**ed** start → start**ed**
stay → stay**ed** live → liv**ed** dance → danc**ed**

These verbs are *regular* verbs.

- I brush my teeth every morning. This morning I **brushed** my teeth.
- Lee **worked** in a bank from 1989 to 1992.
- Yesterday it **rained** all morning. It **stopped** at noon.
- We **enjoyed** the party last night. We **danced** a lot and **talked** to a lot of people. The party **ended** at midnight.

Spelling:

stud**y** → stud**ied** worr**y** → worr**ied**
sto**p** → sto**pp**ed pla**n** → pla**nn**ed

See Appendix 4 (4.2 and 4.4).

B

Some verbs are *irregular* (not regular). For irregular verbs, the simple past is *not* **-ed**.
Here are some important irregular verbs (see also Appendixes 1 and 2):

begin →	**began**	fall →	**fell**	leave →	**left**	sell →	**sold**
break	**broke**	find	**found**	lose	**lost**	sit	**sat**
bring	**brought**	fly	**flew**	make	**made**	sleep	**slept**
buy	**bought**	forget	**forgot**	meet	**met**	speak	**spoke**
catch	**caught**	get	**got**	pay	**paid**	stand	**stood**
come	**came**	give	**gave**	put	**put**	take	**took**
cost	**cost**	go	**went**	read	**read***	tell	**told**
do	**did**	have	**had**	ring	**rang**	think	**thought**
drink	**drank**	hear	**heard**	say	**said**	win	**won**
eat	**ate**	know	**knew**	see	**saw**	write	**wrote**

* The past tense of **read** sounds like "red."

- I usually get up early, but this morning I **got** up at 9:30.
- We **did** a lot of housework yesterday.
- Ann **went** to the movies three times last week.
- Mr. Wood **came** into the room, **took** off his coat, and **sat** down.

For the simple past, see also Unit 10.

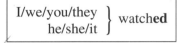

Exercises

9.1 Complete these sentences. Use one of these verbs in the simple past:

brush die end enjoy happen live open play rain start stay turn want ~~watch~~

1. Yesterday evening I watched television.
2. I .... my teeth three times yesterday.
3. It was dark, so I .... on the light.
4. The concert last night .... at 7:30 and .... at 10 o'clock.
5. The accident .... last Sunday afternoon.
6. When I was a child, I .... to be a doctor.
7. Mozart .... from 1756 to 1791.
8. We .... our vacation last year. We .... at a very good hotel.
9. Today the weather is nice, but yesterday it ....
10. It was hot in the room, so I .... the window.
11. The weather was good yesterday afternoon, so we .... tennis.
12. William Shakespeare .... in 1616.

9.2 Write the past of these verbs.

1. get got	7. leave	13. buy	19. put ....
2. eat	8. arrive	14. know	20. tell ....
3. pay	9. see	15. snow	21. call ....
4. try	10. go	16. stand	22. lose ....
5. make	11. hear	17. take	23. think ....
6. give	12. find	18. do	24. speak ....

9.3 Write sentences about the past (**yesterday** / **last week**, etc.).

1. He always goes to work by car. Yesterday he went to work by car.
2. They always get up early. This morning they ....
3. Bill often loses his keys. He .... last Saturday.
4. I write a letter to Jane every week. Last week ....
5. She meets her friends every evening. She .... last evening.
6. I usually read two newspapers every day. .... yesterday.
7. They come to my house every Friday. Last Friday ....
8. We usually go to the movies on Sunday. .... last Sunday.
9. Tom always has fruit for breakfast. .... this morning.
10. They buy a new car every year. Last year ....
11. I eat an orange every day. Yesterday ....
12. We usually do our shopping on Monday. .... last Monday.
13. Ann often takes photographs. Last weekend ....
14. We leave home at 8:30 every morning. .... this morning.

9.4 Write sentences about yourself. What did you do yesterday or what happened yesterday?

1. ....
2. ....
3. ....
4. ....
5. ....

UNIT 10 I didn't . . . Did you . . .? (simple past negative and questions)

A We use **did** in simple past negative and questions:

Base form
watch
clean
play
do
go
have
begin

Positive	
I	watch**ed**
we	clean**ed**
you	play**ed**
they	**did**
he	**went**
she	**had**
it	**began**

Negative		
I		watch
we		clean
you		play
they	**did not (didn't)**	do
he		go
she		have
it		begin

Question		
	I	watch . . .?
	we	clean . . .?
	you	play . . .?
did	they	do . . .?
	he	go . . .?
	she	have . . .?
	it	begin . . .?

B **do/does** *(present)* → **did** *(past)*:

- I **don't** watch television very often.
- I **didn't** watch television **yesterday**.
- **Does** she go out very often?
- **Did** she go out **last night**?

C We use **did/didn't** + *base form* (**watch/clean/do**, etc.):

I watch**ed** *but* I didn't **watch** (*not* "I didn't watched")
he **went** *but* did he **go**? (*not* "did he went?")

- I play**ed** tennis yesterday, but I **didn't win**.
- Don **didn't have** breakfast this morning. (*not* "Don hadn't breakfast")
- They **went** to a movie, but they **didn't enjoy** it.
- We **didn't do** much work yesterday.

D Note the word order in questions with **did**:

	did +	*subject* +	*base form*	
	Did	**Sue**	**give**	you a birthday present?
What	**did**	**you**	**do**	last night?
How	**did**	**the accident**	**happen**?	
Where	**did**	**your parents**	**go**	on their vacation?

Short answers	
Yes, { I/we/you/they, she/he/it } **did**.	No, { I/we/you/they, she/he/it } **didn't**.

- "**Did you** see Joe yesterday?" **"No, I didn't."**
- "**Did it** rain on Sunday?" **"Yes, it did."**
- "**Did Mary** come to the party?" **"No, she didn't."**
- "**Did your friends** have a good vacation?" **"Yes, they did."**

For the simple past (positive), see Unit 9.

Exercises

10.1 Complete these sentences with the verb in the negative.

1. I saw John, but I *didn't see*.......... Mary.
2. They worked on Monday, but they .... on Tuesday.
3. We went to the store, but we .... to the bank.
4. She had a pen, but she .... any paper.
5. Jack did the laundry, but he .... the shopping.

10.2 You are asking somebody questions. Write questions with **Did . . . ?**

1. I watched TV last night. How about you? *Did you watch TV last night*.............................. ?
2. I enjoyed the party. How about you? .... you .... ?
3. I had a good vacation. How about you? .... ?
4. I got up early this morning. How about you? .... ?
5. I slept well last night. How about you? .... ?

10.3 What did *you* do yesterday? (Your sentence can be positive or negative.)

1. (watch TV) *I watched TV yesterday.*.......... (*or* *I didn't watch TV yesterday.*................)
2. (get up before 7:30) I ....
3. (have breakfast) I ....
4. (buy a magazine) ....
5. (speak English) ....
6. (take an exam) ....
7. (talk on the phone) ....
8. (go to bed before 10:30) ....

10.4 Write questions with **Who/What/How/Why . . . ?**

1. I met somebody. Who *did you meet*... ?
2. Tom arrived. What time .... Tom .... ?
3. I saw somebody. Who .... you .... ?
4. They wanted something. What .... ?
5. The meeting ended. What time .... ?
6. Ann went home early. Why .... ?
7. We had dinner. What .... for dinner?
8. It cost a lot of money. How much .... ?

10.5 Put the verb in the correct form of the past (positive, negative, or question).

1. I *played*.......... (play) tennis yesterday, but I *didn't win*............... (not/win).
2. We .... (wait) a long time for the bus, but it .... (not/come).
3. That's a nice shirt. Where .... (you/buy) it?
4. She .... (see) me, but she .... (not/speak) to me.
5. "............................. (it/rain) yesterday?" "No, it was a nice day."
6. That was a strange thing to do. Why .... (you/do) it?
7. I .... (not/buy) anything because I .... (not/have) any money with me.

UNIT 11

was/were

Now Bill **is** at work.

At midnight last night he **wasn't** at work.

He **was** in bed.
He **was** asleep.

am/is *(present)* → **was** *(past)*:

■ I **am** tired (now).	I **was** tired **last night**.
■ **Is** she at home (now)?	**Was** she at home **yesterday morning**?
■ The weather **is** nice today.	The weather **was** nice **yesterday**.

are *(present)* → **were** *(past)*:

■ You **are** late (now).	You **were** late **yesterday**.
■ They **aren't** here (now).	They **weren't** here **last Sunday**.

Positive	
I he she it	**was**
we you they	**were**

Negative	
I he she it	**was not** **(wasn't)**
we you they	**were not** **(weren't)**

Question	
was	I? he? she? it?
were	we? you? they?

- Last year she **was** 22, so she **is** 23 now.
- When I **was** a child, I **was** afraid of dogs.
- We **were** tired after the trip, but we **weren't** hungry.
- The hotel **was** very comfortable, and it **wasn't** expensive.
- Where **were** you at 3 o'clock yesterday afternoon?
- **Was** the weather nice when you **were** on vacation?
- Those shoes are nice. **Were** they expensive?
- Why **was** he angry yesterday?

Short answers	
Yes, { I/he/she/it **was**. we/you/they **were**.	No, { I/he/she/it **wasn't**. we/you/they **weren't**.

- "**Were you** late?" "**No, I wasn't.**"
- "**Was Ted** at work yesterday?" "**Yes, he was.**"
- "**Were they** at the party?" "**No, they weren't.**"

Exercises

11.1 Look at the pictures. Where were these people at 3 o'clock yesterday afternoon?

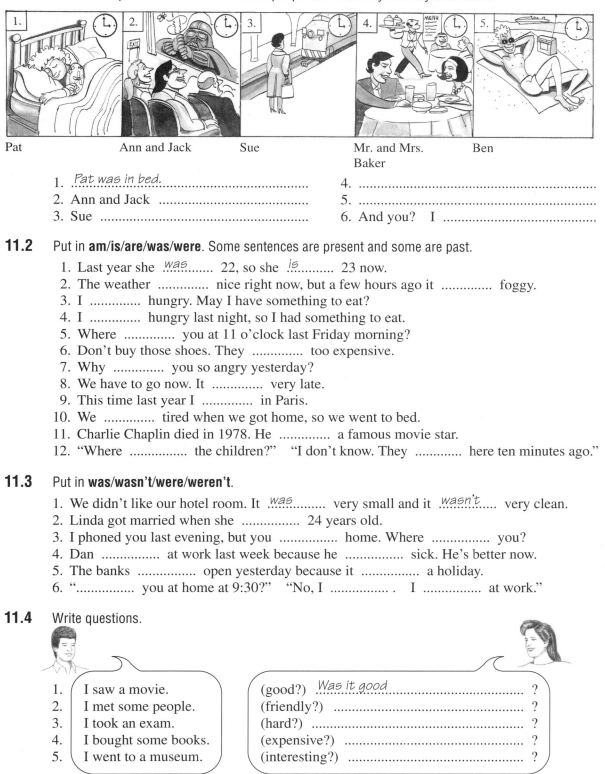

1. Pat
2. Ann and Jack
3. Sue
4. Mr. and Mrs. Baker
5. Ben

1. *Pat was in bed.* ....
2. Ann and Jack ....
3. Sue ....
4. ....
5. ....
6. And you? I ....

11.2 Put in **am/is/are/was/were**. Some sentences are present and some are past.

1. Last year she *was*....... 22, so she *is*......... 23 now.
2. The weather .... nice right now, but a few hours ago it .... foggy.
3. I .... hungry. May I have something to eat?
4. I .... hungry last night, so I had something to eat.
5. Where .... you at 11 o'clock last Friday morning?
6. Don't buy those shoes. They .... too expensive.
7. Why .... you so angry yesterday?
8. We have to go now. It .... very late.
9. This time last year I .... in Paris.
10. We .... tired when we got home, so we went to bed.
11. Charlie Chaplin died in 1978. He .... a famous movie star.
12. "Where .... the children?" "I don't know. They .... here ten minutes ago."

11.3 Put in **was/wasn't/were/weren't**.

1. We didn't like our hotel room. It *was*......... very small and it *wasn't*..... very clean.
2. Linda got married when she .... 24 years old.
3. I phoned you last evening, but you .... home. Where .... you?
4. Dan .... at work last week because he .... sick. He's better now.
5. The banks .... open yesterday because it .... a holiday.
6. "................ you at home at 9:30?" "No, I .... I .... at work."

11.4 Write questions.

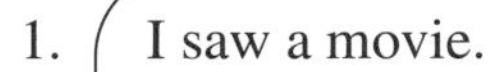

1. I saw a movie. — (good?) *Was it good* .... ?
2. I met some people. — (friendly?) .... ?
3. I took an exam. — (hard?) .... ?
4. I bought some books. — (expensive?) .... ?
5. I went to a museum. — (interesting?) .... ?

UNIT 12

I was doing (past continuous)

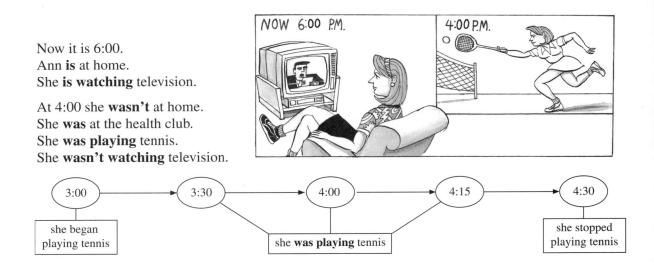

Now it is 6:00.
Ann **is** at home.
She **is watching** television.

At 4:00 she **wasn't** at home.
She **was** at the health club.
She **was playing** tennis.
She **wasn't watching** television.

3:00 → 3:30 → 4:00 → 4:15 → 4:30

3:00: she began playing tennis
3:30–4:15: she **was playing** tennis
4:30: she stopped playing tennis

A

was/were -ing (do**ing**/play**ing**/work**ing**, etc.) is the *past continuous* tense:

Positive	
I he she it	**was -ing**
we you they	**were -ing**

Negative		
I he she it	**was not (wasn't)**	**-ing**
we you they	**were not (weren't)**	**-ing**

Question		
was	I he she it	**-ing**?
were	we you they	**-ing**?

- "What **were** you do**ing** at 11:30 yesterday?" "I **was** work**ing**."
- "What did he say?" "I don't know. I **wasn't** listen**ing**."
- It **was** rain**ing**, so we didn't go out.
- In 1990 they **were** liv**ing** in Japan.
- Today she's wearing a skirt, but yesterday she **was** wear**ing** pants.
- I woke up early yesterday. It was a beautiful morning. The sun **was** shin**ing** and the birds **were** sing**ing**.

B

am/is/are -ing *(present)* → **was/were -ing** *(past)*:

- **I'm** work**ing** (now). — I **was** work**ing** at 10:30 last night.
- It **isn't** rain**ing** (now). — It **wasn't** rain**ing** when we went out.
- What **are** you do**ing** (now)? — What **were** you do**ing** at 3 o'clock?

For spelling (mak**e** → mak**ing**, run → ru**nning**, **lie** → **lying**, etc.), see Appendix 4.
For the past continuous, see also Unit 13.

Exercises

12.1 Look at the pictures. Where were these people at 3 o'clock yesterday afternoon? And what were they doing? Write *two* sentences for each picture.

Ann	Sue and Jack	Tom	Linda	Sam and Liz
1.	2.	3.	4.	5.
at home / watch TV	at the theater / watch a movie	in his car / drive	at the station / wait for a train	in the park / walk

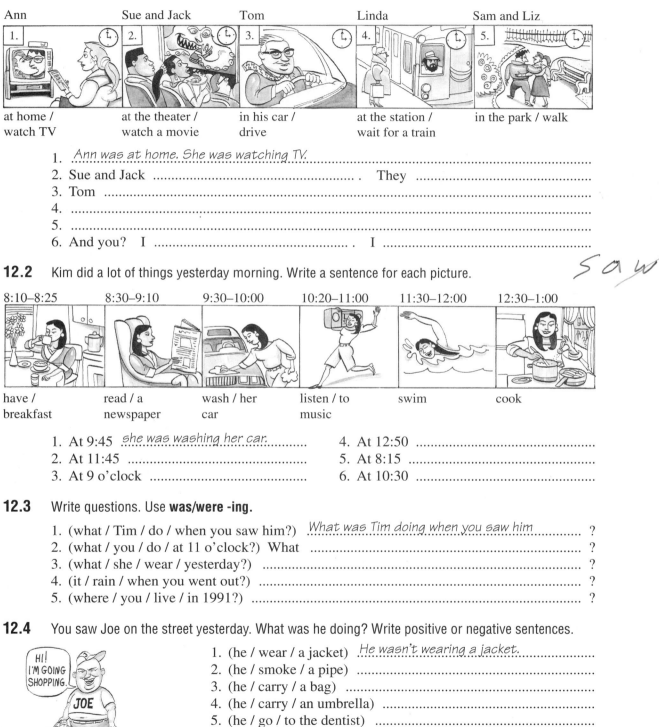

1. *Ann was at home. She was watching TV.*
2. Sue and Jack .... They ....
3. Tom ....
4. ....
5. ....
6. And you? I .... I ....

12.2 Kim did a lot of things yesterday morning. Write a sentence for each picture.

8:10–8:25	8:30–9:10	9:30–10:00	10:20–11:00	11:30–12:00	12:30–1:00
have / breakfast	read / a newspaper	wash / her car	listen / to music	swim	cook

1. At 9:45 *she was washing her car.*
2. At 11:45 ....
3. At 9 o'clock ....
4. At 12:50 ....
5. At 8:15 ....
6. At 10:30 ....

12.3 Write questions. Use **was/were -ing.**

1. (what / Tim / do / when you saw him?) *What was Tim doing when you saw him* ?
2. (what / you / do / at 11 o'clock?) What .... ?
3. (what / she / wear / yesterday?) .... ?
4. (it / rain / when you went out?) .... ?
5. (where / you / live / in 1991?) .... ?

12.4 You saw Joe on the street yesterday. What was he doing? Write positive or negative sentences.

1. (he / wear / a jacket) *He wasn't wearing a jacket.*
2. (he / smoke / a pipe) ....
3. (he / carry / a bag) ....
4. (he / carry / an umbrella) ....
5. (he / go / to the dentist) ....
6. (he / wear / a hat) ....

UNIT 13 **I was doing** (past continuous) and **I did** (simple past)

Jack was reading a book.

The phone rang.

He stopped reading.

He answered the phone.

What **happened**? The phone **rang**. *(simple past)*
What **was Jack doing** when the phone rang?
He **was reading** a book. *(past continuous)*
What **did he do** when the phone rang?
He **stopped** reading and **answered** the phone. (*simple past*)

Jack began reading *before* the phone rang. So:
When the phone rang, he **was reading**.

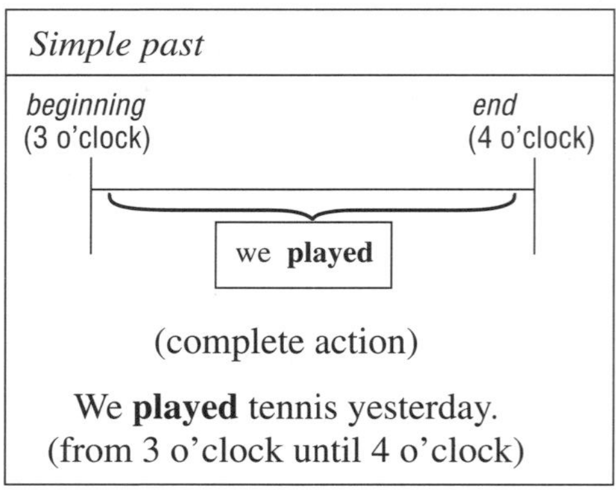

(complete action)

We **played** tennis yesterday.
(from 3 o'clock until 4 o'clock)

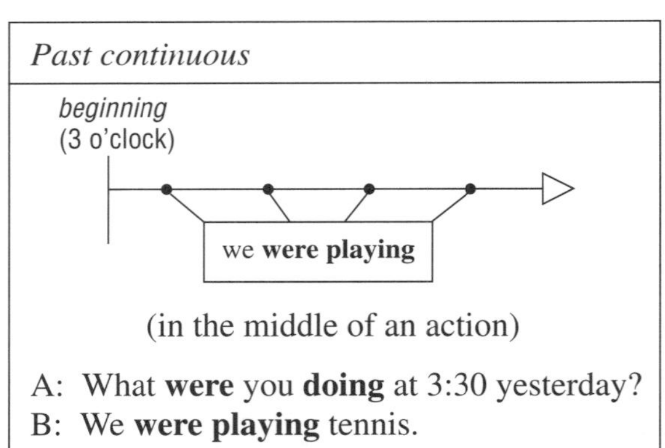

(in the middle of an action)

A: What **were** you **doing** at 3:30 yesterday?
B: We **were playing** tennis.

- Jack **was reading** the newspaper when the phone **rang**.
  but Jack **read** the newspaper yesterday.
- **Were you watching** television when I **called** you?
  but **Did you watch** the movie on television last night?
- I **started** work at 9:00 and **finished** at 4:30. At 2:30 I **was working**.
- When we **went** out, it **was raining**. (= it started raining *before* we went out)
- I **saw** Sue and Tom this morning. They **were standing** at the bus stop.
- Ann **fell** asleep while she **was reading**.

For **while**, see Unit 92.

Exercises

13.1 Look at the pictures and write sentences. Use the past continuous or simple past.

Example (see the pictures on page 26): (Jack / read / a book) *Jack was reading a book.*
(the phone / ring) *The phone rang.*
(he / answer / the phone) *He answered the phone.*

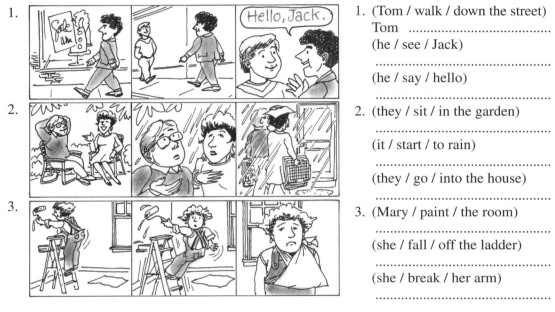

1. (Tom / walk / down the street)
Tom ....
(he / see / Jack)
....
(he / say / hello)
....

2. (they / sit / in the garden)
....
(it / start / to rain)
....
(they / go / into the house)
....

3. (Mary / paint / the room)
....
(she / fall / off the ladder)
....
(she / break / her arm)
....

13.2 Put the verb into the past continuous (**I was doing**) or simple past (**I did**).

1. When we *went* (go) out, it *was raining* (rain).
2. I wasn't hungry last night. I *didn't eat* (not/eat) anything.
3. *Were you watching* (you/watch) television when I *phoned* (phone) you?
4. Jane was busy when I went to see her. She .... (work).
5. I .... (get) up early this morning. I .... (wash), ... (get) dressed, and then I .... (have) breakfast.
6. The mail .... (come) while I .... (have) lunch.
7. We .... (meet) Joan at the party. She .... (wear) a red dress.
8. The boys .... (break) a window when they .... (play) baseball.
9. I was late, but my friends .... (wait) for me when I .... (arrive).
10. I .... (get) up at 7 o'clock. The sun .... (shine), so I .... (go) for a walk.
11. He .... (not/drive) fast when the accident .... (happen).
12. Ann .... (not/go) to work yesterday. She was sick.
13. "What .... (you/do) on Saturday evening?" "I went to the movies."
14. "What .... (you/do) at 9:30 on Saturday night?"
"I .... (watch) a movie on TV."

UNIT 14

I have done (present perfect 1)

His shirt is dirty.

He is washing his shirt.

He **has washed** his shirt.
(= his shirt is clean *now*)

They are at home.

They are going out.

They **have gone** out.
(= they are not at home *now*)

A

has washed / have gone, etc. is the *present perfect* (**have/has** + *past participle**):

I / we / you / they	**have** (**'ve**) / **have not** (**haven't**)	wash**ed** / arriv**ed** / **done** / **been** / **bought** / **taken** / **begun**
he / she / it	**has** (**'s**) / **has not** (**hasn't**)	

have	I / we / you / they	wash**ed**? / arriv**ed**? / **done**? / **been**? / **bought**? / **taken**? / **begun**?
has	he / she / it	

B

We use the present perfect for *an action in the past* with a result *now*:

- **I've lost** my passport. (= I can't find my passport *now*)
- She**'s** (= she **has**) **gone** to bed. (= she is in bed *now*)
- We**'ve bought** a new car. (= we have a new car *now*)
- It's Mary's birthday tomorrow and I **haven't bought** her a present.
- "Bob is on vacation." "Oh, where **has he gone**?"
- "Are they still having dinner?" "No, they**'ve finished**."

Sometimes you can use the present perfect or the simple past – see Unit 18.

C

*The past participle of *regular* verbs is **-ed**:
wash → have wash**ed** arrive → have arriv**ed** stop → have stopp**ed**

The past participle of *irregular* verbs is sometimes the same as the simple past and sometimes different. For example:

the same:	lose → have **lost**	make → have **made**	have → have **had**
different:	do → have **done**	see → have **seen**	write → have **written**

For a list of irregular past participles, see Appendixes 1 and 2.

For the present perfect, see also Units 15, 16, and 18. For the present perfect + **yet**, see Unit 86.

Exercises

14.1 Look at the pictures. What has happened?

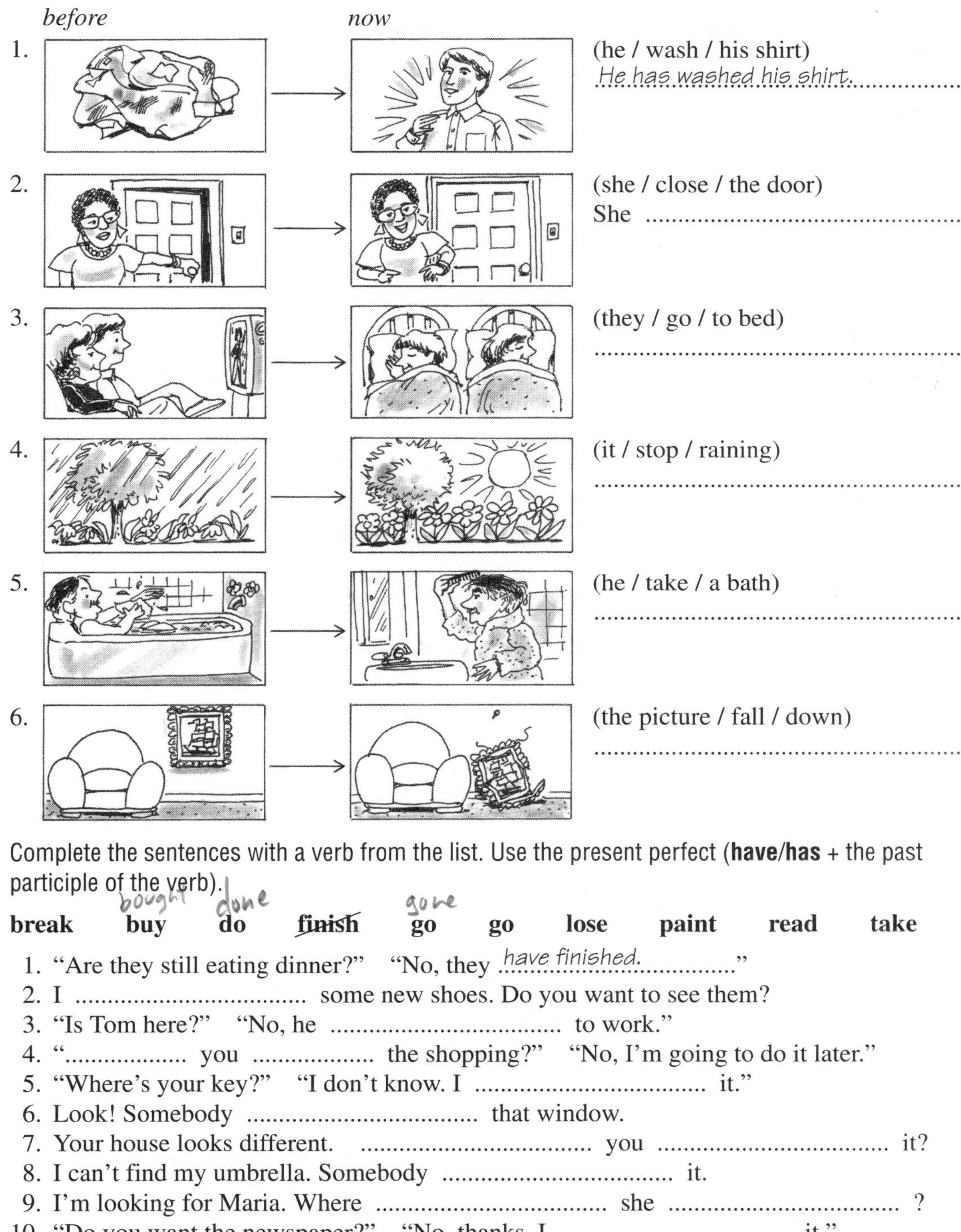

before *now*

1. (he / wash / his shirt) He has washed his shirt.
2. (she / close / the door) She ....
3. (they / go / to bed) ....
4. (it / stop / raining) ....
5. (he / take / a bath) ....
6. (the picture / fall / down) ....

14.2 Complete the sentences with a verb from the list. Use the present perfect (**have/has** + the past participle of the verb).

break **buy** **do** **~~finish~~** **go** **go** **lose** **paint** **read** **take**

1. "Are they still eating dinner?" "No, they have finished."
2. I .... some new shoes. Do you want to see them?
3. "Is Tom here?" "No, he .... to work."
4. ".................. you .... the shopping?" "No, I'm going to do it later."
5. "Where's your key?" "I don't know. I .... it."
6. Look! Somebody .... that window.
7. Your house looks different. .... you .... it?
8. I can't find my umbrella. Somebody .... it.
9. I'm looking for Maria. Where .... she .... ?
10. "Do you want the newspaper?" "No, thanks. I .... it."

UNIT
15

Have you ever . . .? (present perfect 2)

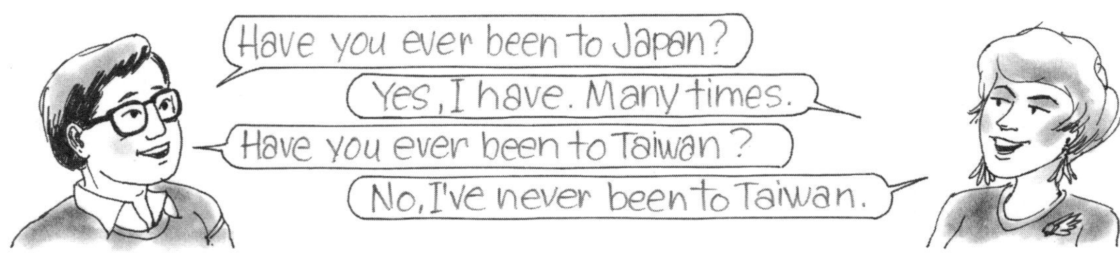

A

We use the *present perfect* (**have been / have played / have done**, etc.) when we talk about a time from the past until now – for example, your life:

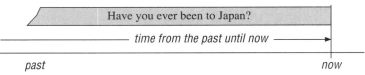

Have you ever been to Japan?

time from the past until now

past *now*

- "**Have you been** to France?" *(in your life)* "No, I **haven't**."
- **I've been** to Canada, but I **haven't been** to the United States.
- She is an interesting person. She **has had** many different jobs and **has visited** many countries.
- **I've seen** that woman before, but I can't remember when.
- How many times **has Brazil won** the World Cup?
- "**Have you read** this book?" "Yes, **I've read** it twice." (= two times)

B

You can use the *present perfect* + **ever** *(in questions)* and **never**:

- "**Has** Ann **ever been** to Hungary?" "No, never."
- "**Have** you **ever played** golf?" "Yes, once." (= one time)
- My mother **has never traveled** by air.
- **I've never ridden** a horse.

C

gone and **been**

He's **gone** to Spain.
(= he is in Spain *now*)

He's **been** to Spain.
(= he went to Spain but *now he is back*)

Compare:

- I can't find Sue. Where **has she gone**? (= Where is she now?)
- Oh, hello, Sue. I was looking for you. Where **have you been**?

For the present perfect, see also Units 14, 16, and 18.

Exercises

15.1 You are asking Ann questions beginning **Have you ever . . .?** Write the questions.

You | Ann

1. (Montreal?) *Have you ever been to Montreal* ? — No, never.
2. (play / golf?) *Have you ever played golf* ? — Yes, twice.
3. (Poland?) Have .... ? — No, never.
4. (lose / your passport?) .... ? — Yes, once.
5. (ride / a horse?) .... ? — No, never.
6. (eat / Chinese food?) .... ? — Yes, a few times.
7. (travel / train?) .... ? — Yes, many times.
8. (win / a lot of money?) .... ? — No, never.
9. (break / your leg?) .... ? — Yes, once.

15.2 Look at Ann's answers in Exercise 1. Write sentences about Ann and yourself.

Ann	*You*
1. *Ann has never been to Montreal.*	*I have been to Montreal twice.*
2. *Ann has played golf twice.*	I ....
3. She	I ....
4. She	....
5.	....
6.	....
7.	....
8.	....
9.	....

15.3 Mary is 65 years old. She has had an interesting life. Write sentences about the things she has done. Use the present perfect.

1. (she / has / many different jobs) *She has had many different jobs.*
2. (she / travel / to many places) She ....
3. (she / do / a lot of interesting things) ....
4. (she / write / ten books) ....
5. (she / meet / a lot of interesting people) ....
6. (she / be / married five times) ....

15.4 Put in **gone** or **been**.

1. He's on vacation right now. He's *gone* .... to Puerto Rico.
2. "Where's Pat?" "She's not here. I think she's .... to the bank."
3. "Hello, Pat. Where have you .... ?" "I've .... to the bank."
4. "Have you ever .... to Mexico?" "No, never."
5. My parents aren't home this evening. They've .... out.
6. There's a new restaurant in town. Have you .... to it?
7. Paris is a wonderful city. I've .... there many times.
8. Helen was here earlier, but I think she's .... now.

UNIT 16

How long have you . . . ? (present perfect 3)

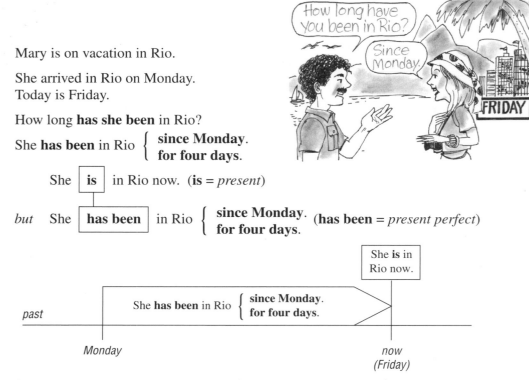

Mary is on vacation in Rio.

She arrived in Rio on Monday.
Today is Friday.

How long **has she been** in Rio?

She **has been** in Rio { **since Monday**. / **for four days**. }

She **is** in Rio now. (**is** = *present*)

but She **has been** in Rio { **since Monday**. / **for four days**. } (**has been** = *present perfect*)

She **is** in Rio now.

past — She **has been** in Rio { **since Monday**. / **for four days**. } — *Monday* — *now (Friday)*

Compare:

Simple present		*Present perfect*
Mark **is** in Canada.	*but*	He **has been** in Canada **since April**. (*not* "He is in Canada since April.")
Are you married?	*but*	**How long have** you **been** married? (*not* "How long are you married?")
Do you **know** Sue?	*but*	**How long have** you **known** her? (*not* "How long do you know her?") **I've known** her **for a long time**.
Linda **lives** in Hong Kong.	*but*	**How long has** she **lived** in Hong Kong? She **has lived** there **all her life**.
We **have** a car.	*but*	**How long have** you **had** your car? We**'ve had** it **for a year**.

Present continuous		*Present perfect continuous* (**have been -ing**)
I'm study**ing** German.	*but*	**How long have** you **been** study**ing** German? **I've been** study**ing** German **for six weeks**.
It**'s** rain**ing**.	*but*	It**'s been** (= it **has been**) rain**ing since I got up this morning**.

For **for** and **since**, see Unit 17.

Exercises

16.1 Complete these sentences.

1. Mary is in Rio. She *has been*.................. in Rio since Monday.
2. I know Bob. I *have known*.................. him for a long time.
3. They are married. They .... married since 1988.
4. Ted is sick. He .... sick for a week.
5. We live in this house. We .... here for ten years.
6. I know Tom very well. I .... him since we were children.
7. We are waiting for you. We .... waiting since 8 o'clock.
8. Jane works in a bank. She .... in a bank for five years.
9. I'm studying English. I .... studying English for six months.
10. She has a headache. She .... a headache since she got up.

16.2 Make questions with **How long . . . ?**

1. Mary is in Rio. *How long has she been in Rio*..................................?
2. I know Bob. *How long have you known him*..................................?
3. Mike and Judy are in Indonesia. How long ....?
4. Ann is studying Italian. How long ....?
5. My brother lives in Greece. ....?
6. It is raining. ....?
7. Bill is a teacher. ....?
8. I know Nancy. ....?
9. I have a motorcycle. ....?
10. Linda and Frank are married. ....?
11. Alan works in Vancouver. ....?

16.3 Write a sentence for each picture. Use the words below each picture.

for ten years | since Sunday | for two hours | all day | all her life | for five years

1. *They have been married for ten years.*..................................
2. He .... since Sunday.
3. They .... television ....
4. It .... all day.
5. She ....
6. He ....

UNIT 17

for since ago

A

for and **since**:
We use **for** and **since** to say *how long*:

- Mary has been in Rio { **for four days**. / **since Monday**.

We use **for** + *a period of time* (**four days / two years**, etc.):

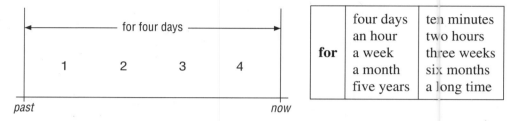

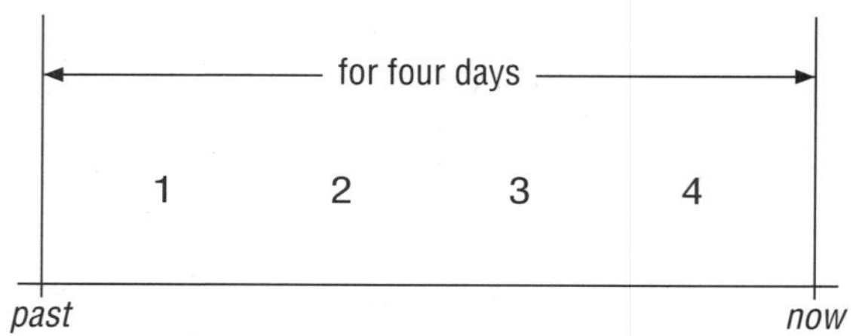

for	four days an hour a week a month five years	ten minutes two hours three weeks six months a long time

We use **since** + *the start of the period* (**Monday / 9 o'clock**, etc.):

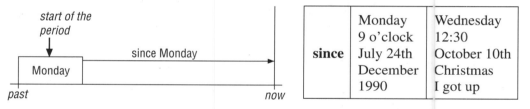

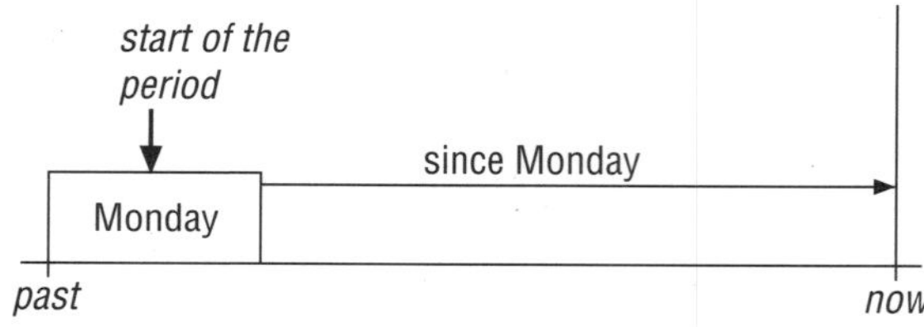

since	Monday 9 o'clock July 24th December 1990	Wednesday 12:30 October 10th Christmas I got up

Compare:

- Dan has been in Canada **since January**. (= from January to now)
  Dan has been in Canada **for six months**. (*not* "since six months")
- I've known her **since 1990**. (= from 1990 to now)
  I've known her **for a long time**. (*not* "since a long time")

B

ago = *before now*:

- Sue **started** her new job **two weeks ago**. (= two weeks before now)
- "When **did Tom go** out?" **"Ten minutes ago."** (= ten minutes before now)
- I **had** dinner **an hour ago**. (= an hour before now)
- Life **was** very different **a hundred years ago**.

We use **ago** with the *simple past* (**did/had/started**, etc.).

Compare **ago** and **for**:

- **When did she arrive** in Rio?
  She **arrived** in Rio **four days ago**.
- **How long has she been** in Rio?
  She **has been** in Rio **for four days**.

For the present perfect + **for** and **since**, see Unit 16.
For **from . . . to / until / since / for**, see Unit 91.

Exercises

17.1 Write **for** or **since**.

1. She's been in Rio since Monday.
2. She's been in Rio for four days.
3. Mike has been sick .... a long time. He's been in the hospital .... October.
4. My aunt has lived in the United States .... 15 years.
5. Nobody lives in those houses. They have been empty .... many years.
6. Mrs. Harris is in her office. She's been there .... 7 o'clock.
7. India has been an independent country .... 1947.
8. The bus is late. We've been waiting .... 20 minutes.

17.2 When was . . . ? Use **ago** in your answers.

1. your last vacation? 6 months ago
2. your last meal? ....
3. your 10th birthday? ....
4. the last time you were sick? ....
5. the last time you went to the movies? ....
6. the last time you drank coffee? ....
7. the last time you were in a car? ....
8. the last time you read a newspaper? ....

17.3 Answer the questions. Use the words in parentheses ( ) + **for** or **ago**.

1. (four days) When did she arrive in Rio? four days ago
2. (four days) How long has she been in Rio? for four days
3. (20 years) How long have they been married? ....
4. (20 years) When did they get married? ....
5. (ten minutes) When did Dan arrive? ....
6. (two months) When did you buy those shoes? ....
7. (two months) How long has she been studying English? ....
8. (a long time) How long have you known Pat? ....
9. (an hour) What time did you have lunch? ....

17.4 Complete the sentences with **for . . .** or **since . . .**

1. She is in Rio now. She arrived there four days ago. She has been there for four days.
2. Jack is here. He arrived here on Thursday. He has ....
3. It is raining. It started an hour ago. It's been ....
4. I know Sue. I first met Sue two years ago. I've ....
5. I have a camera. I bought it in 1992. I've ....
6. They are married. They got married six months ago. They've ....
7. Liz is studying medicine at the university. She started three years ago. She has ....

17.5 Write sentences about yourself. Begin with the words in parentheses ( ).

1. (I've lived) ....
2. (I've been) ....
3. (I've been studying) ....
4. (I've had) ....
5. (I've known) ....

UNIT 18 I have done (present perfect) and I did (simple past)

A

Sometimes you can use the *present perfect* or the *simple past* ("I **have lost**" or "I **lost**," "he **has gone**" or "he **went**," "they **have seen**" or "they **saw**," etc.):

- "Where's your key?" "**I've lost** it." *or* "I **lost** it."
- "Is Jack here?" "No, he**'s gone** home." *or* "He **went** home."

B

With a *finished time* (for example: **yesterday / last week / in 1988 / six months ago**), you can only use the past (*not* the present perfect):

Past +	*Finished time*
We **arrived** (*not* "we have arrived")	yesterday last week at 3 o'clock in 1986 six months ago

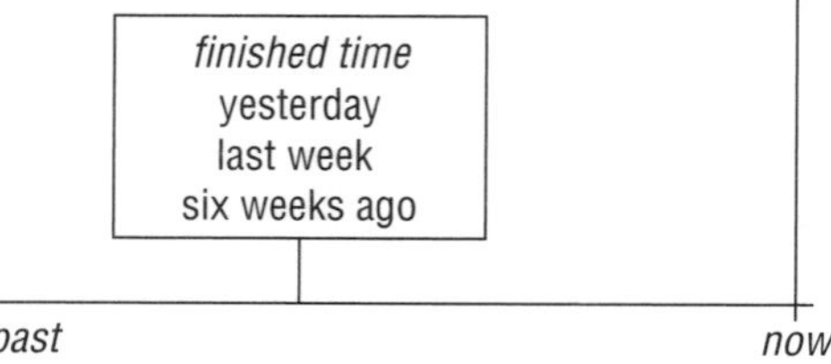

Do *not* use the present perfect (**have done / have lost / have been**, etc.) with a finished time:

- I **saw** Jack **yesterday**. (*not* "I have seen Jack yesterday.")
- Where **were** you **last night**? (*not* "Where have you been last night?")
- We **didn't take** a vacation **last year**. (*not* "We haven't taken")
- I **got** up **at 7:15**. I **washed**, **got** dressed, and then I **had** breakfast.
- William Shakespeare (1564–1616) **was** a writer. He **wrote** many plays and poems. (*not* ". . . has been a writer . . . has written many plays")

Use the *simple past* to ask **When?** or **What time?**:

- **When did** they **arrive**? (*not* "When have they arrived?")

C

Compare:

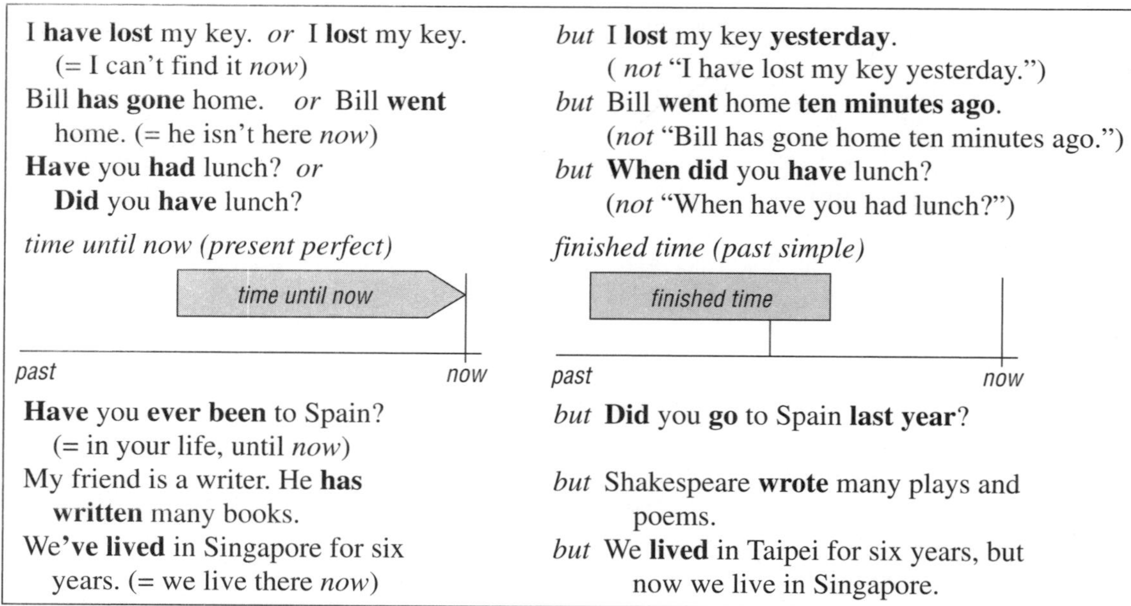

I **have lost** my key. *or* I **lost** my key. (= I can't find it *now*)	*but* I **lost** my key **yesterday**. (*not* "I have lost my key yesterday.")
Bill **has gone** home. *or* Bill **went** home. (= he isn't here *now*)	*but* Bill **went** home **ten minutes ago**. (*not* "Bill has gone home ten minutes ago.")
Have you **had** lunch? *or* **Did** you **have** lunch?	*but* **When did** you **have** lunch? (*not* "When have you had lunch?")
time until now (present perfect)	*finished time (past simple)*
Have you **ever been** to Spain? (= in your life, until *now*)	*but* **Did** you **go** to Spain **last year**?
My friend is a writer. He **has written** many books.	*but* Shakespeare **wrote** many plays and poems.
We**'ve lived** in Singapore for six years. (= we live there *now*)	*but* We **lived** in Taipei for six years, but now we live in Singapore.

For the present perfect, see Units 14–16. For the simple past, see Units 9–10.

Exercises

18.1 Use the words in parentheses ( ) to answer the questions.

1. Have you lost your key? — (yesterday) Yes, I lost it yesterday.
2. Have you seen Bob? — (ten minutes ago) Yes, I .... ten minutes ago.
3. Have you painted the room? — (last week) Yes, we .... it ....
4. Has Jane gone to France? — (on Friday) Yes, she ....
5. Have the children had dinner? — (at 7 o'clock) ....
6. Has he started his new job? — (yesterday) ....

18.2 Write questions with **When . . . ?** and **What time . . . ?**

1. They have arrived. — What time did they arrive ?
2. Bill has gone out. — What time .... ?
3. I've seen Ann. — When .... you .... ?
4. She's left her job. — When .... ?

18.3 In these sentences the verbs are underlined. Are they right or wrong? Correct the verbs that are wrong.

1. Tom arrived last week. RIGHT
2. Have you seen Pam last week? WRONG Did you see
3. I have finished my work. ....
4. I have finished my work at 2 o'clock. ....
5. When have you finished your work? ....
6. George has graduated from school three years ago. ....
7. "Where's Ann?" "She's gone to the movies." ....
8. Napoleon Bonaparte has died in 1821. ....
9. Have you ever been to Argentina? ....
10. I haven't seen you at the party on Saturday. ....
11. The weather has been very bad last week. ....

18.4 Put the verb in the present perfect (**I have done**) or the simple past (**I did**).

1. My friend is a writer. She has written (write) many books.
2. We didn't take (not/take) a vacation last year.
3. Did you see (you/see) Tony last week?
4. I .... (play) tennis yesterday afternoon.
5. What time .... (you/go) to bed last night?
6. .... (you/ever/be) to Australia?
7. I .... (wash) my hair before breakfast this morning.
8. When I was a child, I .... (not/like) sports.
9. Kathy loves traveling. She .... (visit) many countries.
10. John works in a bookstore. He .... (work) there for three years.
11. Last year we .... (go) to Thailand for vacation. We .... (stay) there for three weeks.

UNIT 19

it is done / it was done (passive)

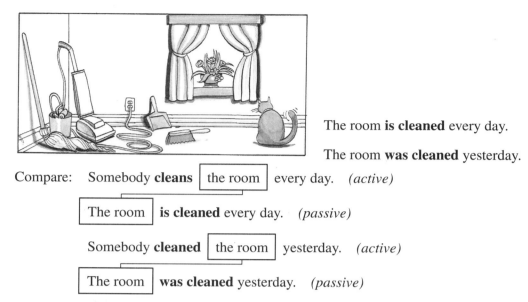

The room **is cleaned** every day.

The room **was cleaned** yesterday.

Compare: Somebody **cleans** the room every day. *(active)*

The room **is cleaned** every day. *(passive)*

Somebody **cleaned** the room yesterday. *(active)*

The room **was cleaned** yesterday. *(passive)*

A

The passive is:

				Past participle	
Present	**am/is/are**			clean**ed**	**done**
		(not)	+	export**ed**	**made**
Past	**was/were**			damag**ed**	**broken**

The past participle of *regular* verbs is **-ed** (clean**ed**/damag**ed**, etc.). For a list of *irregular* past participles (**made/seen**, etc.), see Appendixes 1 and 2.

- Butter **is made** from milk.
- Oranges **are imported** into Canada.
- How often **are** these rooms **cleaned**?
- I **am** never **invited** to parties.

- This house **was built** 100 years ago.
- These houses **were built** 100 years ago.
- When **was** the telephone **invented**?
- I **wasn't invited** to the party last week.
- Six people **were injured** in the accident yesterday.

Two trees **were blown** down in the storm last night.

B

We say **was/were** born:

- I **was born** in Los Angeles in 1974. (*not* "I am born")
- Where **were you born**?

C

passive + **by . . .** :

- We were woken up **by the noise**. (= The noise woke us up.)
- The telephone was invented **by Alexander Graham Bell** in 1876.
- My brother was bitten **by a dog** last week.

Exercises

19.1 Write sentences from the words in parentheses ( ). All the sentences are present.

1. (this room / clean / every day) *This room is cleaned every day.*
2. (how often / the room / clean?) *How often is the room cleaned* ?
3. (glass / make / from sand) Glass ....
4. (stamps / sell / in a post office) ....
5. (soccer / play / in most countries) ....
6. (this machine / not / use / very often) ....
7. (what language / speak / in Ethiopia?) What .... ?
8. (what / this machine / use / for?) .... ?

19.2 Write sentences from the words in parentheses ( ). All the sentences are past.

1. (the room / clean / yesterday) *The room was cleaned yesterday.*
2. (when / the room / clean?) *When was the room cleaned* ?
3. (this room / paint / last month) This room ....
4. (these houses / build / about 50 years ago) ....
5. (Ann's bicycle / steal / last week) ....
6. (three people / injure / in the accident) ....
7. (when / this church / build?) When .... ?
8. (when / television / invent?) .... ?
9. (how / the window / break?) .... ?
10. (anybody / injure / in the accident?) .... ?
11. (why / the letter / send / to the wrong address?) .... ?

19.3 Complete the sentences. Use the passive (present or past) of these verbs:

~~blow~~ build ~~clean~~ damage find invent make make show speak steal

1. The room *is cleaned* every day.
2. Two trees *were blown* down in the storm last night.
3. Paper .... from wood.
4. There was a fire at the hotel last week. Two rooms ....
5. Many different languages .... in India.
6. These houses are very old. They .... about 100 years ago.
7. Many foreign movies .... on television.
8. "Is this an old movie?" "Yes, it .... in 1949."
9. My car .... last week. The next day it .... by the police.
10. The transistor .... in 1948.

19.4 Where were they born?

1. (Tony / Rome) *Tony was born in Rome.*
2. (Noriko / Osaka) Noriko ....
3. (her parents / Tokyo) Her ....
4. (you / ???) I ....
5. (your mother / ???) My ....

UNIT 20

What are you doing tomorrow? (present for the future)

They **are playing** tennis **now**.

She **is playing** tennis **tomorrow**.

A

We use **am/is/are -ing** *(present continuous)* for something happening now.

- "Where are Bob and Sue?" "They**'re playing** tennis in the park."
- Please be quiet. **I'm working**.

We also use **am/is/are -ing** for the *future* (tomorrow / next week, etc.):

- Ann **is playing** tennis **tomorrow**.
- **I'm not working next week**.

I am doing something tomorrow = I have *arranged* to do something, I have a plan to do something:

- Carla **is going** to the dentist on Friday.
  (= she has an appointment with the dentist)
- They **are going** to a concert tomorrow night.
  (= they have tickets for the concert)
- **Are you meeting** Bill this evening?
  (= have you and Bill arranged to meet?)
- What **are you doing** this weekend?
- **I'm not going out** tonight. **I'm staying** home.

You can also say "**I'm going to do** something."
For **I am going to . . .**, see Unit 21.

B

Do *not* use the simple present (**I go / do you go**?, etc.) for arrangements:

- **I'm going** out this evening. (*not* "I go")
- **Are you going** out tonight? (*not* "do you go")
- Ann **isn't coming** to the party next week. (*not* "Ann doesn't come")

But we use the simple present for timetables, trains, programs, schedules, etc.:

- The concert **starts** at 7:30.
- What time **does the train leave**?

C

Study the difference:

- **I'm going** to a concert this evening.
  The concert **starts** at 7:30.

I'm going – *present continuous*: usually for people
The concert starts – *simple present*: for programs, trains, etc.

For the present continuous, see Units 3 and 4.

Exercises

20.1 Look at the pictures. What are these people doing next Friday?

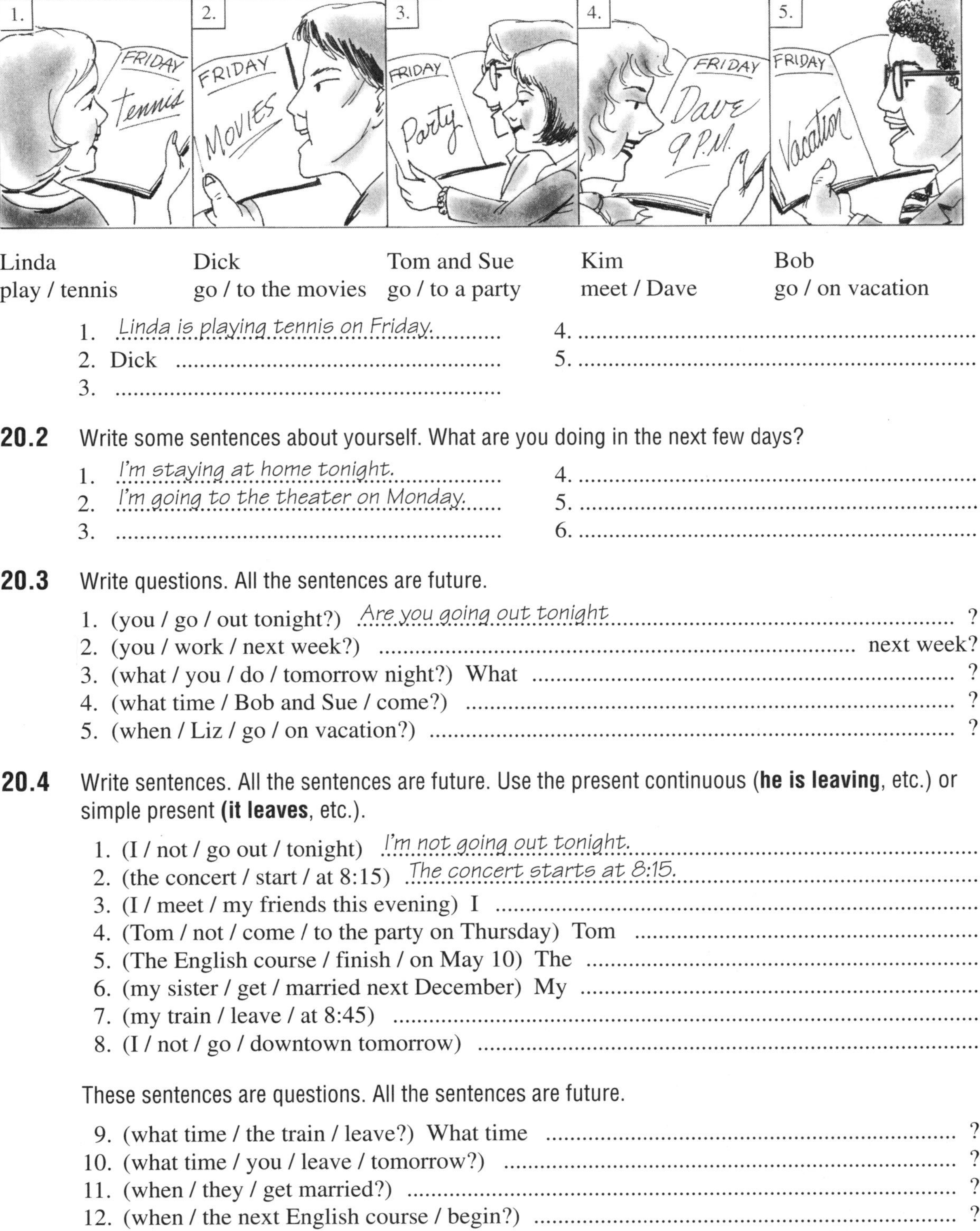

Linda	Dick	Tom and Sue	Kim	Bob
play / tennis	go / to the movies	go / to a party	meet / Dave	go / on vacation

1. *Linda is playing tennis on Friday.*
2. Dick ....
3. ....
4. ....
5. ....

20.2 Write some sentences about yourself. What are you doing in the next few days?

1. *I'm staying at home tonight.*
2. *I'm going to the theater on Monday.*
3. ....
4. ....
5. ....
6. ....

20.3 Write questions. All the sentences are future.

1. (you / go / out tonight?) *Are you going out tonight* ?
2. (you / work / next week?) .... next week?
3. (what / you / do / tomorrow night?) What .... ?
4. (what time / Bob and Sue / come?) .... ?
5. (when / Liz / go / on vacation?) .... ?

20.4 Write sentences. All the sentences are future. Use the present continuous (**he is leaving**, etc.) or simple present (**it leaves**, etc.).

1. (I / not / go out / tonight) *I'm not going out tonight.*
2. (the concert / start / at 8:15) *The concert starts at 8:15.*
3. (I / meet / my friends this evening) I ....
4. (Tom / not / come / to the party on Thursday) Tom ....
5. (The English course / finish / on May 10) The ....
6. (my sister / get / married next December) My ....
7. (my train / leave / at 8:45) ....
8. (I / not / go / downtown tomorrow) ....

These sentences are questions. All the sentences are future.

9. (what time / the train / leave?) What time .... ?
10. (what time / you / leave / tomorrow?) .... ?
11. (when / they / get married?) .... ?
12. (when / the next English course / begin?) .... ?

UNIT 21 I'm going to . . .

morning . . .

She **is going to watch** TV this evening.

A

We use **am/is/are going to . . .** for the *future*:

I	**am**		do . . .
he/she/it	**is** (not)	**going to**	drink . . .
we/you/they	**are**		watch . . .

am	I		buy . . . ?
is	he/she/it	**going to**	eat . . . ?
are	we/you/they		wear . . . ?

I am going to do something = I have already decided to do something, my intention is to do something:

- **I'm going to buy** some books tomorrow.
- Pam **is going to sell** her car.
- **I'm not going to have** breakfast this morning. I'm not hungry.
- What **are you going to wear** to the party on Saturday?
- "Your hair is dirty." "Yes, I know. **I'm going to wash** it."
- **Are you going to invite** John to your party?

B

You can say that something **is going to happen** when it is clear *now* that it is sure to happen:

- Look at the sky! It**'s going to rain.**
  (black clouds *now* → rain)
- Oh no! It's 9 o'clock and I'm not ready.
  I'm going to be late.
  (9 o'clock *now* and not ready → late)

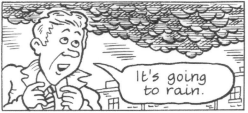

C

We also use the *present continuous* (**I am -ing**) for the future, usually for arrangements:

- I **am playing** tennis with Jack tomorrow.

See also Unit 20.

Exercises

21.1 What are these people going to do?

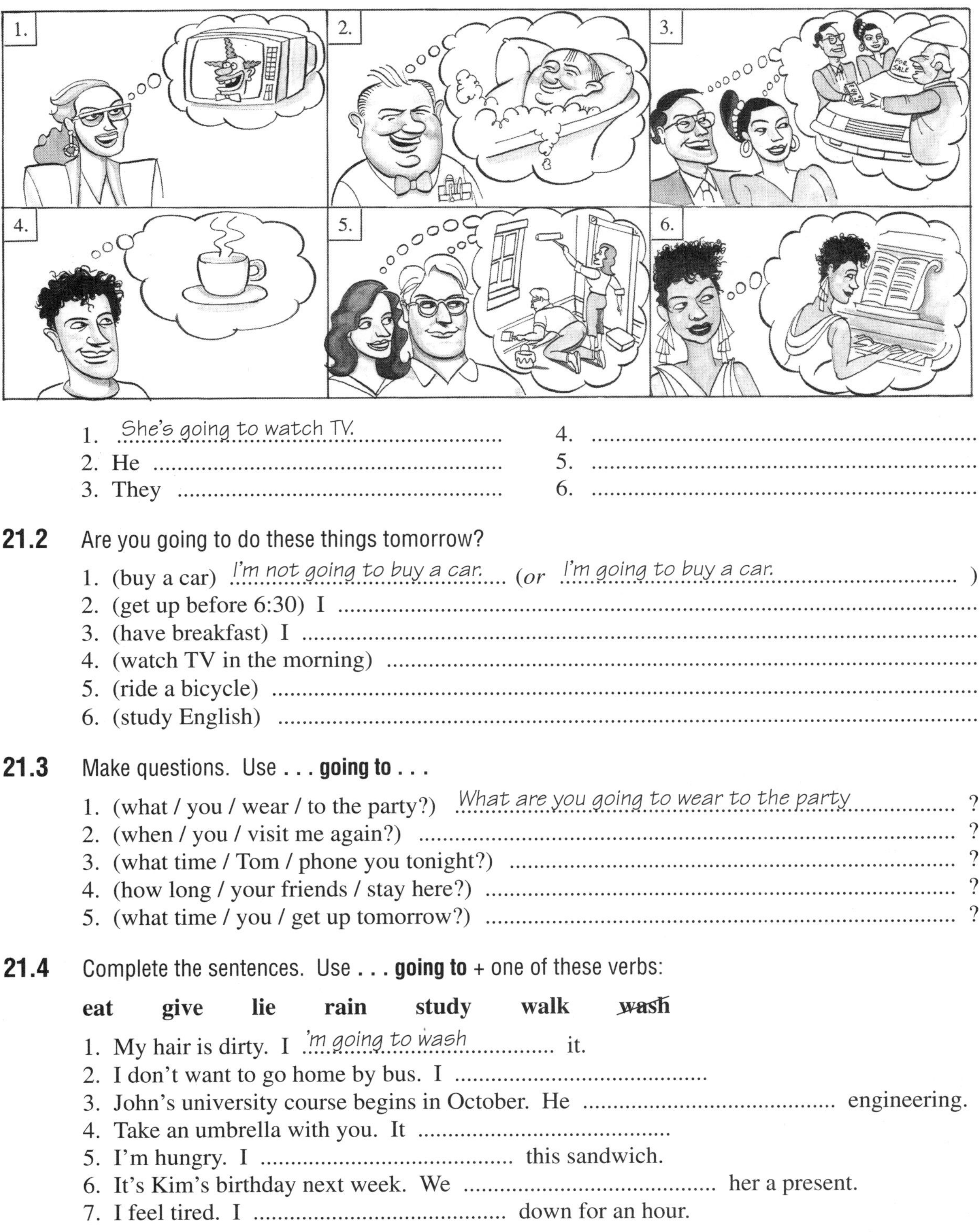

1. *She's going to watch TV.*
2. He ....
3. They ....
4. ....
5. ....
6. ....

21.2 Are you going to do these things tomorrow?

1. (buy a car) *I'm not going to buy a car.* (*or* *I'm going to buy a car.*)
2. (get up before 6:30) I ....
3. (have breakfast) I ....
4. (watch TV in the morning) ....
5. (ride a bicycle) ....
6. (study English) ....

21.3 Make questions. Use . . . **going to** . . .

1. (what / you / wear / to the party?) *What are you going to wear to the party* ?
2. (when / you / visit me again?) .... ?
3. (what time / Tom / phone you tonight?) .... ?
4. (how long / your friends / stay here?) .... ?
5. (what time / you / get up tomorrow?) .... ?

21.4 Complete the sentences. Use . . . **going to** + one of these verbs:

eat give lie rain study walk ~~wash~~

1. My hair is dirty. I *'m going to wash* it.
2. I don't want to go home by bus. I ....
3. John's university course begins in October. He .... engineering.
4. Take an umbrella with you. It ....
5. I'm hungry. I .... this sandwich.
6. It's Kim's birthday next week. We .... her a present.
7. I feel tired. I .... down for an hour.

will

Bill **is** 24 years old now.

Last year he **was** 23.

Next year he **will be** 25.

A

will + *base form* (will **be** / will **win** / will **come**, etc.):

Positive and negative		
I/we/you/they he/she/it	**will ('ll)** **will not (won't)**	**be** **win** **come** **eat**

Question		
will	I/we/you/they he/she/it	**be . . . ?** **win . . . ?** **come . . . ?** **eat . . . ?**

will = **'ll**: **I'll** (= I will) / you**'ll** / she**'ll**, etc.
will not = **won't**: I **won't** (= I will not) / you **won't** / it **won't**, etc.

B

We use **will** for the *future* (**tomorrow / next week**, etc.):

- She travels a lot. Today she is in New York. Tomorrow she**'ll be** in Los Angeles. Next week she**'ll be** in Tokyo.
- Phone me this evening. **I'll be** home.
- Throw the bread on the ground. The birds **will eat** it.
- We**'ll** probably **go** out this evening.
- **Will you be** home this evening?

- I **won't be** here tomorrow. (= I will not be here)
- Don't drink coffee before you go to bed. You **won't sleep**.

We often say **I think . . . will . . .** :

- **I think** Linda **will pass** the exam.
- **I don't think** it **will rain** this afternoon.
- **Do you think** the exam **will be** difficult?

But do *not* use **will** for things you have *already arranged* to do or *decided* to do:

- We**'re going** to the theater on Saturday. (*not* "we will go")
- **Are you working** tomorrow? (*not* "will you work")

See also Units 20–21.
For **will**, see also Unit 23.

Exercise

22.1 Helen is going on a South American tour next month. Look at her plans. Where will she be on these dates?

6 – 9	Buenos Aires
9 – 11	Montevideo
11 – 15	Lima
16 – 22	Rio de Janeiro
23 – 28	Caracas

1. (8th) *She'll be in Buenos Aires.*
2. (10th) She ....
3. (25th) ....
4. (14th) ....
5. (20th) ....

22.2 Where will *you* be? Write sentences about yourself. Use **I'll be . . . / I'll probably be . . . / I don't know where I'll be.**

1. (tomorrow at 10 o'clock) *I'll probably be at the beach.*
   (*or* *I'll be at work.* *or* *I don't know where I'll be.*)
2. (one hour from now) I ....
3. (at midnight) ....
4. (at 3 o'clock tomorrow afternoon) ....
5. (two years from now) ....

22.3 Write the negative.

1. You'll sleep. *You won't sleep.*
2. I'll forget. I ....
3. It will happen. ....
4. You'll find it. ....

22.4 Write sentences with **I think . . .** All the sentences are future.

1. (Barbara / pass the exam) *I think Barbara will pass the exam.*
2. (Jack / win the game) I think ....
3. (Sue / like her present) ....
4. (the weather / be nice tomorrow) ....

Now write two sentences with **I don't think . . .**

5. (they / get married) I don't ....
6. (I / be home this evening) ....

22.5 The verbs in these sentences are underlined. Which are right? Study Unit 20 before you do this exercise.

1. ~~We'll go~~ / We are going to the theater tonight. We have tickets.
   (We are going is *right*.)
2. "What will you do / are you doing tomorrow evening?" "Nothing. I'm free."
3. I'll go / I'm going away tomorrow morning. My train is at 8:40.
4. I'm sure he'll lend / he's lending you some money. He's very rich.
5. "Why are you putting on your coat?" "I'll go out / I'm going out."
6. Do you think Pat will phone / is phoning us tonight?
7. She can't meet us on Saturday. She'll work / She's working.

UNIT 23

I'll . . . shall I . . . ? shall we . . . ?

A

You can use **I'll . . .** (= I will) when you *offer* or *decide* to do something:

- "My suitcase is very heavy." "**I'll carry** it for you."
- "**I'll call** you tomorrow, okay?" "Okay. Bye."

We often say **I think I'll / I don't think I'll . . .** when we decide to do something:

- I'm tired. **I think I'll go** to bed early tonight.
- It's a nice day. **I think I'll sit** in the sun.
- It's raining. **I don't think I'll go** out.

Don't use the simple present (**I go / I call**, etc.) in sentences like these:

- **I'll call** you tomorrow, okay? (*not* "I call you")
- I think **I'll go** to bed early. (*not* "I go to bed")

Don't use **I'll . . .** for something you decided *before*:

- **I'm working** tomorrow. (*not* "I'll work")
- **I'm going to watch** TV tonight. (*not* "I'll watch")
- What **are you doing** this weekend? (*not* "what will you do")

See Units 20–21.

B

Shall I . . . ? / Shall we . . . ?

Shall I / Shall we . . . ? = Do you think this is a good thing to do? Do you think this is a good idea?

- It's warm in this room. **Shall I open** the window?
- "**Shall I call** you this evening?" "Okay."
- I'm going to a party tonight. What **shall I wear**?

- It's a nice day. **Shall we go** for a walk?
- Where **shall we go** for our vacation this year?
- "Let's go out this evening." "Okay. What time **shall we meet**?"

For **will**, see also Unit 22.

Exercises

23.1 Complete the sentences. Use **I will (I'll)** + one of these verbs:

~~carry~~ do eat send show sit stay

1. My suitcase is very heavy. — *I'll carry* .... it for you.
2. Enjoy your vacation. — Thank you. I .... you a postcard.
3. I don't want this banana. — Well, I'm hungry. .... it.
4. Are you coming with me? — No, I don't think so. .... here.
5. Did you call Jack? — Oh no, I forgot. .... it now.
6. Do you want a chair? — No, it's okay. .... on the floor.
7. How do you use this camera? — Give it to me and .... you.

23.2 Complete the sentences. Use **I think I'll . . .** or **I don't think I'll . . .** + one of these verbs:

buy ~~**go**~~ **have** **play**

1. It's cold. *I don't think I'll go* .... out.
2. I'm hungry. I think .... something to eat.
3. I feel tired. I don't .... tennis.
4. This camera is too expensive. I .... it.

23.3 Are the underlined words right or wrong? Correct the sentences that are wrong.

1. I phone you tomorrow morning, okay? *WRONG I'll phone*
2. I phone my sister every Friday. *RIGHT*
3. I haven't done the shopping yet. I do it later. ....
4. "I don't want to drive." "Okay, I drive." ....
5. "How do you usually get to work?" "I drive." ....
6. "I don't have any money." "I lend you some." ....

23.4 The verbs in these sentences are underlined. Which is right?

1. "I think it's too warm in this room." "Okay. I'll open / ~~I'm going to open~~ the window." (I'll open is *right.*)
2. "I'd like something to drink." "Me too. I'll make / I'm going to make some coffee."
3. "Where are you going?" "To the kitchen. I'll make / I'm going to make some coffee."
4. Pat will buy / is going to buy a new car. She told me last week.
5. "When you see Tom, can you ask him to phone me?" "Okay, I'll ask / I'm going to ask him."
6. "What would you like to drink? Tea or coffee?" "I'll have / I'm going to have tea, please."
7. "Will you do / Are you doing anything this evening?" "Yes, I'll go / I'm going out with some frien
8. Don't take that newspaper away. I'll read / I'm going to read it.

23.5 Write sentences with **Shall we . . . ?** Choose words from box A and box B.

A **what** ~~**what time**~~ **where** **who**	*B* **buy** **go** **invite** ~~**meet**~~

1. Let's go out tonight. — Okay. *What time shall we meet* .... ?
2. Let's take a vacation. — Okay. .... ?
3. Let's spend some money — Okay. .... ?
4. Let's have a party. — Okay. .... ?

UNIT 24

can and could

He **can play** the piano.

A

can + *base form* (can **do** / can **play** / can **come**, etc.):

Positive and negative		
I/we/you/they he/she/it	**can** **can't** (**cannot**)	**do** **play** **come** **see**

Question		
can	I/we/you/they he/she/it	**do . . .** ? **play . . .** ? **come . . .** ? **see . . .** ?

B

I can do something = I *know how* to do it or *it is possible* for me to do it:

- I **can play** the piano. My brother **can play** the piano too.
- Ann **can speak** Portuguese, but she **can't speak** Spanish.
- **"Can you swim?"** "Yes, but not very well."
- "**Can you change** a ten-dollar bill?" "I'm sorry, **I can't.**"
- Mary and Andy **can't come** to the party next week.

C

In the *past* (**yesterday / last week**, etc.):

can (do) →	**could** (do)
can't (do) →	**couldn't** (do)

- When I was young, I **could run** very fast.
- Before she came to Canada, she **couldn't speak** English. Now she **can speak** English very well.
- I was tired last night, but I **couldn't sleep**.
- Mary and Andy **couldn't come** to the party last week.

We use **Can you . . . ?** *or* **Could you . . . ?** when we ask people to do things:

- "**Can** (*or* **Could**) **you open** the door, please?" "Sure."
- **Can** (*or* **Could**) **you tell** me the time, please?

We use **Can I . . . ?** when we ask if it is okay to do something:

- *(in a restaurant)* "**Can I take** your order?" "Yes, we're ready."
- *(on the phone)* Hello. **Can I speak** to Don, please?
  You can also say **May I . . . ?** See Unit 25.

We use **Can I have . . . ?** to ask for something:

- *(in a store)* **Can I have** these postcards, please?

Exercises

24.1 Ask someone if he or she can do these things:

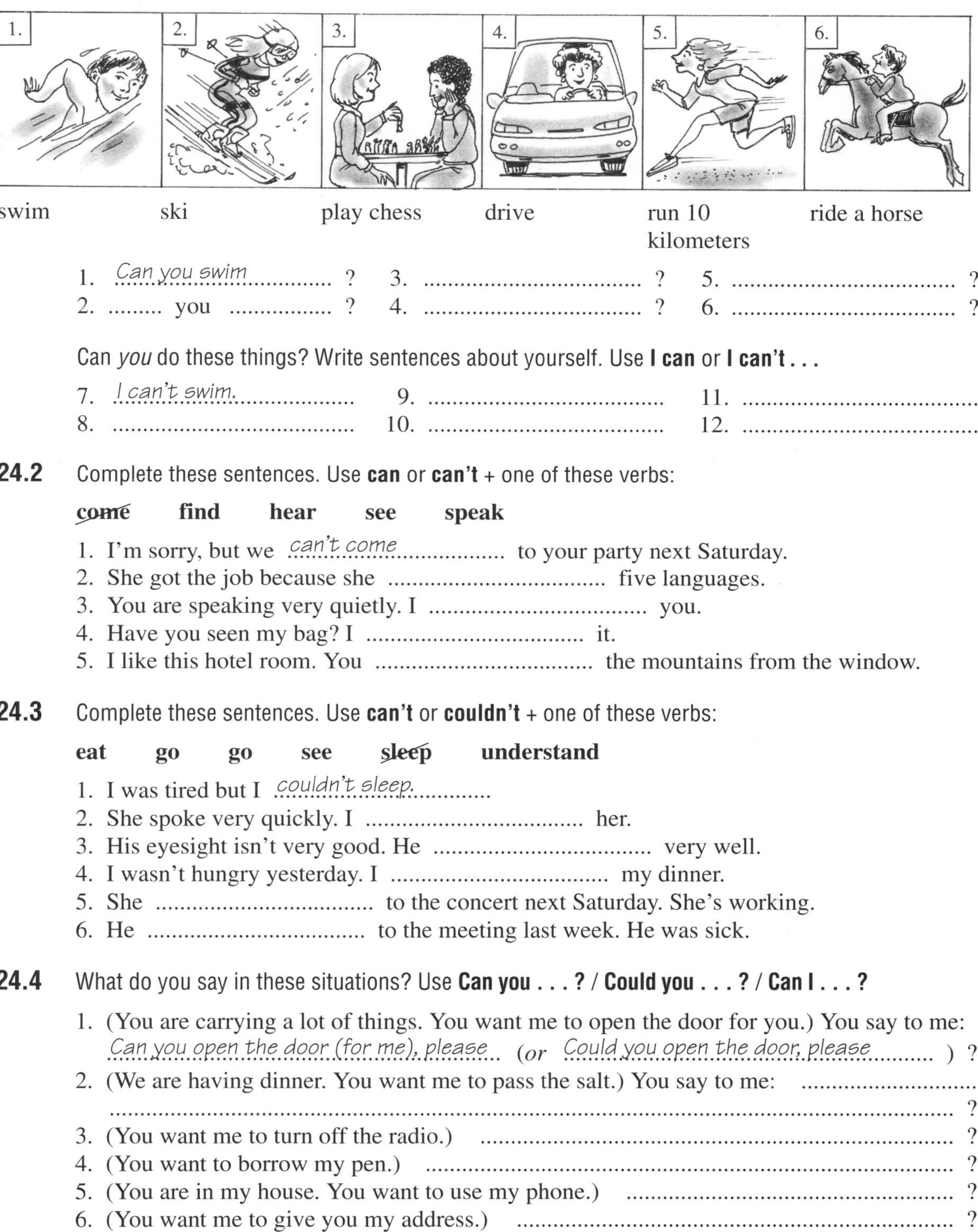

swim	ski	play chess	drive	run 10 kilometers	ride a horse

1. Can you swim .... ?
2. .... you .... ?
3. .... ?
4. .... ?
5. .... ?
6. .... ?

Can *you* do these things? Write sentences about yourself. Use **I can** or **I can't . . .**

7. I can't swim. ....
8. ....
9. ....
10. ....
11. ....
12. ....

24.2 Complete these sentences. Use **can** or **can't** + one of these verbs:

~~come~~ find hear see speak

1. I'm sorry, but we can't come .... to your party next Saturday.
2. She got the job because she .... five languages.
3. You are speaking very quietly. I .... you.
4. Have you seen my bag? I .... it.
5. I like this hotel room. You .... the mountains from the window.

24.3 Complete these sentences. Use **can't** or **couldn't** + one of these verbs:

eat go go see ~~sleep~~ understand

1. I was tired but I couldn't sleep. ....
2. She spoke very quickly. I .... her.
3. His eyesight isn't very good. He .... very well.
4. I wasn't hungry yesterday. I .... my dinner.
5. She .... to the concert next Saturday. She's working.
6. He .... to the meeting last week. He was sick.

24.4 What do you say in these situations? Use **Can you . . . ? / Could you . . . ? / Can I . . . ?**

1. (You are carrying a lot of things. You want me to open the door for you.) You say to me:
Can you open the door (for me), please (*or* Could you open the door, please ....) ?
2. (We are having dinner. You want me to pass the salt.) You say to me: ....
.... ?
3. (You want me to turn off the radio.) .... ?
4. (You want to borrow my pen.) .... ?
5. (You are in my house. You want to use my phone.) .... ?
6. (You want me to give you my address.) .... ?

UNIT 25

may and **might**

I **may go** to Paris.
(= Perhaps I will go to Paris.)

It **might rain**.
(= Perhaps it will rain.)

A

may *or* **might** + *base form* (may **go** / might **go** / may **play** / might **play**, etc.):

I/we/you/they he/she/it	**may** (not) **might** (not)	**be** **go** **play** **come**

B

may/might = it is possible that something will happen.
You can use **may** *or* **might**:

- I **may go** to the movies tonight.
  or I **might go** to the movies tonight. (= perhaps I will go)
- "When is Pam going to phone you?" "I don't know. She **may phone** this afternoon."
- Take an umbrella with you. It **might rain**.
- "Do you think Jack will come to the party?" "I'm not sure. **He may**."
  (= He may come.)
- "Are you going out tonight?" **"I might."** (= I might go out.)

Study the difference:

- **I'm playing** tennis tomorrow. *(sure)*
  I **may play** tennis tomorrow. *(possible)*
- Barbara **is going** to France next week. *(sure)*
  Barbara **might go** to France next week. *(possible)*

C

The negative is **may not** *or* **might not**:

- I **might not go** to work tomorrow. (= perhaps I will not go)
- Sue **may not come** to the party. (= perhaps she will not come)

D

May I . . . ? = Is it okay to do something?:

- **May I smoke?** (= Is it okay if I smoke? / Can I smoke?)
- "**May I sit** here?" "Yes, of course."

Exercises

25.1 Write sentences with **may** or **might**.

1. (perhaps I will go to the movies) *I may go to the movies.* (*or* *I might go to the movies.*)
2. (perhaps I will see Tom tomorrow) I ....
3. (perhaps Kim will be late) Kim ....
4. (perhaps it will snow today) It ....
5. (perhaps I will wear my new jeans) I ....

These sentences are negative.

6. (perhaps they will not come) ....
7. (perhaps I will not go out tonight) I ....

25.2 Somebody is asking you about your plans. You have some ideas but you are not sure. Use **may** or **might** + one of these:

?	**go away**	**some shoes**	**~~Spain~~**	**fish**	?
	this evening	**to a restaurant**	**tomorrow**		

You

1. Where are you going for your vacation next year? — *I'm not sure yet. I might go to Spain.*
2. Where are you going tonight? — I don't know yet. I ....
3. When will you see Ann again? — I'm not sure. ....
4. What are you going to buy when you go shopping? — I haven't decided yet. ....
5. What are you doing this weekend? — ....
6. When are you going to phone John? — ....
7. What are you going to have for dinner tonight? — ....

25.3 What are you doing tomorrow? Write *true* sentences about yourself. Use:

I'm (not) -ing or **I'm (not) going to . . .** or **I may . . .** or **I might . . .**

1. (watch television) *I'm not going to watch television.*
2. (write a letter) *I might write a letter.*
3. (get up early) I ....
4. (go to the movies) ....
5. (take a bath or shower) ....
6. (buy a newspaper) ....
7. (play tennis) ....
8. (make some telephone calls) ....

UNIT 26

have to . . .

A

I have to do something = it is necessary for me to do it *or* I am obliged to do it:

I/we/you/they **have** he/she/it **has**	**to do . . .** **to work . . .** **to go . . .** **to wear . . .**

I HAVE TO TAKE MY MEDICINE FOUR TIMES A DAY.
4 times a day

- I'll be late for work tomorrow. I **have to go** to the dentist. (= it is necessary for me to go to the dentist)
- Sue starts work at 7:00, so she **has to get** up at 6:00.
- You **have to pass** a test before you can get a driver's license.

B

The past (**yesterday / last week**, etc.) is **had to . . .**:

- I was late for work yesterday. I **had to go** to the dentist.
- There was no bus, so we **had to walk** home.

C

In *questions* and *negatives* we use **do/does** *(present)* and **did** *(past)*:

	Questions	*Negative*
present	**do** I/we/you/they **does** he/she/it } **have to . . . ?**	I/we/you/they **don't** he/she/it **doesn't** } **have to . . .**
past	**did** { I/we/you/they he/she/it } **have to . . . ?**	I/we/you/they he/she/it } **didn't have to . . .**

- What time **do you have to get** up tomorrow morning?
- **Does Sue have to work** on Saturdays?
- Why **did they have to leave** the party early?

I **don't have to** do (something) = it is *not* necessary to do it:

- I'm not working tomorrow, so I **don't have to get** up early.
- Mike **doesn't have to work** very hard. He has an easy job.
- We **didn't have to wait** very long. The bus came right on time.

D

must

You can also use **must** to say it is necessary to do something:

- The windows are very dirty. I **must clean** them. (*or* I have to clean them.)
- It's a fantastic movie. You **must see** it. (*or* You have to see it.)

We use **have to** more often than **must**, especially in spoken English.

Exercises

26.1 Complete the sentences. Use **have to** or **has to** + one of these verbs:

hit **read** **speak** **take** **travel** **~~wear~~**

1. My eyesight isn't very good. I *have to wear* .... glasses.
2. At the end of the course, all the students .... a test.
3. Mary is studying literature. She .... a lot of books.
4. He doesn't understand much English, so I .... to him very slowly.
5. Sam is often away from home. He .... a lot in his job.
6. In tennis you .... the ball over the net.

26.2 Complete the sentences. Use **have to** or **had to** + one of these verbs:

answer **buy** **change** **get** **go** **~~walk~~**

1. There were no buses yesterday evening. We *had to walk* .... home.
2. I'm going to bed early tonight. I .... up early tomorrow.
3. It's late. I .... now. I'll see you tomorrow.
4. I went to the supermarket after work because I .... some food.
5. This bus doesn't go downtown. You .... at Maple Street.
6. We took an exam yesterday. We .... six questions out of ten.

26.3 Write questions. Some are present and some are past.

1.	I have to get up early tomorrow.	What time *do you have to get up* .... ?
2.	They had to leave early.	Why .... ?
3.	We had to pay a lot of money.	How much .... you .... ?
4.	I have to go home now.	Why .... ?
5.	He had to wait a long time.	How long .... ?
6.	Sue has to work this evening.	Why .... ?

26.4 Write sentences with **don't / doesn't / didn't have to . . .**

1. Why are you going home now? You *don't have to go home now.* ....
2. Why is she waiting? She doesn't ....
3. Why did you get up so early? You ....
4. Why do you want to decide now? We ....
5. Why does he work so hard? He ....

26.5 Write some things that *you* have to do or had to do.

1. (every day) *I have to travel ten miles to work every day.* ....
2. (every day) .... every day.
3. (tomorrow) ....
4. (last week) ....
5. (when I was younger) ....

should

YOU SHOULDN'T WATCH TV SO MUCH.

should + *base form* (should **do** / should **write**, etc.):

I/we/you/they he/she/it	**should** **shouldn't**	**do** **go** **stop** **write**

A

(Someone) **should** do something = It is a good thing to do or the right thing to do:

- Tom **should go** to bed earlier. He usually goes to bed very late, and he's always tired.
- It's a good movie. You **should go** and see it.
- When you play tennis, you **should** always **watch** the ball.
- Which way **should** we **go**? Left or right.

B

shouldn't (*or* **should not**) = It's *not* a good thing to do or it's not the right thing to do:

- Tom **shouldn't go** to bed so late.
- You work all the time. You **shouldn't work** so hard.

C

We often use **think** with **should**:

I think . . . should . . . :

- **I think** Ann **should buy** some new clothes. (= I think it's a good idea)
- It's late. **I think** we **should go** home now.
- "Should I buy this coat?" "Yes, **I think** you **should**."

I don't think . . . should . . . :

- **I don't think** you **should work** so hard. (= I don't think it's a good idea)
- **I don't think** the police **should carry** guns.

Do you think . . . should . . . ?:

- **Do you think** I **should buy** this jacket?
- What time **do you think** we **should go** home?

DO YOU THINK I SHOULD BUY THIS HAT?

D

ought

ought to = **should**:

- I **ought to go** home now. (= I should go home now.)
- It's a good movie. You **ought to see** it. (= You should see it.)

Remember that we say "**ought to** do" (with **to**), but "**should** do" (without **to**):

- Ann **ought to buy** some new clothes. (*not* "Ann ought buy")

Exercises

27.1 Complete the sentences. Use **should** + one of these verbs:

brush **go** **read** **visit** ~~**watch**~~ **wear**

1. When you play tennis, you *should watch* the ball.
2. You look tired. You .... to bed.
3. You .... your teeth after every meal.
4. The city museum is very interesting. You .... it.
5. When you are driving, you .... a seat belt.
6. It's a good book. You .... it.

27.2 Make sentences with **shouldn't . . . so . . .**

1. (you watch too much TV) *You shouldn't watch TV so much.*
2. (you work too hard) You .... so hard.
3. (he eats too much) He .... much.
4. (she watches TV too often) She ....
5. (you talk too much) You ....

27.3 Ask a friend for advice. Make questions with **Do you think I should . . . ?**

1. (buy this jacket?) *Do you think I should buy this jacket* ?
2. (buy a new camera?) Do you think .... ?
3. (get a new job?) Do .... ?
4. (take an English course?) .... ?
5. (learn to drive?) .... ?

27.4 Write sentences with **I think . . . should . . .** Choose from:

take a vacation **go to college** **sell it** ~~**go home now**~~ **go to the doctor**

1. It's late. *I think we should go home now.*
2. Your car is very old. I think you ....
3. They need a rest. I ....
4. He looks terrible. ....
5. She's very intelligent. ....

Write sentences with **I don't think . . . should . . .** Choose from:

stay there ~~**phone them now**~~ **go to work today** **get married**

6. It's very late. *I don't think you should phone them now.*
7. They're too young. I don't think ....
8. That hotel is too expensive for us. I ....
9. You're still sick. ....

27.5 What do you think? Write sentences with **should**.

1. I think everybody should *learn another language.*
2. I think .... should ....
3. I don't think ....
4. I think I should ....

UNIT 28 Would you like . . . ?

A

Would you like . . . ? = Do you want . . . ?
We use **Would you like . . . ?** to *offer* things:

- "**Would you like** some coffee?"
  "Yes, please."
- "**Would you like** a cigarette?"
  "No, thank you. I don't smoke."
- "What **would you like**, tea or coffee?"
  "Tea, please."

We use **Would you like to . . . ?** to *invite* someone:

- **Would you like to come** to a party?
- "**Would you like to have** dinner with me on Sunday?"
  "Yes, **I'd love to**." (= I would love to have dinner with you.)
- Where **would you like to go** this evening?

B

I'd like (**I would like**) is a polite way of saying "I want" :

- *(in a restaurant)* **I'd like fish**, please.
- I'm thirsty. **I'd like** a drink.
- **I'd like to watch** the news on television.

C

Study the difference:

Would you like . . . ? / I'd like . . .

"**Would you like** some tea?" =
Do you want some tea? *(an offer)*

Do you like . . . ? / I like . . .

"**Do you like** tea?" =
Do you enjoy drinking tea?"

- "**Would you like to go** to the movies tonight?" *(tonight)*
  "Yes, I'd love to go."

but "**Do you like to go** to the movies?" *(in general)*
"Yes, I go to the movies a lot."

- "**I'd like** an orange. (= I want an orange now.)

but **I like** oranges. *(in general)*

For **Do you like going . . . ?** and **Would you like to go . . . ?**, see Unit 47.

Exercises

28.1 Look at the pictures. What are the people saying? Use **Would you like . . . ?** + one of these:

an apple **a cookie** **some cake** **some cheese** ~~**a cup of coffee**~~ **a sandwich**

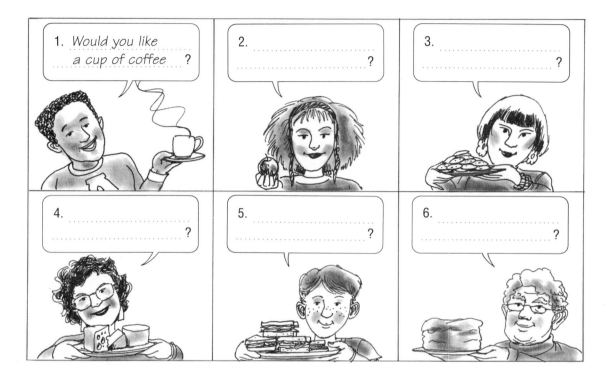

1. *Would you like a cup of coffee* ?
2. .... ?
3. .... ?
4. .... ?
5. .... ?
6. .... ?

28.2 Invite people to do things. Use **Would you like to . . . ?**

1. (invite someone to come to a party next Friday)
   Would you like to come to a party next Friday .... ?
2. (invite someone to go to a concert on Sunday)
   .... on Sunday?
3. (invite someone to play tennis tomorrow)
   .... ?
4. (invite someone to dance) .... ?

28.3 Choose the correct form.

1 "~~Do you like~~ / Would you like a glass of juice?" "Yes, please."
  (Would you like is *right.*)
2. "Do you like / Would you like a banana?" "No, thank you."
3. "Do you like / Would you like bananas?" "Yes, I love them."
4. "What do you like / would you like to drink?" "Water, please."
5. "Do you like / Would you like to go for a walk?" "Not now. Maybe later."
6. I like / I'd like ice cream, but I don't eat it very often.
7. I'm tired. I like / I'd like to go to sleep.
8. "Do you like / Would you like something to eat?" "No, thanks. I'm not hungry."

UNIT 29

I'd rather . . .

Would you like to sit here?
No, thanks. I'd rather sit on the floor.

Ann likes to sit on the floor. She doesn't want to sit on a chair. So she says:

I'd rather sit on the floor. (= I would prefer to sit on the floor.)

I'd rather . . . = I **would** rather.

A

I **would rather** (do something) = I would prefer (to do something):

Positive	*Negative*	*Question*
I'd rather (I **would rather**) { do . . . / stay . . . / have . . . / be . . .	**I'd rather not** (I **would rather not**) { do . . . / stay . . . / have . . . / be . . .	**would** you **rather** { do . . .? / stay . . . ? / have . . . ? / be . . . ?

- I don't really want to go out. I'**d rather stay** home. (= I'd prefer to stay home)
- "Shall we go now?" "No, not yet. I'**d rather wait** until later."
- I want to go now but Tom **would rather wait** until later.

- I'm feeling tired. I'**d rather not go** out this evening. (= I'd prefer not to go out)
- Sue is feeling tired. She'**d rather not go** out this evening.
- We're not hungry. We'**d rather not eat** yet.
- "Do you want to go out this evening?" "I'**d rather not**." (= I'd rather not go out)

- "**Would you rather have** milk or juice?" "Juice, please."
- What **would you rather do**? Go to the movies or watch a video at home?

B

We say "I'd rather **do** something" (*not* "to do something"):

- I'd rather **sit** on the floor. (*not* "I'd rather to sit")
- Sue would rather not **go** out. (*not* "would rather not to go")

But we say "I'd **prefer to do** something":

- I'd prefer **to sit** on the floor.
- Sue would prefer not **to go** out.

See also Unit 47.

C

You can say **"I'd rather do . . . than . . ."**:

- **I'd rather** go out **than** stay home.
- **I'd rather** have a dog **than** a cat.
- We'**d rather** go to the movies **than** watch a video at home.

Exercises

29.1 Look at the pictures and complete B's sentences. Use **I'd rather . . .**

A
B
1.
Would you like to sit here?
No, thanks. I'd rather sit on the floor.
2.
Do you want to watch TV?
No, I .... my book.
3.
Would you like some tea?
TEA
TEA
COFFEE
Well, ... if you have some.
4.
Shall we go out now?
.... until it stops raining.

29.2 Answer these questions about yourself. Use **I'd rather . . .**

1. Which would you like to be: a bus driver or an airline pilot? *I'd rather be a bus driver.*
2. Which would you like to be: a journalist or a school teacher? ....
3. Where would you like to live: in a big city or a small town? ....
4. Which would you like to have: a helicopter or a yacht? ....
5. Which would you like to study: electronics or philosophy? ....

29.3 Complete these questions. Use **would you rather . . .**

1. Do you want to go out or *would you rather stay home* ?
2. Shall we have dinner now or .... later?
3. Would you like a glass of water or .... ?
4. Do you want to go to the movies or .... ?

29.4 Complete the sentences with a verb. Sometimes you need **to**.

1. I'd rather *stay* home this evening. I'd prefer not *to go* out.
2. Shall we walk home or would you rather .... a taxi?
3. Do you want me to come with you or would you prefer .... alone?
4. Mary doesn't want to go to college. She'd rather .... a job.
5. "Can I help you with your suitcase?" "No, thank you. I'd rather .... it myself."
6. I'd rather not .... him. I'd prefer .... him a letter.

29.5 Write sentences about yourself with **I'd rather . . . than . . .** Use the verb in parentheses ( ).

1. (be) *I'd rather be an airline pilot than a bus driver.*
2. (be) ....
3. (have) ....
4. (live) ....
5. (travel) ....

UNIT 30

Do this! Don't do that! Let's do this!

A

We use the *base form* (**come/go/do/wait/be**, etc.) when we tell someone to do something:

- "**Come** here and **look** at this!" "What is it?"
- I don't like you. **Go** away!
- Please **wait** for me!
- **Be** quiet. I'm working.
- Goodbye. **Have** a nice time!

The negative is **don't . . .** (**don't come/go/do/wait/be**, etc.). **Don't** = do not:

- **Stay** here! Please **don't go**!
- **Don't be** silly!
- **Be** careful! **Don't fall.**

B

You can say **Let's . . .** when you want people to do things *with you*:

- It's a nice day. **Let's go** out. (= *you and I* can go out)

Let's = let us. We use **let's** + *base form* (**let's go/do/have**, etc.):

- Come on! **Let's dance.**
- Are you ready? **Let's go!**
- **Let's have** fish for dinner tonight.
- "Shall we go out tonight?" "No, I'm tired. **Let's stay** home."

C

The negative is **let's not . . .** :

- It's cold. **Let's not go** out. Let's stay home.
- **Let's not have** fish for dinner. Let's have chicken.

Exercises

30.1 Look at the pictures. What are the people saying? Sometimes the sentence is positive (**go**/**eat**, etc.) and sometimes it is negative (**don't go** / **don't eat**, etc.). Use these verbs:

buy ~~**come**~~ **drink** **make** **sit** **sleep** **smile** **turn**

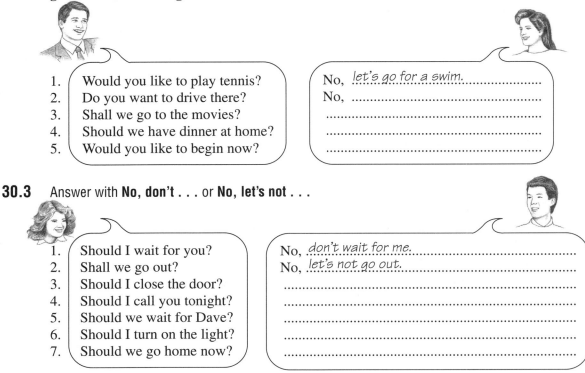

1. *Come* in!
2. It's too expensive. .... it.
3. .... please!
4. .... the water.
5. .... left.
6. .... down!
7. .... any noise.
8. .... well.

SALE $10,000

SHH!

I'm going to bed.

30.2 Complete the sentences. Use **No, let's . . .** + one of these:

go to a restaurant ~~**go for a swim**~~ **wait** **take the bus** **watch TV**

1. Would you like to play tennis? — No, *let's go for a swim.*
2. Do you want to drive there? — No, ...
3. Shall we go to the movies? — ....
4. Should we have dinner at home? — ....
5. Would you like to begin now? — ....

30.3 Answer with **No, don't . . .** or **No, let's not . . .**

1. Should I wait for you? — No, *don't wait for me.*
2. Shall we go out? — No, *let's not go out.*
3. Should I close the door? — ....
4. Should I call you tonight? — ....
5. Should we wait for Dave? — ....
6. Should I turn on the light? — ....
7. Should we go home now? — ....

UNIT 31

there is there are

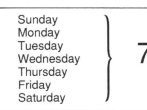

There's a man on the roof.

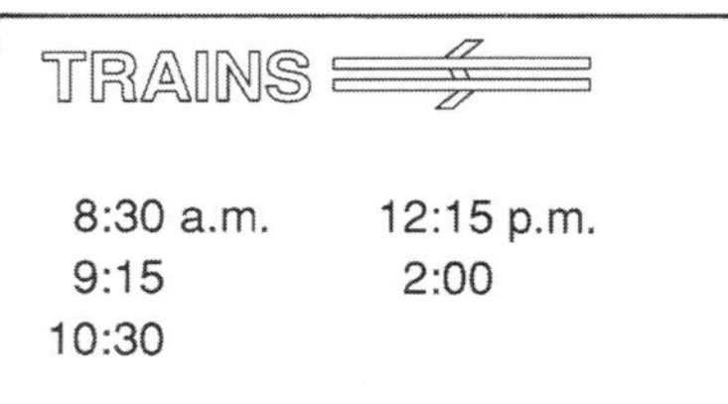

There's a train at 10:30.

Sunday
Monday
Tuesday
Wednesday
Thursday
Friday
Saturday
} 7

There are seven days in a week.

A there is / there are

Singular	
there is . . .	**(there's)**
there is not . . .	**(there isn't** *or* **there's not)**
is there . . . ?	

- **There's** a big tree in the park.
- **There's** a good movie on TV tonight. I'm going to watch it.
- Excuse me, **is there** a hotel near here?
- "Do you have any money?" "Yes, **there's** some in my bag."
- We can't go skiing. **There isn't** any snow.
- Look at this crowd! **There's not** a free seat in the theater.

Plural	
there are . . .	
there are not . . .	**(there aren't)**
are there . . . ?	

- **There are** some big trees in the park.
- **Are there** any letters for me today?
- This is a modern town. **There aren't** many old buildings here.
- **How many players are there** on a soccer team?
- **There are 11 players** on a soccer team.

B there is and it is

there is

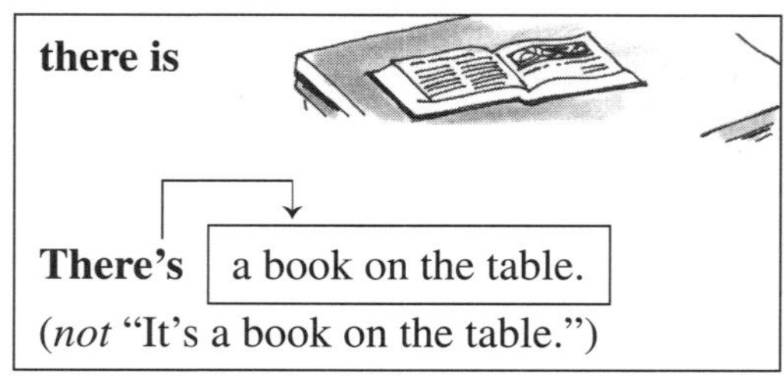

There's a book on the table.
(*not* "It's a book on the table.")

it is

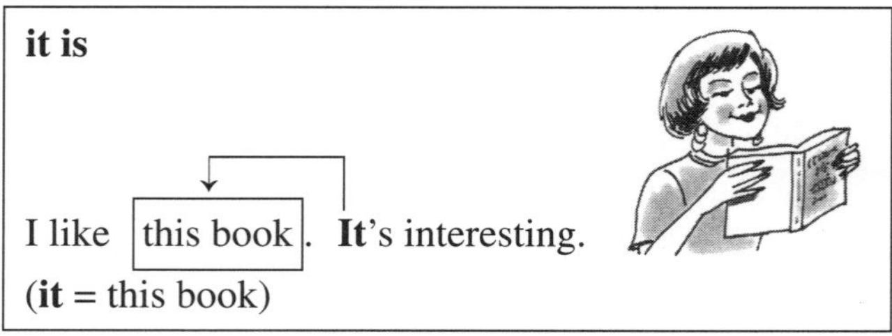

I like this book. **It**'s interesting.
(**it** = this book)

Compare:

- A: What's that noise? B: **It**'s a train. (**it** = that noise)
- **There's** a train at 10:30. **It**'s a fast train. (**it** = the 10:30 train)
- **There is** a lot of salt in this soup.
  I don't like this soup. **It**'s too salty. (**it** = this soup)

Exercises

31.1 What's in the box? Ask questions with **Is there . . . ?** and **Are there . . . ?**

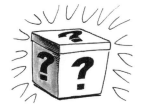

1. (any pencils?) Are there any pencils in the box ?
2. (any books?) .... in the box?
3. (a person?) .... ?
4. (any money?) .... ?
5. (any clothes?) .... ?
6. (a key?) .... ?

31.2 Springfield is a small town. Look at the information in the box and write sentences with **There is/isn't/are/aren't . . .**

golf course	Yes
swimming pool	No
hospital	Yes
movie theaters	Yes (two)
university	No
big hotels	No
park	Yes

1. There is a golf course in Springfield.
2. .... in Springfield.
3. ....
4. ....
5. ....
6. ....
7. ....

31.3 Put in **there is / there isn't / is there / there are / there aren't / are there**.

1. This is a very modern town. There aren't many old buildings.
2. Look! .... a photograph of Bill in the newspaper!
3. Excuse me, ... a restaurant near here?
4. .... five people in my family: my parents, my two sisters, and me.
5. We can't take any photographs. .... any film in the camera.
6. How many students .... in your class?
7. Where can we sit? .... any chairs.
8. .... a bus from the city center to the airport?

31.4 Write sentences with **There are . . .** Choose the right number: ~~7~~ **9 26 30 50 60**.

1. (days / a week). There are seven days in a week.
2. (states / the USA) ....
3. (minutes / hour) ....
4. (planets / the solar system) ....
5. (letters / the English alphabet) ....
6. (days / September) ....

31.5 Put in **there** or **it**.

1. There's a train at 10:30. It's a fast train.
2. I'm not going to buy this shirt. ....'s very expensive.
3. "What's wrong?" "................'s something in my eye."
4. ....'s a car in front of the house. Is .... your car?
5. "Is .... anything interesting on TV?" "Yes, ...'s a movie at 8:15."
6. ....'s a letter in the mailbox. Is .... for you?

UNIT 32 there was / were / has been / will be

there	is/are	See Unit 31.
	was/were	For **was/were**, see Unit 11.
	has been / have been	For **has / have been**, see Units 14–16.
	will be	For **will**, see Unit 22.

A there was/were

TRAINS
8:30 a.m.
9:15
10:30
12:15 p.m.
2:00

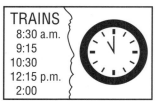

The time is now 11:00.

There was a train at 10:30.

Compare:

there is/are *(present)*

- **There is** a good movie on TV tonight.
- We are staying at a very big hotel. **There are** 250 rooms.
- I'm hungry but **there isn't** anything to eat.
- **Are there** any packages for me this morning?

there was/were *(past)*

- **There was** a good movie on TV last night.
- We stayed at a very big hotel. **There were** 250 rooms.
- When I got home, I was hungry but **there wasn't** anything to eat.
- **Were there** any packages for me yesterday morning?

B there has been / there have been

There's been an accident.

- Look! **There's been** an accident. (there**'s** been = there **has** been)
- This road is very dangerous. **There have been** lots of accidents on it.
  but There **was** an accident **last night**. (*not* "has been . . . last night")
  See Unit 18.

C there will be

- Do you think **there will be** a lot of people at the party on Saturday?
- *(from the weather forecast)* Tomorrow the weather will be cold. **There will be** some rain in the afternoon.

Exercises

32.1 Look at the two pictures. Now the room is empty, but before it was full of things. Write sentences about the things in the list. Use **There was/were . . .**

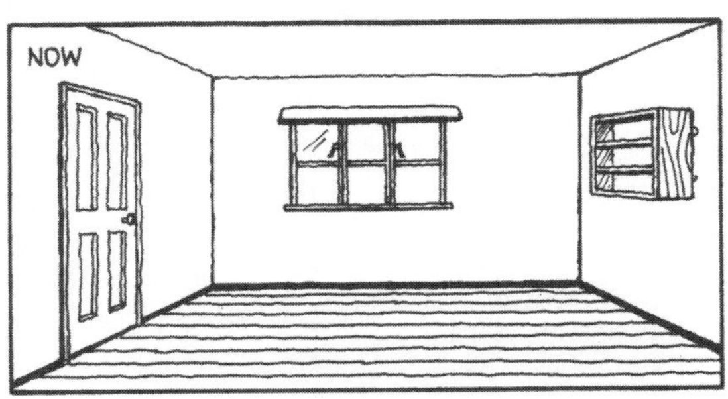

an armchair **some books** **a rug** ~~**a clock**~~ **some flowers** **some pictures** **a sofa** **a small table**

1. *There was a clock* .... on the wall near the window.
2. .... on the floor.
3. .... on the wall near the door.
4. .... in the middle of the room.
5. .... on the table.
6. .... on the shelves.
7. .... in the corner near the door.
8. .... opposite the door.

32.2 Put in **there was / there wasn't / was there / there were / there weren't / were there**.

1. I was hungry but *there wasn't* .... anything to eat.
2. *Were there* .... any packages for me yesterday?
3. .... a soccer match on TV last night, but I didn't see it.
4. "We stayed at a nice hotel." "Really? .... a swimming pool?"
5. The suitcase was empty. .... any clothes in it.
6. I found a wallet on the street, but .... any money in it.
7. ".............................. many people at the meeting?" "No, very few."
8. We didn't visit the museum. .... enough time.
9. I'm sorry I'm late. .... a lot of traffic.
10. The radio wasn't working because .... any batteries in it.

32.3 Put in **there is / there are / there was / there were / there has been / there will be**.

1. *There was* .... a good movie on TV last night.
2. Look! *There has been* .... an accident. Call an ambulance!
3. .... 24 hours in a day.
4. .... a party at school last Friday, but I didn't go.
5. Look! This bag is empty. .... nothing in it.
6. "Why are the police outside the bank?" ".............................. a robbery."
7. When we arrived at the theater, ... a long line outside.
8. .... somebody at the station to meet you when you arrive tomorrow.
9. Ten years ago .... 500 children at the school. Now .... over a thousand.

UNIT 33

it . . .

A it for *time/day/distance/weather*

time

What time is **it**?
It's 10:30.
It's late.
It's time to go home.

day

What day is **it**?
It's March 16th.
It's Thursday today.
It's my birthday today.

distance

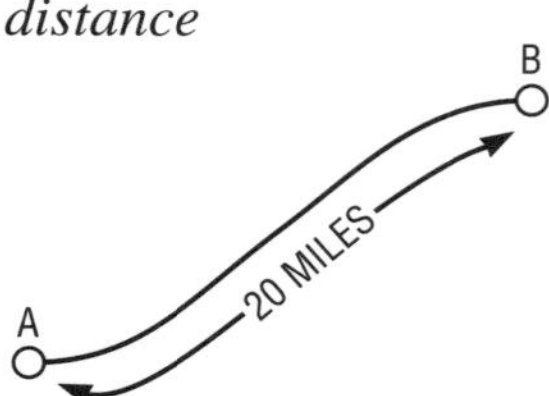

How far is **it** from California to Japan?
It's a long way from here to the airport.
We can walk home. **It** isn't far.*
It's 20 miles from our town to the nearest city.

* Use **far** in *questions* **(is it far?)** and negatives **(it isn't far)**.
Use **a long way** in *positive sentences* **(it's a long way)**.

weather

It's raining. **It** isn't raining. Is **it** snowing?
It rains/snows/rained/snowed.
It's warm/hot/cold/cloudy/windy/sunny/foggy/dark, etc.
It's a nice day today.

Compare **it** and **there**:

- **It rains** a lot in the winter. (**rains** is a *verb*)
  but **There is a lot of rain** in the winter. (**rain** is a *noun*)
- **It** was very **windy**. (**windy** is an *adjective*)
  but **There was a** strong **wind** yesterday. (**wind** is a *noun*)

For **there is** and **it is**, see also Unit 31.

B it's nice to . . . , etc.

It's	**easy/difficult/foolish/hard/impossible/dangerous/safe/ cheap/expensive/nice/good/wonderful/terrible**, etc.	**to . . .**

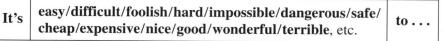

- **It 's nice to see** you again. (**it** = to see you again)
- **It's impossible to understand** her. (**it** = to understand her)
- **It wasn't easy to find** your house. (**it** = to find your house)

C

Don't forget **it**:

- **It**'s raining again. (*not* "Is raining again.")
- Is **it** true that you are married? (*not* "Is true that . . . ?")

Exercises

33.1 Put in **it is** (**it's**) or **is it.**

1. What time *is it* ...... ?
2. *It's* ...... raining again.
3. .... very late. We have to go home.
4. ".......... cold out?" "Yes, put on your coat."
5. .... true that Bill can fly a helicopter?
6. "What day .... today? .... Thursday?" "No, Friday."
7. .... about three miles from the airport to the city center.
8. .... possible for me to phone you at your office?
9. "Should we walk to the restaurant?" "I don't know. How far .... ?"
10. .... Jack's birthday today. He's 27.
11. .... too bad that Ann can't come to the party on Saturday.
12. I don't believe it! .... impossible!

33.2 Write questions with **How far . . . ?**

1. (here / the airport?) *How far is it from here to the airport* ...... ?
2. (New York / Washington?) How .... Washington?
3. (your house / the station?) .... ?
4. (the hotel / the beach?) .... ?

33.3 Put in **it** or **there**.

1. *It* ...... rains a lot in the winter.
2. *There* ...... was a stong wind yesterday.
3. Look! ....'s snowing.
4. We can't go skiing. .... isn't any snow.
5. "Did .... rain yesterday?" "No, ... was sunny."
6. ....'s dark in this room. Can you turn on the light?
7. ....'s a big black cloud in the sky. ....'s going to rain.
8. .... was a thunderstorm last night. Did you hear it?
9. ....'s a long way from here to the nearest gas station.

33.4 Complete the sentences. Use **it's** + *(box 1)* + **to** + *(box 2)*.

1 it's			*2* to		
	difficult	**foolish**		**see you again**	**go out alone**
	~~**easy**~~	**impossible**		**wear**	**sleep**
	easy	**nice**		~~**understand him**~~	**save**
	dangerous			**meet people**	

1. *It's easy to understand him* .... because he speaks very slowly.
2. ...., Ann. How are you?
3. .... at night. There is always a lot of noise.
4. A lot of cities are not safe. .... at night.
5. If you don't have a job that pays well, ... money.
6. .... warm clothes in hot weather.
7. Everybody is very friendly in this town. ....

UNIT 34

go/going work/working play/playing, etc.

A

go/work/play, etc. *(base form)*
We use the *base form* (**go/work/play/be**, etc.) after:

will	Tom **will be** here tomorrow.	(See Units 22 and 23.)
shall	**Shall** I **open** the window?	(See Units 22 and 23.)
can	I **can't play** tennis.	(See Unit 24.)
could	**Could** you **pass** the salt, please?	(See Unit 24.)
may	**May** I **smoke**?	(See Unit 25.)
might	I **might be** late tonight.	(See Unit 25.)
must	You **must taste** this delicious soup!	(See Unit 26.)
should	You **shouldn't work** so hard.	(See Unit 27.)
would	**Would** you **like** some coffee?	(See Unit 28.)

We use the *base form* with **do/does/did**:

do	**Do** you **work**?	I **don't work**.
does	How much **does** it **cost**?	She **doesn't play** tennis.
did	What time **did** they **leave**?	We **didn't sleep** very well.

For the simple present, see Units 6 and 7.
For the simple past, see Unit 10.

B

to go / to work / to play, etc. *(infinitive)*
We use **to . . . (to go / to work / to play / to be**, etc.) after:

(I'm) **going (to . . .)**	**I'm going to play** tennis tomorrow.	
	What **are** you **going to do**?	(See Unit 21.)
(I) **have (to . . .)**	I **have to go** now.	
	Everybody **has to eat**.	(See Unit 26.)
(I) **want (to . . .)**	Do you **want to go** out?	
	They don't **want to come** with us.	(See Unit 47.)
(I) **would like (to . . .)**	**I'd like to be** rich.	
	Would you **like to go** out?	(See Unit 28.)

C

going/working/playing, etc.
We use **-ing** with **am/is/are/was/were**:

am/is/are } + **-ing** *present continuous*
was/were } + **-ing** *past continuous*

- Please be quiet. **I'm working**.
- Tom **isn't working** today.
- What time **are** you **going** out?
- We didn't go out because it **was raining**.
- What **were** you **doing** at 11 o'clock yesterday morning?

For the present continuous, see Units 3 and 4 and Unit 20.
For the past continuous, see Unit 12.
For **to . . . (I want to do)** and **-ing (I enjoy doing)**, see Unit 47.

Exercises

34.1 Finish each of these sentences. Write "**. . . call Jack**" or "**. . . to call Jack**."

1. I'll *call Jack.*
2. I'm going *to call Jack.*
3. Can you .... Jack?
4. Shall I .... ?
5. I'd like ....
6. I have ....
7. You should ....
8. I want ....
9. I might ....
10. You must ....

34.2 Complete the sentences with a verb from the box. Sometimes you need the base form (**go/work**, etc.) and sometimes you need **-ing** (**going/working**, etc.).

do/doing	**get/getting**	**rain/raining**	**wait/waiting**	~~**work/working**~~
drive/driving	**go/going**	~~**sleep/sleeping**~~	**watch/watching**	
eat/eating	**listen/listening**	**stay/staying**	**wear/wearing**	

1. Please be quiet. I'm *working.*
2. I feel tired. I didn't *sleep* very well last night.
3. What time do you usually .... up in the morning?
4. "Where are you .... ?" "To the store."
5. Did you .... television last night?
6. Open your umbrella. It's ....
7. The police stopped her because she was .... the car too fast.
8. You can turn off the radio. I'm not .... to it.
9. They didn't .... anything because they weren't hungry.
10. "What are you .... tonight?" "I'm .... home."
11. "Does she always .... glasses?" "No, only for reading."
12. My friends were .... for me when I arrived.

34.3 Put in the correct form. Choose the base form (**go/open**, etc.), infinitive (**to go/to open**, etc.), or **-ing** (**going/opening**, etc.).

1. Should I *open* the window? (open)
2. It's late. I have *to go* now. (go)
3. Tom isn't *working* this week. He's on vacation. (work)
4. Do you want .... out tonight? (go)
5. "Where are you .... for your vacation this year?" (go)
   "We're not sure, but we may .... to Australia." (go)
6. I'm afraid I can't .... you. (help)
7. It's a really great movie. You must .... it. (see)
8. What time do you have .... tomorrow morning? (leave)
9. Do you think it will .... this afternoon? (rain)
10. I'm hungry. I'm going .... something to eat. (have)
11. My brother is .... physics at college. (study)
12. He spoke very quietly. I couldn't .... him. (hear)
13. I'm very tired. I think I'll .... down for a few minutes. (lie)
14. I was very tired. I had .... down for a few minutes. (lie)
15. Would you like .... out for dinner this evening? (go)
16. You don't look well. I don't think you should .... out. (go)

UNIT 35

be/have/do in present and past tenses

A

be (am/is/are/was/were) -ing (cleaning/working/doing, etc.)
present continuous and past continuous

am/is/are -ing *present continuous* (See Units 3 and 4 and Unit 20.)	▪ Please be quiet. **I'm working**. ▪ It **isn't raining** right now. ▪ What **are** you **doing** tonight?
was/were -ing *past continuous* (See Unit 12.)	▪ I **was working** when she arrived. ▪ It **wasn't raining**, so we went out. ▪ What **were** you **doing** at 3 o'clock?

B

be (am/is/are/was/were) + *past participle* (**cleaned/made/eaten**, etc.)
passive

am/is/are + *past participle* *present passive* (See Unit 19.)	▪ The room **is cleaned** every day. ▪ I **am invited** to lots of parties. ▪ Oranges **are imported** into Canada.
was/were + *past participle* *past passive* (See Unit 19.)	▪ The room **was cleaned** yesterday. ▪ These houses **were built** 100 years ago. ▪ How **was** the window **broken**?

C

have/has + *past participle* (**cleaned/lost/eaten/been/gone**, etc.)
present perfect

have/has + *past participle* *present perfect* (See Units 14–16.)	▪ I **have cleaned** my room. ▪ Tom **has lost** his passport. ▪ Barbara **hasn't been** to Mexico. ▪ Where **have** they **gone**?

D

do/does/did + *base form* (**clean/like/eat/go**, etc.)
simple present and simple past – negatives and questions

do/does + *base form* *simple present negatives and questions* (See Units 6 and 7.)	▪ I like coffee but I **don't like** tea. ▪ Tom **doesn't smoke**. ▪ What **do** you usually **do** on weekends? ▪ **Does** Barbara **live** alone?
did + *base form* *simple past negatives and questions* (See Unit 10.)	▪ I **didn't watch** TV yesterday. ▪ It **didn't rain** last week. ▪ What time **did** Barbara **go** out?

Exercises

35.1 Put in **is/as/do/does**.

1. *Do*........ you brush your teeth every day?
2. Where *are*...... they going?
3. Why .... you looking at me?
4. .... Bill live in a house?
5. .... you like dancing?
6. .... the sun shining?
7. What time .... the stores close?
8. .... you working tomorrow?
9. .... Pat work on Saturdays?
10. What .... this word mean?
11. What time .... you going out?
12. What time .... you usually go out?
13. .... it raining?
14. .... you feeling all right?

35.2 Put in **am not / isn't / aren't / don't / doesn't**. All these sentences are negative.

1. Tom *doesn't*.................... smoke.
2. It *isn't*......................... raining right now.
3. I .... want to go out tonight.
4. I .... going out tonight.
5. Bob .... working this week.
6. My parents .... watch television very often.
7. Tom and Ann .... coming to the party next week.
8. Sue .... speak a foreign language.
9. I'm sorry, I .... understand. Can you say that again, please?
10. You can turn off the television. I .... watching it.

35.3 Put in **was/were/did/have/has**.

1. Where *were*.... your shoes made?
2. *Did*....... you go out last night?
3. What .... you doing at 10:30?
4. Where .... he buy his new coat?
5. Where .... she born?
6. Where .... you born?
7. .... Kim gone home?
8. What time .... she go?
9. What .... she wearing yesterday?
10. When .... this road built?
11. Why .... they go home early?
12. How long .... they been married?
13. .... you see Jim last night?
14. .... you ever seen a ghost?

35.4 Put in **is/are/was/were/have/has**.

1. Oranges *are*....... imported into Canada.
2. Joe *has*...... lost his passport.
3. Glass .... made from sand.
4. Rita is my best friend. I .... known her for ten years.
5. This shopping center .... built ten years ago.
6. The streets in this town .... cleaned every day.
7. .... you finished your work?
8. Mary .... gone to Japan for vacation.
9. These are very old photographs. They .... taken a long time ago.
10. Ted and Linda are here. They .... just arrived.
11. She's Italian but she .... born in France.
12. Can you tell me how this word .... pronounced?

UNIT 36 Regular and irregular verbs

A

Simple past and *past participle*
The simple past and past participle of *regular* verbs is **-ed**:

clean → clean**ed** live → liv**ed** paint → paint**ed** study → stud**ied**

simple past

- I **cleaned** my room yesterday.
- Tom **studied** engineering in college.

We use the *past participle* for the *present perfect* and the *passive.*

present perfect = **have/has** + *past participle*:

- I **have cleaned** my room.
- Joan **has lived** in San Francisco for ten years.

passive = **be** (**am/is/are/was/were**) + *past participle*:

- These rooms **are cleaned** every day.
- My car **was repaired** last week.

For the simple past, see Unit 9.
For the present perfect, see Units 14–16.
For the passive, see Unit 19.

B

Irregular verbs:
The simple past and past participle of *irregular* verbs are *not* **-ed**:

	make	break	cut
simple past	**made**	**broke**	**cut**
past participle	**made**	**broken**	**cut**

Sometimes the simple past and past participle are the same. For example:

	make	find	buy	cut
simple past	**made**	**found**	**bought**	**cut**
past participle	**made**	**found**	**bought**	**cut**

- I **made** a cake yesterday. (*simple past*)
- I'**ve** just **made** some coffee. *(past participle – present perfect)*
- Butter **is made** from milk. *(past participle – present passive)*

Sometimes the simple past and past participle are different. For example:

	break	know	begin	go
simple past	**broke**	**knew**	**began**	**went**
past participle	**broken**	**known**	**begun**	**gone**

- Somebody **broke** this window last night. (*simple past*)
- Sombody **has broken** this window. *(past participle – present perfect)*
- This window **was broken** last night. *(past participle – past passive)*

For irregular verbs, see also Appendixes 1 and 2.

Exercises

36.1 Write the simple past / past participle of these verbs. (The simple past and past participle are the same for all the verbs in this exercise.)

1. make *made*
2. cut *cut*
3. find ....
4. think ....
5. pay ....
6. sit ....
7. leave ....
8. build ....
9. put ....
10. buy ....
11. hear ....
12. cost ....
13. catch ....
14. lose ....
15. understand ....

36.2 Write the simple past and past participle of these verbs.

1. break *broke* *broken*
2. begin ....
3. eat ....
4. drink ....
5. give ....
6. run ....
7. speak ....
8. write ....
9. come ....
10. drive ....
11. take ....
12. go ....
13. know ....
14. throw ....
15. forget ....

36.3 Put the verb into the right form.

1. I *washed* my hands because they were dirty. (wash)
2. I've just .... some coffee. (make)
3. I feel good. I .... very well last night. (sleep)
4. We .... a really good movie yesterday. (see)
5. It .... a lot when we were on vacation. (rain)
6. I've .... my bag. (lose) Have you .... it? (see)
7. Dan's bicycle was .... last week. (steal)
8. I .... to bed early because I was tired. (go)
9. Have you .... your book yet? (finish)
10. These houses were .... about 20 years ago. (build)
11. Ann .... to drive when she was 18. (learn)
12. I've never .... a horse in my life. (ride)
13. Yesterday I .... off my bicycle and .... my leg. (fall/hurt)
14. She's a good friend of mine. I've .... her a long time. (know)

36.4 Complete these sentences with a verb from the list. Put the verb into the correct form: simple past or past participle.

cost drive fly ~~make~~ meet sell speak swim tell wake

1. You don't need to make coffee. I have already *made* some.
2. I know Sam, but I've never .... his wife.
3. We were .... up by a loud noise in the middle of the night.
4. She jumped into the river and .... to the other side.
5. Many different languages are .... in the Philippines.
6. Our vacation .... a lot of money because we stayed in an expensive hotel.
7. Have you ever .... a very fast car?
8. All the tickets for the concert were .... very quickly.
9. Have you .... John about your new job?
10. A bird .... in through the open window while we were eating dinner.

UNIT 37 I am / I don't, etc. . . . are you? / . . . don't you?, etc.

A

am/is/are	can	will
was/were	could	would
have/has	must	may
do/does/did	should	might

She **isn't** tired but he **is**. (= he is tired)

We use these verbs with other verbs (**am going / has seen / can't come**, etc.), but we can also use them alone:

- A: Are you tired?
  B: I **was** but I'**m not** now. (= I was tired but I'm not tired now.)
- "Please help me." "I'm sorry. I **can't**." (= I can't help you.)
- "Do you think Ann will come?" "She **might**." (= She might come.)

B

We use **do/does** for the *simple present* and **did** for the *simple past*:

- She works very hard, but I **don't**. (= I don't work very hard)
- I don't have a car, but my sister **does**. (= she has a car)
- "Did you and John enjoy the movie?" "I **did**, but John **didn't**."

C

You can use these verbs in this way with **Yes . . .** and **No . . .** :

- "Have you ever been to Canada?" "Yes, I **have**." *or* "No, I **haven't**."
- "Will Tom be here tomorrow?" "Yes, he **will**." *or* "No, he **won't**."
- "Do you enjoy your work?" "Yes, I **do**." *or* "No, I **don't**."
- "Did it rain yesterday?" "Yes, it **did**." *or* "No, it **didn't**."

D

You can use **. . . have you? / . . . can't she?**, etc. at the end of a sentence. These endings are *tag questions*:

A *positive* sentence → a *negative* tag question
A *negative* sentence → a *positive* tag question

For example:

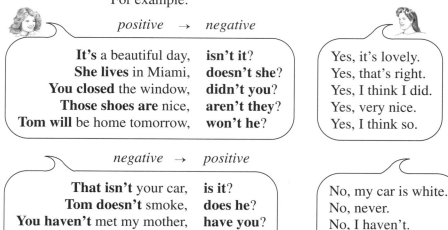

positive	→ *negative*	
It's a beautiful day,	**isn't it**?	Yes, it's lovely.
She lives in Miami,	**doesn't she**?	Yes, that's right.
You closed the window,	**didn't you**?	Yes, I think I did.
Those shoes are nice,	**aren't they**?	Yes, very nice.
Tom will be home tomorrow,	**won't he**?	Yes, I think so.

negative	→ *positive*	
That isn't your car,	**is it**?	No, my car is white.
Tom doesn't smoke,	**does he**?	No, never.
You haven't met my mother,	**have you**?	No, I haven't.
You won't be late,	**will you**?	No, don't worry.

Exercises

37.1 Complete these sentences with **do/does/did** or **don't/doesn't/didn't**.

1. I don't like hot weather, but Sue *does*.
2. Sue likes hot weather, but I *don't*.
3. You don't know John well, but I ....
4. Ann lives in Rio, but her parents ....
5. I like golf, but my brother ....
6. I don't want to go out, but Peter ....
7. I wanted to go out last night, but Mary ....
8. I didn't enjoy the party, but my friends ....
9. Liz doesn't have a car, but most of her friends ....

37.2 Complete these sentences. Use a positive verb (**is/have/can**, etc.) or a negative verb (**isn't/haven't/can't**, etc.).

1. Lee wasn't hungry, but we *were*.
2. My sister can play the piano, but I *can't*.
3. I'm not very patient, but you ....
4. I don't know much about computers, but my brother ....
5. Judy watches TV a lot, but I ....
6. I'll be here tomorrow, but Ann ....
7. I've seen the movie, but Bill ....
8. Ann is going out tonight, but I ....
9. I got up early this morning, but Bob ....
10. I wasn't tired, but Ted and Liz ....
11. I don't have a video camera, but I know somebody who ....
12. Tom has never been to South America, but I ....

37.3 Answer these questions about yourself. Use **Yes, I have** / **No, I'm not**, etc.

1. Are you British *No, I'm not.*
2. Do you have a car? ....
3. Is it raining? ....
4. Do you feel all right? ....
5. Are you tired? ....
6. Do you like chocolate? ....
7. Will you be in Paris tomorrow? ....
8. Have you ever played tennis? ....
9. Did you buy anything yesterday? ......
10. Were you born in Europe? ....

37.4 Complete these sentences with a tag question (**isn't it? / haven't you?**, etc.).

1.	It's a beautiful day *isn't it* ?	Yes, it's lovely.
2.	They're on vacation, ... ?	Yes, they're in Hawaii.
3.	She was angry, ... ?	Yes, very angry.
4.	You've been to Buenos Aires, ... ?	Yes, many times.
5.	You play tennis, ... ?	Yes, but not often.
6.	He looks very tired, ... ?	Yes, he works too hard.
7.	You'll help me, ... ?	Yes, of course I will.

37.5 Complete these sentences with a tag question, positive (**is it? / do you?**, etc.) or negative (**isn't it? / don't you?**, etc.).

1.	You don't have a car, *do you* ?	No, I can't drive.
2.	You aren't tired, ... ?	No, I'm fine.
3.	Sue is a very nice person, ... ?	Yes, I like her very much.
4.	You can play the piano, ... ?	Yes, but not very well.
5.	You don't know Mr. Bond, ... ?	No, I've never met him.
6.	Ann went to college, ... ?	Yes, she studied history.
7.	The movie wasn't very good, ... ?	No, it was terrible.

UNIT 38

too / either so am I / neither do I, etc.

A too and either

I'm happy.
I am too.
I'm not happy.
I'm not either.

We use **too** and **either** at the end of a sentence.

We use **too** after a *positive* verb:

- "I'm happy." "I **am too**." (= I am happy too.)
- "I enjoyed the movie." "I **did too**." (= I enjoyed it too.)
- Mary is a doctor. Her husband **is too**. (= Her husband is a doctor too.)

We use **either** after a *negative* verb (am **not** / is**n't** / ca**n't**, etc.):

- "I'm not happy." "I'm **not either**." (*not* "I'm not too")
- "I can't cook." "I ca**n't either**."
- Bill doesn't watch TV. He does**n't** read newspapers **either**.

B So am I / Neither do I, etc.

	am/is/are	...
	was/were	...
so	**do/does**	...
	did	...
	have/has	...
neither	**can**	...
	will	...
	must	...

So am I (= I am too), **So have I** (= I have too), etc.:

- "**I'm** tired." **"So am I."** (*not* "So I am.")
- "**I was** late for work today." **"So was John."**
- "**I work** in a bank." **"So do I."**
- "**We went** to the movies last night." **"So did we."**

Neither am I (= I'm not either), **Neither have I** (= I haven't either), etc.:

- "**I don't have** a key." **"Neither do I."** (*not* "Neither I do")
- "**Ann can't** cook." **"Neither can Tom."**
- "**I won't** (= will not) be here tomorrow." **"Neither will I."**
- "**I never eat** meat." **"Neither do I."**

For **am/was/do**, etc., see Unit 37.

Exercises

38.1 Put in **too** or **either**.

1. I'm happy. — I am *too.*
2. I'm not hungry. — I'm not ....
3. I'm tired. — I am ....
4. It rained on Saturday. — It rained on Sunday ....
5. Ann can't drive a car. — She can't ride a bicycle ....
6. I don't smoke. — I don't smoke ....
7. Jane's mother is a teacher. — Her father is ....

38.2 Answer with **So . . . I** (**So am I** / **So do I** / **So can I**, etc.).

1. I went to bed late last night. — *So did I.*
2. I'm hungry. — ....
3. I've been to Rome. — ....
4. I want to go home now. — ....
5. I'll be late tomorrow. — ....
6. I was surprised at the news. — ....

Answer with **Neither . . . I**.

7. I can't play the piano. — ....
8. I didn't buy a newspaper. — ....
9. I haven't eaten lunch yet. — ....
10. I'm not working tomorrow. — ....
11. I don't know them very well. — ....

38.3 You are talking to Maria. Write *true* answers about *yourself*. Where possible, use **So . . . I** or **Neither . . . I**. Look at the examples carefully.

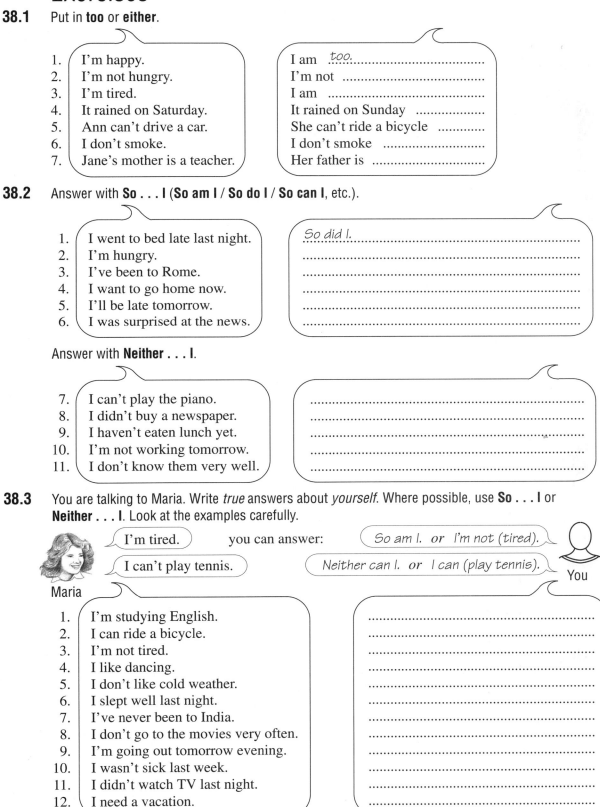

Maria: I'm tired. — you can answer: *So am I. or I'm not (tired).*

Maria: I can't play tennis. — *Neither can I. or I can (play tennis).*

You

1. I'm studying English. — ....
2. I can ride a bicycle. — ....
3. I'm not tired. — ....
4. I like dancing. — ....
5. I don't like cold weather. — ....
6. I slept well last night. — ....
7. I've never been to India. — ....
8. I don't go to the movies very often. — ....
9. I'm going out tomorrow evening. — ....
10. I wasn't sick last week. — ....
11. I didn't watch TV last night. — ....
12. I need a vacation. — ....

UNIT 39

Negatives: **isn't/haven't/don't**, etc.

A

We use **not** (**n't**) in negative sentences.

positive → negative		
am	**am not** (**'m not**)	I'**m not** tired.
is	**is not** (**isn't** *or* **'s not**)	It **isn't** (*or* It'**s not**) raining.
are	**are not** (**aren't** *or* **'re not**)	They **aren't** (*or* They'**re not**) here.
was	**was not** (**wasn't**)	Jack **wasn't** hungry.
were	**were not** (**weren't**)	The shops **weren't** open.
have	**have not** (**haven't**)	I **haven't** finished my work.
has	**has not** (**hasn't**)	Sue **hasn't** been to Europe.
will	**will not** (**won't**)	They **won't** be here tomorrow.
would	**would not** (**wouldn't**)	I **wouldn't** like to be an actor.
can	**cannot** (**can't**)	Tim **can't** drive.
could	**could not** (**couldn't**)	I **couldn't** sleep last night.
should	**should not** (**shouldn't**)	You **shouldn't** work so hard.

B

Simple present negative:

I/we/you/they **do not** (**don't**)
he/she/it **does not** (**doesn't**) } + *base form* (**work/live/have**, etc.)

Simple past negative:

I/they/he/she, etc. **did not** (**didn't**) + *base form*

positive	→	*negative*
I **smoke**.	→	I **don't smoke**.
They **work** hard.	→	They **don't work** hard.
Tom **plays** the guitar.	→	Tom **doesn't play** the guitar.
Sue **has** a car.	→	Sue **doesn't have** a car.
I **got** up early.	→	I **didn't get** up early.
We **worked** hard.	→	We **didn't work** hard.
They **saw** the movie.	→	They **didn't see** the movie.
She **had** breakfast.	→	She **didn't have** breakfast.

For the simple present, see Unit 6. For the simple past, see Unit 10.

C

The negative of "**Look!**," "**Go away!**," etc. is "**Don't . . . !**" :

Look! → **Don't look!** **Go** away! → **Don't go** away!

D

Do can also be the main verb (**don't do / didn't do**, etc.):

positive	→	*negative*
Do it.	→	**Don't do** it.
He **does** a lot of work.	→	He **doesn't do** much work.
I **did** what you said.	→	I **didn't do** what you said.

Exercises

39.1 Make these sentences negative.

1. I'm tired. *I'm not tired.*
2. He has a car. *He doesn't have a car.*
3. They are married. ....
4. I've had dinner. ....
5. It's cold today. ....
6. I can see you. ....
7. We were late. ....
8. I'm going out. ....
9. She has gone out. ....
10. I'll be late tonight. ....
11. It was expensive. ....
12. You should go. ....

39.2 Make negatives with **don't/doesn't/didn't**.

1. He saw me. *He didn't see me.*
2. Do it! *Don't do it.*
3. I like fish. ....
4. She smokes. ....
5. Look at me. ....
6. I got up early. ....
7. They understood. ....
8. Call me tonight. ....
9. I did the shopping. ....
10. He lives near here. ....
11. It rained yesterday. ....
12. They did the work. ....

39.3 Make these sentences negative.

1. It's raining. *It isn't raining.*
2. She saw the movie. *She didn't see the movie.*
3. She can swim. ....
4. They're on vacation. ....
5. He speaks German. ....
6. I enjoyed the movie. ....
7. It's important. ....
8. We watched TV. ....
9. They were angry. ....
10. He'll be pleased. ....
11. I went to the bank. ....
12. She has a camera. ....
13. Open the door. ....
14. I could hear them. ....

39.4 Complete these sentences with a negative verb (**isn't/haven't/don't**, etc.).

1. The sun is shining. It *isn't* raining.
2. She isn't rich. She *doesn't* have much money.
3. "Would you like something to eat?" "No, thank you. I .... hungry."
4. I .... hear you. Please speak louder.
5. Bob .... write letters very often. He prefers to call.
6. I don't like this book. It .... very interesting.
7. "Where is Sue?" "I .... know. I .... seen her today."
8. She .... go to work yesterday because she .... feeling well, but she's better today.
9. Be careful! .... fall!
10. We .... take an umbrella with us because the sun was shining.
11. I've been to Japan many times, but I .... been to Korea.
12. When we were in Rio, we stayed with friends. We .... stay at a hotel.
13. She .... be here tomorrow. She's going away.
14. "Who broke that window?" "Not me! I .... do it."
15. The box was too heavy. We tried to lift it but we ....
16. We didn't see what happened. We .... looking at the time.

UNIT 40

Questions (1): **is it . . . ? have you . . . ? do they . . . ?**, etc.

positive	**you**	**are**	**You are** eating.
question	**are**	**you**	**Are you** eating? What **are you** eating?

A

In questions, the first verb (**is/are/have**, etc.) is *before* the subject:

Positive			*Question*		
subject +	*verb*			*verb* +	*subject*
I	**am** late.	→		**Am**	**I** late?
That seat	**is** free.	→		**Is**	**that seat** free?
She	**was** angry.	→	Why	**was**	**she** angry?
David	**has** gone.	→	Where	**has**	**David** gone?
They	**will** be here.	→	When	**will**	**they** be here?
Tom	**can** swim.	→		**Can**	**Tom** swim?

Be careful with word order. The subject is after the first verb:

- Where **has David** gone? (*not* "Where has gone David?")
- Why **are those people** waiting? (*not* "Why are waiting those people?")

B

Simple present questions: **do** (I/we/you/they) / **does** (he/she/it) } + *base form* (**work/live/have**, etc.)

Simple past questions: **did** (you/they/she, etc.) + *base form*

Positive			*Question*		
You	**have** a car.	→		**Do you**	**have** a car?
They	**live** in Vancouver.	→	Where	**do they**	**live**?
Jack	**plays** the piano.	→		**Does Jack**	**play** the piano?
She	**gets** up early.	→	What time	**does she**	**get** up?
They	**worked** hard.	→		**Did they**	**work** hard?
You	**had** dinner.	→	What	**did you**	**have** for dinner?
She	**got** up early.	→	What time	**did she**	**get** up?

Do can also be the main verb (**do you do / did she do**, etc.):

- What **do you** usually **do** on weekends?
- "What **does your sister do**?" "She works in a bank."
- "I broke my leg." "How **did you do** that?" (*not* "How did you that?")

C

Negative questions with **Why . . . ?** (**Why isn't . . . ? / Why don't . . . ?**, etc.).
Be careful with word order in these questions:

- Where's John? **Why isn't he** here? (*not* "Why he isn't here?")
- **Why can't Paula** come to the meeting tomorrow? (*not* "Why Paula can't . . . ?")
- **Why didn't you** call me last night?

For the simple present and simple past, see Units 7 and 10.
For questions, see also Units 41 and 42.

Exercises

40.1 Write questions.

1. I can swim. (and you?) Can you swim ?
2. I jog. (and Jim?) Does Jim jog ?
3. I was late this morning. (and you?) .... ?
4. I've had lunch. (and Ann?) .... ?
5. I'll be here tomorrow. (and you?) .... ?
6. I'm going out tonight. (and Tom?) .... ?
7. I've finished my work. (and you?) .... ?
8. I like my job. (and you?) .... ?
9. I live near the city center. (and Pam?) .... ?
10. I enjoyed the movie. (and you?) .... ?
11. I had a nice vacation. (and you?) .... ?

40.2 You are asking somebody questions. Write the full answers.

You

You	
1. (tired?) Are you tired ?	Yes, a little.
2. (play the piano?) .... ?	Yes, but not very well.
3. (married?) .... ?	No, I'm single.
4. (live in a city?) .... ?	No, in a small town.
5. (been to China?) .... ?	No, never.
6. (go out last night?) .... ?	No, I stayed home.
7. (like chocolate?) .... ?	Yes, I love it.
8. (watch TV yesterday?) .... ?	No, I never watch TV.
9. (sleep well last night?) .... ?	No, not very well.

40.3 Ask questions.

1. I want to go.	Where do you want to go ?
2. They aren't here.	Why aren't they here ?
3. It's important.	Why .... ?
4. I'm reading.	What .... you .... ?
5. Jane went home.	What time .... ?
6. Dave and Mary are going away.	When .... ?
7. I like music.	What kind of music .... ?
8. I met Tim.	Where .... ?
9. He is going to stay here.	How long .... ?
10. The children have gone.	Where .... ?
11. I can't come to the party.	Why .... ?
12. I broke the window.	How .... ?
13. I need some money.	How much money .... ?
14. She did her homework.	When .... ?
15. I don't like her.	Why .... ?
16. It rains a lot.	How often .... ?

UNIT 41

Questions (2): **Who saw you? Who did you see?**

Fred saw Mary.

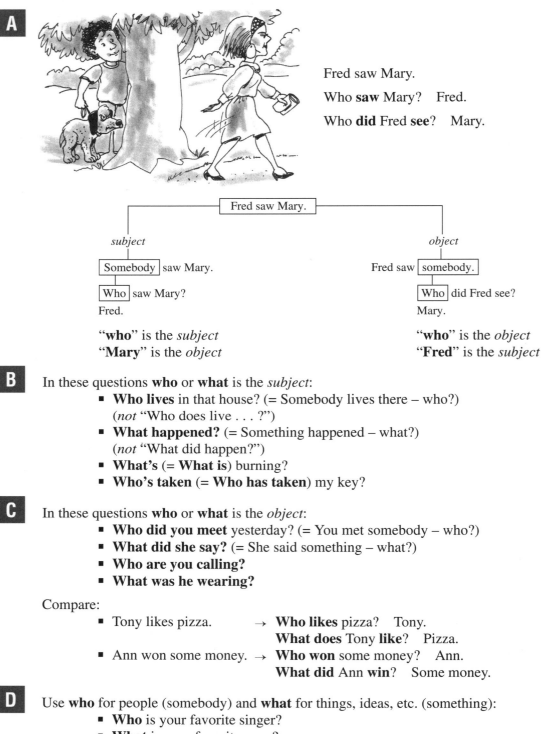

Who **saw** Mary? Fred.

Who **did** Fred **see**? Mary.

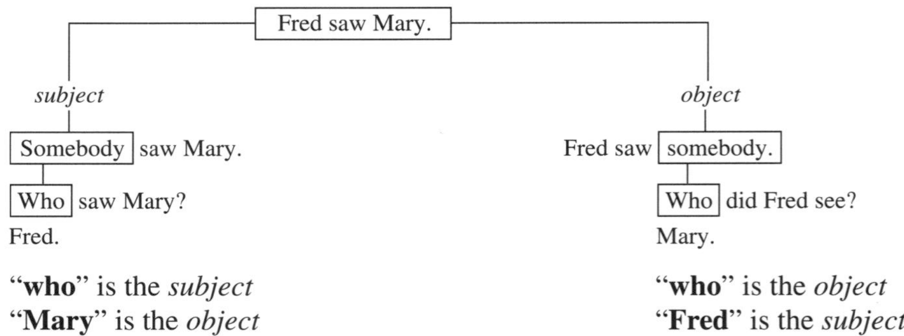

"**who**" is the *subject*
"**Mary**" is the *object*

"**who**" is the *object*
"**Fred**" is the *subject*

B

In these questions **who** or **what** is the *subject*:

- **Who lives** in that house? (= Somebody lives there – who?)
  (*not* "Who does live . . . ?")
- **What happened?** (= Something happened – what?)
  (*not* "What did happen?")
- **What's** (= **What is**) burning?
- **Who's taken** (= **Who has taken**) my key?

C

In these questions **who** or **what** is the *object*:

- **Who did you meet** yesterday? (= You met somebody – who?)
- **What did she say?** (= She said something – what?)
- **Who are you calling?**
- **What was he wearing?**

Compare:

- Tony likes pizza. → **Who likes** pizza? Tony.
  What does Tony **like**? Pizza.
- Ann won some money. → **Who won** some money? Ann.
  What did Ann **win**? Some money.

D

Use **who** for people (somebody) and **what** for things, ideas, etc. (something):

- **Who** is your favorite singer?
- **What** is your favorite song?

Exercises

41.1 Make questions with **who** and **what**. In these sentences **who/what** is the subject.

1. Somebody broke the window. — *Who broke the window* ?
2. Something happened. — *What happened* ?
3. Somebody is coming. — Who .... ?
4. Somebody took my umbrella. — .... your umbrella?
5. Something made me angry. — .... you angry?
6. Somebody wants to see you. — .... me?
7. Somebody told me about the accident. — .... you .... ?
8. Something went wrong. — .... ?

41.2 Make questions with **who** and **what**. In these sentences **who/what** is the object.

1. I met somebody. — *Who did you meet* ?
2. I'm doing something. — *What are you doing* ?
3. I'm reading something. — What .... you .... ?
4. I saw somebody. — Who .... ?
5. I want something. — .... ?
6. I called somebody. — .... ?
7. I'm going to cook something. — .... ?
8. I bought something. — .... ?

41.3 Make questions with **who** and **what.** Sometimes **who/what** is the subject, sometimes **who/what** is the object.

1. Somebody lives in that house. — Who *lives in that house* ?
2. Tom said something. — What *did Tom say* ?
3. They lost something. — What .... ?
4. Somebody cleaned the kitchen. — Who .... ?
5. I asked somebody for money. — Who .... you .... money?
6. Somebody asked me for money. — Who .... ?
7. Something happened last night. — What .... ?
8. Jack bought something. — What .... ?
9. Somebody called me yesterday. — Who .... ?
10. I called somebody yesterday. — Who .... ?
11. Somebody knows the answer. — Who .... ?
12. Something woke me up this morning. — What .... ?
13. Somebody has my pen. — Who .... pen?
14. Tom and Ann saw something. — What .... ?
15. Somebody saw the accident. — Who .... ?
16. Somebody did the dishes. — Who .... ?
17. Joan did something. — What .... ?
18. This word means something. — What .... ?

UNIT 42 Questions (3): Who is she talking to? What is it like?

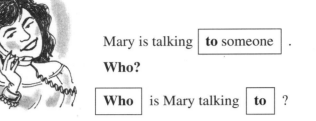

Mary is talking **to** someone.

Who?

Who is Mary talking **to** ?

A Questions (**Who . . . ? / What . . . ? / Where . . . ? / Which . . . ?**) often end with a *preposition* (**to/for/about/with**, etc.):

- "I'm thinking." "**What** are you thinking **about**?"
- "I'm afraid." "Why? **What** are you afraid **of**?"
- "**Where** is your friend **from**?" "She's from Peru."
- "**Who** does this book belong **to**?" "It's mine."
- "**Who** did she go on vacation **with**?" "With her parents."
- "**What** does he look **like**?" "He has a beard and wears glasses."
- "This book is very good." "Really? **What** is it **about**?"
- "Tom's father is in the hospital." "**Which hospital** is he **in**?"

B **What (is/are/was/were) . . . like?**

What's your new house like?
It's very big.

"What is it like?" = Tell me something about it; is it good or bad, big or small, old or new?, etc. When we say "**What . . . like?**," **like** is a *preposition*. It is *not* the verb **like** (**Do you like music?**, etc.).

- A: I went to the new restaurant last night.
  B: Really? **What**'s it **like**? Good?
  A: Yes, excellent.
- A: **What**'s your new teacher **like**?
  B: She's very good. We learn a lot.
- A: I met Linda's parents yesterday.
  B: Oh, **what** are they **like**?
  A: They're very friendly.
- A: **What** was the weather **like** when you were on vacation?
  B: It was great!

Exercises

42.1 Write questions.

1.	I'm thinking about something.	What *are you thinking about* ?
2.	He went out with somebody.	Who *did he go out with* ?
3.	I'm waiting for somebody.	Who are you .... ?
4.	She danced with somebody.	Who did she .... ?
5.	He's interested in something.	What .... ?
6.	I had dinner with somebody.	Who .... ?
7.	They're looking for something.	What .... ?
8.	Mike was with somebody.	Who .... ?
9.	I gave the money to somebody.	Who .... ?
10.	I'm looking at something.	What .... ?
11.	They were talking about something.	What .... ?
12.	I dreamed about somebody.	Who .... ?
13.	He was afraid of something.	What .... ?
14.	They're going to a restaurant.	Which restaurant .... ?
15.	She spoke to somebody.	Who .... ?
16.	I stayed at a hotel.	Which hotel .... ?

42.2 You are talking to somebody from another country. You want some information about the country. Ask questions with **What is/are . . . like?**

1. (the houses) *What are the houses like* ?
2. (the food) What .... ?
3. (the weather) .... ?
4. (the people) .... ?
5. (your city) .... ?
6. (the stores) .... ?
7. (the schools) .... ?
8. (TV shows) .... ?

42.3 Ask questions with **What was/were . . . like?**

1. Your friend has just come back from vacation. Ask about the weather.
   What was the weather like ?
2. Your friend has just come back from the movies. Ask about the movie.
   What .... ?
3. Your friend has just arrived at the airport. Ask about the flight.
   .... ?
4. Your friend has just been to a concert. Ask about the concert.
   .... ?
5. Your friend has just finished an English course. Ask about the classes.
   .... ?
6. Your friend has just come back from a business trip. Ask about the hotel.
   .... ?

UNIT 43

What . . . ? Which . . . ? How . . . ?

A

What . . . ?

What + *noun* (**What color . . . ? / What kind . . . ?**, etc.):

- **What color** is your car? **What color** are your eyes?
- **What size** is this shirt? **What kind** of job do you want?
- **What time** is it?

What *without a noun*:

- **What**'s your favorite color?
- **What** do you want to do tonight?

For **What** and **Who**, see Unit 41.

B

Which . . . ?

Which + *noun (things or people)*:

- **Which train** did you catch – the 9:50 or the 10:30?
- **Which doctor** did you see – Doctor Ellis, Doctor Gray, or Doctor Hill?

Which *without a noun (not people)*:

- **Which** is bigger – Canada or Australia?
  but **Who** is taller – Bill or Tom? (**Who** *for people*)

For **Which one(s)**, see Unit 68.

C

What . . . ? and **Which . . . ?**

We say **which** when we are thinking about a small number (perhaps two, three, or four things):

- We can go this way or that way.
  Which way shall we go?
- There are four umbrellas here.
  Which is yours? *or*
  Which one is yours?

? OR ? OR ? OR ?

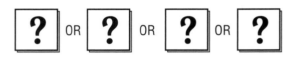

Use **what** in other situations:

- **What** is the capital of Mexico?
- **What kind** of music do you like?

Compare:

- **What color** are your eyes? (*not* "Which color . . . ?")
  but **Which color** do you prefer, **pink or yellow**?

D

How . . . ?

- "**How** was the party last night?" "It was great!"
- "**How** do you usually get to work?" "By bus."

How + *adjective/adverb* (**how old / how big / how fast**, etc.):

- **How old** is your father? **How tall** are you? **How big** is the house?
- **How far** is it to the bus stop from here?
- **How often** do you go on vacation?

Exercises

43.1 Write questions with **Which . . . ?**

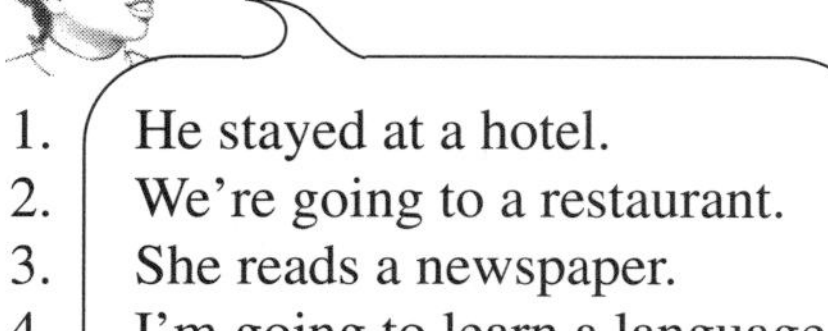

1.	He stayed at a hotel.	Which hotel did he stay at ?
2.	We're going to a restaurant.	.... to?
3.	She reads a newspaper.	.... ?
4.	I'm going to learn a language.	.... ?
5.	They visited many places.	.... ?
6.	I'm waiting for a bus.	.... ?

43.2 Put in **what/which/who**.

1. What is that man's name?
2. Which way should we turn? To the right or the left?
3. You can have tea or coffee. .... do you want?
4. "I can't find my umbrella." ".................. color is it?"
5. .... is your favorite sport?
6. This is a very nice house. .... room is yours?
7. .... is more expensive, meat or fish?
8. .... is older, Ann or Bob?
9. .... is your telephone number?
10. .... kind of TV shows do you like to watch?
11. "She has three cars." ".................. car does she use the most?"
12. ".................. nationality are you?" "I'm Brazilian."

43.3 Write questions with **What . . . ?** or **How . . . ?**

1. Are his eyes blue? Green? Brown? What color are his eyes ?
2. Did you get up at 7:00? 7:30? 8:15? .... ?
3. Are you 20 years old? 21? 22? .... ?
4. Is the door red? Blue? Yellow? .... ?
5. Do you watch TV every day? Once a week? Never? .... ?
6. Are these shoes small? Medium? Large? .... ?
7. Is it 1,000 miles from Paris to Moscow? 1,500? 2,000? .... ?
8. Is your room big? Very big? Not very big? .... ?
9. Do you like classical music? Rock? Folk music? .... ?
10. Can you run one kilometer? Five? Ten? .... ?
11. Is your sweater large or extra large? .... ?
12. Are you 1.75 meters? 1.80? 1.85? .... ?
13. Is it Monday? Tuesday? Wednesday? .... ?
14. Is this box one kilogram? One and a half? Two? .... ?
15. Can this plane fly 500 miles an hour? 600? 700? .... ?
16. Do you like horror movies? Science fiction movies? Thrillers? Comedies? .... ?

How long does it take?

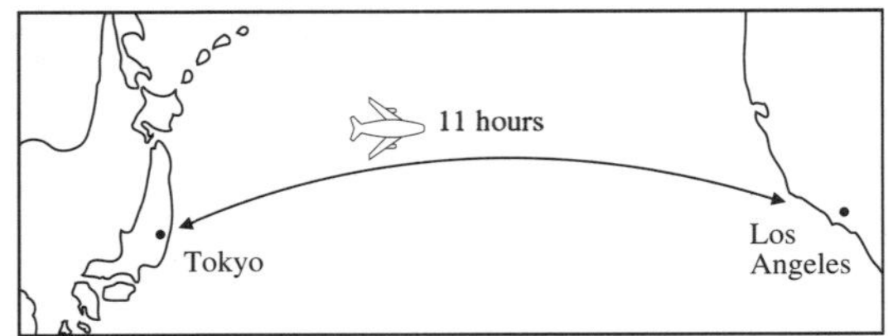

How long **does it take** to get from Tokyo to Los Angeles by plane?

It takes eleven hours.

I started reading the book two weeks ago. I finished it today.

It took me two weeks to read it.

How long **does it take**	to get from . . . to . . .	by plane? by train? by car?

It takes	two hours ten minutes a long time	to get from . . . to . . .	by plane. by train. by car.

- **How long does it take** to get from Tokyo to Osaka by train?
  It takes three hours to get from Tokyo to Osaka by train.
- **How long does it take** to get from your house to the station by car?
  It takes ten minutes to get from my house to the station by car.

How long	**did** **does** **will**	**it take**	(you) (Ann) (them)	**to** (do something)?

It	**took** **takes** **will take**	(me) (Ann) (them)	a week a long time three hours	**to** (do something).

- **How long does it take to cross** the Atlantic Ocean by ship?
- **How long will it take me to learn** to drive?
- "I came by train." "Really? **How long did it take?**"
- **Did it take you a long time to find** a job?
- **It takes a long time to learn** a language.
- **It takes me 20 minutes to get** to work in the morning.
- **It took Tom an hour to do** the shopping.
- **It will take me an hour to cook** dinner.
- **It doesn't take long to cook** an omelet.

Exercises

44.1 Write questions with **How long does it take . . . ?**

1. (London / Madrid / by plane) *How long does it take to get from London to Madrid by plane* ?
2. (São Paulo / Rio / by car) .... ?
3. (the city center / the airport / by bus) .... ?
4. (Taiwan / Singapore / by plane) .... ?
5. (the station / the hotel / by taxi) .... ?
6. (Munich / Prague / by train) .... ?
7. (Florida / Puerto Rico / by ship) .... ?
8. (your house / work / by bicycle) .... ?

44.2 Look at the timetable of flights from New York. How long does it take to get to each place? Write sentences with **It takes . . .**

from NEW YORK	*depart*	*arrive (New York time)*
to MIAMI	8:40 a.m.	11:45 a.m.
LOS ANGELES	10:00 a.m.	3:50 p.m.
TORONTO	9:10 a.m.	10:40 a.m.
PARIS	1:00 p.m.	6:45 p.m.
MEXICO CITY	5:50 p.m.	9:55 p.m.
HONOLULU	8:05 a.m.	8:05 p.m.

How long does it take to fly to:
1. Miami? *It takes three hours and five minutes.*
2. Los Angeles? It ....
3. Toronto? ....
4. Paris? ....
5. Mexico City? ....
6. Honolulu? ....

44.3 Write questions with **How long did it take . . . ?**

1. She found a job. *How long did it take her to find a job* ?
2. I walked to the station. .... you .... ?
3. They cleaned the house. .... ?
4. I learned to swim. .... ?
5. He found an apartment. .... ?

44.4 Write sentences with **It took . . .**

1. (he read the book / two weeks) *It took him two weeks to read the book.*
2. (we walked home / an hour) ....
3. (I learned to drive / a long time) ....
4. (they fixed the car / all day) ....
5. *Write a true sentence about yourself:* ....

44.5 How long does it take (you) to do these things? Write complete sentences.

1. (run five miles / kilometers?) *It takes me about 30 minutes to run five kilometers.*
2. (take a shower?) ....
3. (fly to New York from your country?) ....
....
4. (study to be a doctor in your country?) ....
....
5. (walk from your house to the nearest store?) ....
....

UNIT 45 Can you tell me where . . . ? Do you know what . . . ?, etc.

EXCUSE ME, CAN YOU TELL ME WHERE THE BUS STATION IS, PLEASE?

We say: Where **is** **the bus station**?
but
Can you tell me where **the bus station** **is** ?

(*not* "Can you tell me where is the bus station?")
also:

I know I don't know I can't remember I wonder	**where the station is**.
Do you know (etc.)	**where the station is**?

Who **are those people**?
Where **have they** gone?
How old **is Tom**?
What time **is the bus**?
When **is Ann** going away?
How much **is this camera**?
Why **were they** late?
What **was he** wearing?

but

Do you know **I don't know** **I know** **Can you tell me** **I can't remember**	who **those people are** where **they've** gone how old **Tom is** what time **the bus is** when **Ann is** going away how much **this camera is** why **they were** late what **he was** wearing

A

Questions with **do/does/did** (*simple present* and *simple past*):

Where **does he live** ?

Do you know where **he lives** ? (*not* "Do you know where does he live?")

How **do airplanes fly**?
What **does she want**?
Why **did she go** home?
Where **did I put** the key?

but

Do you know	how **airplanes fly**
I don't know	what **she wants**
I know	why **she went** home
I can't remember	where **I put** the key

B

Questions beginning **Is . . . ? / Do . . . ? / Can . . . ?**, etc. (*yes/no questions*):

Is Jack at home?
Have they gone away?
Can he help us?
Does Ann speak French?
Did anybody see you?

but

Do you know **I don't know**	**if** *or* **whether**	**Jack is** at home **they've** gone away **he can** help us **Ann speaks** French **anybody saw** me

You can use **if** *or* **whether** in these sentences:

- Do you know **if** she smokes? *or* Do you know **whether** she smokes?

Exercises

45.1 You are a tourist. Ask **Excuse me, can you tell me where . . . ?**

1. (the bus station) *Excuse me, can you tell me where the bus station is* .... ?
2. (the museum) Excuse me, ... ?
3. (the information center) .... ?
4. (the nearest bank) .... ?

45.2 Answer these questions with **I don't know where/when/why . . .**, etc.

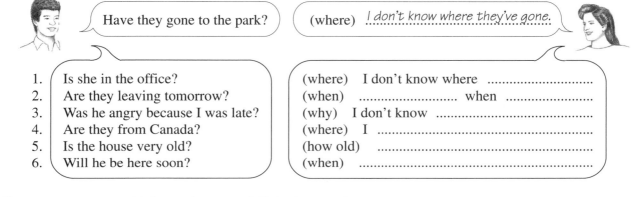

Have they gone to the park?

(where) *I don't know where they've gone.*

1.	Is she in the office?	(where) I don't know where ....
2.	Are they leaving tomorrow?	(when) .... when ....
3.	Was he angry because I was late?	(why) I don't know ....
4.	Are they from Canada?	(where) I ....
5.	Is the house very old?	(how old) ....
6.	Will he be here soon?	(when) ....

45.3 Write sentences with **Do you know . . . ? / I don't remember . . .**, etc.

1. (How do airplanes fly?) Do you know *how airplanes fly* .... ?
2. (Where does Sue work?) I don't know ....
3. (Where do they live?) Do you know .... ?
4. (What did he say?) Do you remember .... ?
5. (What time does the concert begin?) Do you know .... ?
6. (Why did they leave early?) I don't know ....
7. (How did the accident happen?) I don't remember ....

45.4 Ask questions with **Do you know if** (or **whether**) **. . . ?**

1. (Do they have a car?) *Do you know if they have a car* .... ?
2. (Are they married?) Do you know .... ?
3. (Does she like her job?) Do you know .... ?
4. (Will Ted be here tomorrow?) Do .... ?
5. (Did he pass his exam?) .... ?

45.5 Write new questions beginning **Do you know . . . ?**

1. (What does she want?) *Do you know what she wants* .... ?
2. (Where is Ann?) Do you know where .... ?
3. (Is Pat working today?) Do you .... ?
4. (What time do they start work?) Do .... ?
5. (Do they work on Sundays?) .... ?
6. (Why were they so nervous?) .... ?
7. (Where did Jane go?) .... ?
8. (Are the stores open tomorrow?) .... ?

UNIT 46 I went to the store to buy . . .

Ann didn't have any bread.
But she wanted some bread.
So she went to the bakery.

Why did she go to the bakery?
To buy some bread.

She went to the bakery **to buy** some bread.

A

to . . . (**to do / to buy / to see**, etc.) tells us *why* a person does something *(the purpose)*:

- "Why are you going out?" "**To buy** a newspaper."
- Bill went to the airport **to meet** his friend.
- She turned on the TV **to watch** the news.
- I'd like to go to Spain **to learn** Spanish.

money/time to (do something):

- We need some **money to buy** food.
- I don't have **time to watch** television.

B

to . . . and **for . . .** :
to + *verb*: **to buy / to have / to see**, etc.
for + *noun*: **for some bread / for dinner / for a vacation**, etc.

- She went to the store **to buy** some bread. (**to** + *verb*)
  but She went to the store **for some bread**. (**for** + *noun*)
- They are going to Japan **to see** their grandmother. (*not* "for to see")
  but They are going to Japan **for a vacation**.
- We need some money **to buy** food. (*not* "for buy")
  but We need some money **for food**.

C

wait
wait for somebody/something:

- Are you **waiting for the bus**?
- Please wait **for me**.

wait for somebody/something **to . . .** :

- I can't go out yet. **I'm waiting for John to call**.
- I was having dinner when they arrived. They **waited for me to finish** my meal.

For **enough/too + to . . .** , see Units 84 and 85.

Exercises

46.1 Write sentences with **I went to the . . . to . . .** Choose from:

get some aspirin **meet a friend** ~~**catch a train**~~ **buy some food**
get some money **mail a letter**

1. (the station) *I went to the station to catch a train.*
2. (the bank) I went ....
3. (the supermarket) I ....
4. (the post office) ....
5. (the drugstore) ....
6. (the coffee shop) ....

46.2 Finish the sentences with the best ending. Choose from:

to open this door **to let some fresh air into the room** **to wake them up**
~~**to watch the news**~~ **to tell him about the party** **to get some gas**
to see the pyramids **to read the newspaper** **to clean it**
to see who it was

1. I turned on the television *to watch the news.*
2. She sat down in an armchair ....
3. Do I need a key .... ?
4. The house is dirty but they don't have time ....
5. She opened the window ....
6. I knocked on their bedroom door ....
7. We stopped at a gas station ....
8. A lot of people go to Egypt ....
9. I called Tom ....
10. The doorbell rang, so I looked out of the window ....

46.3 Put in **to** or **for**.

1. She went to the store *to* buy some bread.
2. We stopped at a gas station .... some gas.
3. I'm going to walk home. I don't have any money .... a taxi.
4. We went to a restaurant .... have dinner.
5. He wants to go to college .... study economics.
6. I'm going to Toronto .... a job interview next week.
7. I'm going to Hong Kong .... visit a friend of mine.
8. I got up late this morning. I didn't have time .... read the paper.
9. Everybody needs money .... live.
10. The office is very small. There's space only .... a table and a chair.

46.4 Finish these sentences. Use the words in parentheses ( ).

1. I can't go out yet. I'm waiting *for John to call.* (John / call)
2. We're not going out yet. We're waiting .... (the rain / stop)
3. We called the police and then we waited .... (them / come)
4. I sat down in the theater and waited .... (the movie / begin)

UNIT 47

to . . . (I want to do) and -ing (I enjoy doing)

A

verbs + **to . . .** (I **want to do**)

want	**decide**	**hope**	**try**
need	**offer**	**expect**	**forget**
plan	**refuse**	**promise**	**learn**

+ **to . . .** (**to do** / **to work** / **to be**, etc.)

- What do you **want to do** tonight?
- I **hope to go** to college next year.
- We have **decided to leave** tomorrow morning.
- You **forgot to turn** off the lights when you went out.
- My brother is **learning to drive**.
- I **tried to work** but I was too tired.

B

verbs + **-ing** (I **enjoy doing**)

enjoy	**mind**	**stop**
finish	**suggest**	

+ **-ing** (do**ing**/work**ing**/be**ing**, etc.)

- I **enjoy** danc**ing**. (*not* "enjoy to dance")
- Has it **stopped** rain**ing**? (*not* "stopped to rain")
- Mary **suggested** go**ing** to the zoo.
- I don't **mind** be**ing** alone.

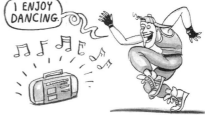

C

verbs + **to . . .** *or* **-ing**:

like	**love**	**start**	**continue**
prefer	**hate**	**begin**	

+ **to . . .** (**to do**, etc.)
or **-ing** (do**ing**, etc.)

- I **like to dance**. *or* I **like dancing**.
- Do you **prefer to travel** by car? *or* Do you **prefer traveling** by car?
- Ann **loves to go** to the movies. *or* Ann **loves going** to the movies.
- I **hate to get** up in the morning. *or* I **hate getting** up in the morning.
- It started **to rain**. *or* It **started raining**.

But you can only use **to . . .** (*not* **-ing**) after **would** like / **would** love, etc.:

would like	**would** love
would prefer	**would** hate

- Jean **would like to meet** you. (*not* "would like meeting")
- **I'd love to go** to Turkey. (*not* "I'd love going") **I'd** = I would
- "**Would** you **like to sit** down?" "No, **I'd prefer to stand**, thank you."
- I **wouldn't like to be** a teacher. / **I'd hate to be** a teacher.

For **would like**, see Unit 28.
For **would rather**, see Unit 29.

Exercises

47.1 Put the verb in the right form, **to . . .** or **-ing**. Sometimes either form is possible.

1. I enjoy *dancing* (dance).
2. Where do you want *to go* (go)?
3. What have you decided .... (do)?
4. I learned .... (swim) when I was five years old.
5. Would you prefer .... (leave) now or later?
6. I'm trying .... (work). Please stop .... (talk).
7. Have you finished .... (clean) the kitchen?
8. I'm tired. I want .... (go) to bed.
9. The weather was nice, so I suggested .... (go) for a walk by the river.
10. Don't forget .... (send) me a postcard when you're on vacation.
11. I'd love .... (help) you, but it's impossible.
12. Where's Bill? He promised .... (be) here on time.
13. Do you enjoy .... (read) books?
14. I don't mind .... (travel) by train, but I prefer .... (fly).
15. We invited Jane to the party, but she didn't want .... (come).
16. Goodbye. I hope .... (see) you again soon.
17. You should stop .... (work) so hard. It's bad for you.
18. This ring is beautiful. I'd hate .... (lose) it.
19. They were very angry and refused .... (speak) to me.
20. Where is Ann? I need .... (talk) to her.
21. Why did you start .... (cry)?
22. Do you like .... (cook)?
23. I enjoy .... (visit) other countries.
24. He wasn't happy when he lost the game. He hates .... (lose).

47.2 Do you like to do these things? Use **I like / I don't like / I hate / I don't mind . . .**

1. (get up early) *I don't mind getting up early.* (*or* *I like . . . / I don't like . . . / I hate . . .*)
2. (write letters) ....
3. (travel by train) ....
4. (visit museums) ....
5. (eat in restaurants) ....

47.3 Write sentences about yourself. Use the verbs given in parentheses ( ).

1. (I'd like / go) *I'd like to go to Mexico.*
2. (I'd like / go) ....
3. (I'd like / have) ....
4. (I'd love / meet) ....
5. (I'd hate / be) ....

47.4 Complete these sentences. Write about yourself.

1. One day I'd like ....
2. On weekends I like ....
3. When I'm on vacation, I like ....
4. In the mornings I don't like ....
5. I wouldn't like ....

UNIT 48

I want you to . . . / I told you to . . .

Sue **wants to study**.

Tom **doesn't want Sue to study**.
He **wants her to go out**.

(I) **want to . . .**

(I) **want (somebody) to . . .**

A

We say **I want (you) to . . .** :

- I **want you to be** happy. (*not* "I want that you are happy.")
- They didn't **want anybody to know** their secret.

We also use this structure (*verb* + somebody + **to . . .**) with:

tell	I	**told**	**you**	**to be**	careful.
ask	She	**asked**	**her friend**	**to help**	her.
advise	What do you	**advise**	**me**	**to do**?	
persuade	We	**persuaded**	**Jack**	**to come**	with us.
expect	I didn't	**expect**	**you**	**to be**	here.
teach	I	**taught**	**my brother**	**to swim**.	

B

I told (somebody) **to . . . / I told** (somebody) **not to . . .** :

- Ann said (to Tom): "**Wait** for me!"
  → Ann **told** Tom **to wait** for **her**.
- Ann said (to Tom): "**Don't wait** for me."
  → Ann **told** Tom **not to wait** for **her**.

C

make and **let**

After **make** and **let** we do *not* use **to**:

- He's very funny. He **makes us laugh**. (*not* "makes us to laugh")
- I don't want you to go alone. **Let me go** with you. (*not* "Let me to go")

Let's (**do** something)

You can say **Let's . . .** (= **let us**) when you want people to do things with you:

- Come on! **Let's dance!**

See Unit 30.

D

help

You can say **help** somebody **do** *or* **help** somebody **to do**:

- Ann **helped me carry** the box. *or* Ann **helped me to carry** the box.

Exercises

48.1 Write sentences beginning **I (don't) want you . . . / Do you want me . . . ?**

1. (you have to come with me) *I want you to come with me.*
2. (should I come with you?) *Do you want me to come with you* ?
3. (listen carefully) I want ....
4. (please don't be angry) I don't ....
5. (shall I wait for you?) Do you .... ?
6. (don't call me tonight) ....
7. (you must meet Chris) ....
8. (should I make some coffee?) .... ?

48.2 Write sentences with **advised/persuaded/let**, etc.

1. (Bob came with us / we persuaded him) *We persuaded Bob to come with us.*
2. (I stayed in bed / the doctor advised me) The doctor ....
3. (she called me / I asked her) I ....
4. (I went to the party / Tom persuaded me) Tom ....
5. (I used their phone / they let me) They ....
6. (Ann plays the piano / her mother taught her) Ann's ....

48.3 Write sentences with **told**.

1. Ann said to Tom: "Wait for me!" *Ann told Tom to wait for her.*
2. I said to you: "Don't wait for me." *I told you not to wait for me.*
3. Sue said to me: "Hurry up." Sue told ....
4. I said to the children: "Be quiet." I ....
5. She said to me: "Don't lose the key." She ....
6. Tom said to me: "Call me later." ....
7. I said to Tom: "Don't say anything." ....

48.4 Complete these sentences with the verbs in the list. Sometimes **to** is necessary (**to get** / **to arrive**, etc.) and sometimes **to** is not necessary (**get** / **arrive**, etc.)

arrive clean cry do explain get ~~go~~ hear know sleep wait walk

1. Please stay here. I don't want you *to go*.
2. Tony's parents didn't want him .... married.
3. She didn't understand the story, so she asked me .... it to her.
4. Don't wake me up tomorrow morning. Let me ....
5. Please talk quietly. I don't want anybody .... us.
6. "Do you want to go by car?" "No, let's ...."
7. You're here early. I expected you .... later.
8. It was a very sad movie. It made me ....
9. Please don't tell Sue about my plan. I don't want her ....
10. The kitchen is very dirty. Can you help me .... it?
11. "Should we begin?" "No, let's .... a few minutes."
12. What do you think about my problem? What do you advise me .... ?

UNIT 49

He said that . . . / He told me that . . .

He said that he was happy.

She told me that she had won the lottery.

A

After **said that / told** (somebody) **that . . .** a verb is usually *past*:

am/is → **was**	(she said) "**I'm** working." → She said that she **was** working. (they said to us) "The hotel **isn't** very good." → They told us that the hotel **wasn't** very good.
are → **were**	(I said) "The stores **are** open." → I said that the stores **were** open.
have/has → **had**	(I said to him) "**I've** finished my work." → I told him that I **had** finished my work.
can → **could**	(Tom said) "I **can't** come to the party." → Tom said that he **couldn't** come to the party.
will → **would**	(my friends said to me) "The exam **will** be easy." → My friends told me that the exam **would** be easy.
do/does → **did**	(I said) "It **doesn't** matter." → I said that it **didn't** matter. (he said) "I **don't** know your address." → He said that he **didn't** know my address.
like → **liked** **go** → **went** (etc.)	(Mary said) "I **like** bananas." → Mary said that she **liked** bananas. (they said) "We **go** to the movies every week." → They said that they **went** to the movies every week.

B

say (→ **said**) and **tell** (→ **told**)

say something (**to** somebody): They **said that** . . . (*not* "They said me that . . .")

tell somebody something: They **told me that** . . . / They **told Ann that** . . .

- He **said** that he was happy. (*not* "He said *me* that he was happy.")
  but He **told me** that he was happy. (*not* "He told that he was happy.")
- What did he **say to you**? (*not* "say you")
  but What did he **tell you**? (*not* "tell to you")

C

that is not necessary in the sentences above. You can say:

- He said **that** he was happy. *or* He said he was happy. (*without* **that**)

Exercises

49.1 A is talking to B about other people. Finish A's second sentence.

1. A: She likes you. B: Really? Are you sure?
   A: Yes, she told me that *she liked you.*
2. A: He is married. B: Really? Are you sure?
   A: Yes, he told me that he ....
3. A: She can play tennis. B: Oh, really? Are you sure?
   A: Yes, she said that ....
4. A: They are from Egypt. B: I didn't know that. Are you sure?
   A: Yes, they told me that ....
5. A: She has a new job. B: Really? Are you sure?
   A: Yes, she told me that ....
6. A: They will help us. B: Oh, really? Are you sure?
   A: Yes, they said that ....
7. A: He is going to India. B: Really? Are you sure?
   A: Yes, he said that ....
8. A: She works in a bank. B: Oh, really? Are you sure?
   A: Yes, she told me that ....
9. A: They live in Budapest. B: Oh, really? Are you sure?
   A: Yes, they told me that ....
10. A: She is studying art. B: I didn't know that. Are you sure?
    A: Yes, she said that ....

49.2 Read what these people say and then write sentences with **She/He said that . . .**

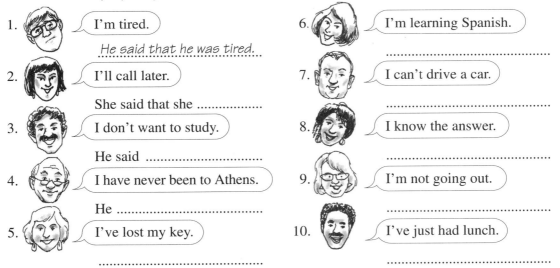

1. I'm tired.
   He said that he was tired.

2. I'll call later.
   She said that she ....

3. I don't want to study.
   He said ....

4. I have never been to Athens.
   He ....

5. I've lost my key.
   ....

6. I'm learning Spanish.
   ....

7. I can't drive a car.
   ....
8. I know the answer.
   ....
9. I'm not going out.
   ....

10. I've just had lunch.
    ....

49.3 Put in **say/said** or **tell/told**.

1. She *said* .... she was tired.
2. He *told* .... me he was tired.
3. I .... her that it was important.
4. Jack .... me you were sick.
5. She .... she didn't like Peter.
6. Did Pat .... that she would be late?
7. I didn't .... the police anything.
8. The man .... us he was a reporter.
9. He .... he was a reporter.
10. Did they .... you their names?

UNIT 50

get

A

get something/somebody = receive/buy/find

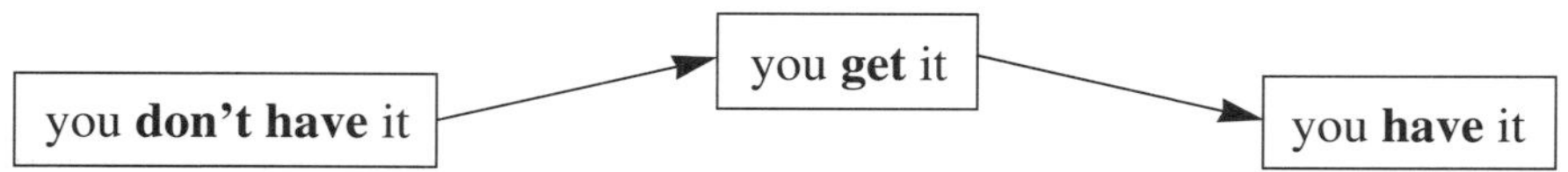

- Did you **get my letter** last week? (= *receive*)
- I like your sweater. Where did you **get it**? (= *buy*)
- *(on the phone)* "Hello, can I speak to Ann, please?" "Sure. I'll **get her**." (= *find and bring back*)
- Is it difficult to **get a job** in your country? (= *find*)

B

get cold/hungry/tired/better, etc. (**get** + *adjective*) = become

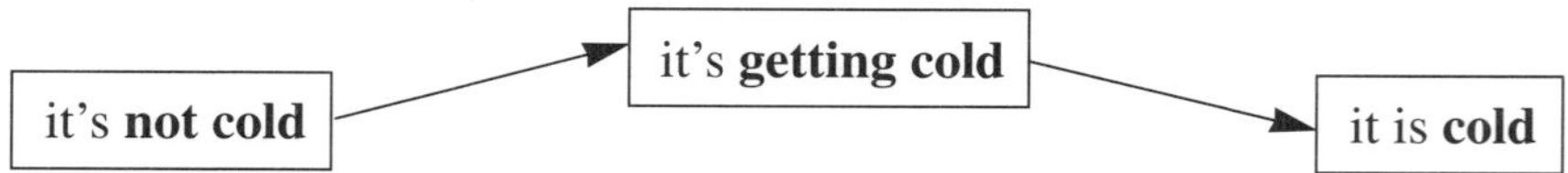

- Drink your coffee. It**'s getting cold**.
- If you don't eat, you **get hungry**.
- I'm sorry he's sick. I hope he **gets better** soon.

also: **get married** and **get lost**:

- Linda and Jack **are getting married** next month.
- I went for a walk and **got lost**. (= I lost my way)

C

get to a place (**get to work / get to Washington / get home**, etc.) = arrive

- I usually **get to work** before 8:30. (= *arrive at work*)
- We went to Washington yesterday. We left Boston at 8:00 and **got to Washington** at 9:30.
- Can you tell me how to **get to the city center**?

get to

but **get home** (*not* "get to home"):

- What time did you **get home** last night?

D

get in/out/on/off

get in (a car)
get out (of a car)

get on
get off } (a bus, a train, a plane)

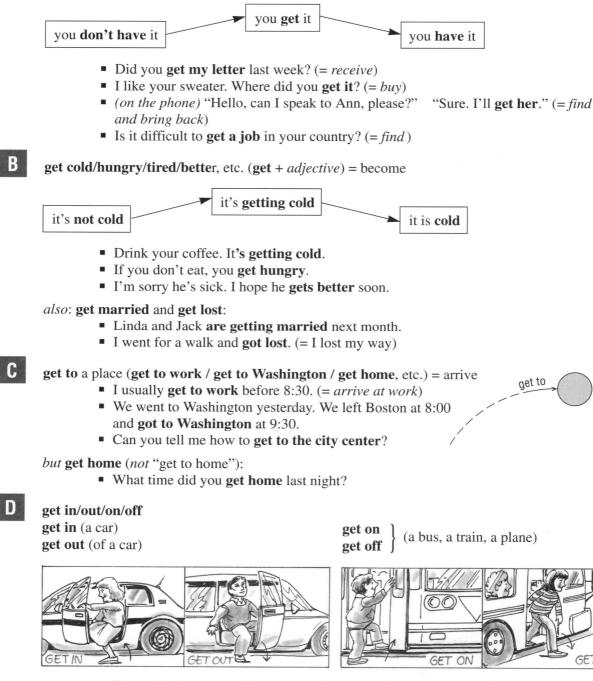

- She **got in the car** and drove away. (*you can also say* "got **into** the car")
- A car stopped and a man **got out**. (*but* "got out **of the car**" *not* "got out the car")
- They **got on** the bus outside the hotel and **got off** at Main Street.

Exercises

50.1 Finish these sentences. Use **get(s)** + the best ending.

your shoes ~~**my letter**~~ **some milk** **a ticket** **a doctor** **the job** **some gas** **a very good salary**

1. I wrote to you last week. Did you *get my letter* ?
2. We stopped at the gas station to ....
3. Quick! This man is sick. We have to ....
4. Where did you .... ? They're very nice.
5. "Are you going to the concert?" "Yes, if I can ...."
6. I had an interview with the manager, but I didn't ....
7. When you go to the store, can you .... ?
8. She has a good job. She ....

50.2 Complete these sentences. Use **getting** + one of these words:

dark **late** ~~**cold**~~ **ready** **married**

1. Drink your coffee. It's *getting cold.*
2. It's .... It's time to go home.
3. "I'm .... next week." "Oh, really? Congratulations!"
4. "Where's Sally?" "She's in her room. She's .... to go out."
5. Turn on the light. It's ....

50.3 Complete the sentences. Use **get/got** + one of these words:

tired **older** ~~**hungry**~~ **married** **better** **wet** **lost**

1. If you don't eat, you'll *get hungry.*
2. If you work too hard, you ....
3. Don't go out in the rain. You'll ....
4. My brother .... last month. His wife's name is Mary.
5. We didn't know the way home, so we ....
6. Everybody wants to stay young, but we all ....
7. The beginning of the movie wasn't very good, but it ....

50.4 Write sentences with **I left . . . and got to . . .**

1. (home / 7:30 → work / 8:15) *I left home at 7:30 and got to work at 8:15.*
2. (Toronto / 11:00 → New York / 12:25) I left Toronto at 11:00 and ....
3. (home / 8:30 → the airport / 9:30) I left home ....
4. (the party / 11:15 → home / midnight) I ....

50.5 Put in **got** + **in** / **out (of)** / **on** / **off**.

1. She *got in* .... the car and drove away.
2. I .... the bus and walked to my house from the bus stop.
3. She .... the car, locked the doors, and went into a store.
4. I made a stupid mistake. I .... the wrong train.

UNIT 51

go

A

go to . . . (**go to China / go to work / go to a concert**, etc.)

- I'm **going to France** next week.
- What time do you usually **go to work**?
- Tom didn't want to **go to the concert**.
- I **went to the dentist** on Friday.
- What time did you **go to bed** last night?

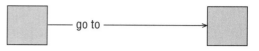

go home (*without* **to**):

- I'm **going home** now. (*not* "going to home")

B

go on vacation / a **tour / a cruise**

- We **go on vacation** (**to** the mountains) every year.
- When we were in Egypt, we **went on a tour of** the pyramids.
- My parents are **going on a cruise** this summer.

C

go for a walk / a run / a swim / a drink

- I'm hot. Let's **go for a swim**.
- "Where's Ann?" "She **went for a walk** in the park."
- Linda **goes for a run** before breakfast every morning.

go out for dinner

- Last night we **went out for dinner**. The restaurant was very good.

go (to a place) for (a) vacation (*with or without* **a**)

- They've gone to Europe **for a vacation**. *or* . . . **for vacation**.

D

go swimming / go shopping, etc.

We use **go -ing** for sporting activities (**go swimming / go skiing / go jogging / go fishing**, etc.) and also **shopping** (**go shopping**):

I **go**	shopp**ing**
he **is going**	swimm**ing**
we **went**	fish**ing**
they **have gone**	sail**ing**
she wants **to go**	ski**ing**
	(etc.)

- We live near the mountains. In the winter we **go skiing** every weekend. (*not* "go to skiing")
- She has a small boat and she often **goes sailing**.
- Are you **going shopping** this afternoon?
- It's a nice day. Let's **go swimming**. (*or* Let's **go for a swim**.)
- Dave **went fishing** last Sunday. He caught a lot of fish.

Exercises

51.1 Put in **to/on/for** where necessary.

1. I'm going ..*to*........ France next week
2. She has a small boat, so she often goes ..—........ sailing. *(no preposition)*
3. Sue went .... New York last year.
4. Would you like to go .... the movies tonight?
5. Jack goes .... jogging every morning before breakfast.
6. I'm going out .... a walk. Do you want to come?
7. I'm tired because I went .... a party last night and went .... bed very late.
8. They're going .... vacation .... Brazil next week.
9. The weather was warm and the river was clean, so we went .... a swim.
10. Excuse me, I have to go .... class now.
11. It's late. I have to go .... home now.
12. I need some stamps, so I'm going .... the post office.
13. Someday I'd like to go .... a tour of the Greek islands.
14. She isn't feeling well, so she went .... the doctor.

51.2 What did these people do yesterday afternoon? Look at the pictures and write a sentence with **went -ing**.

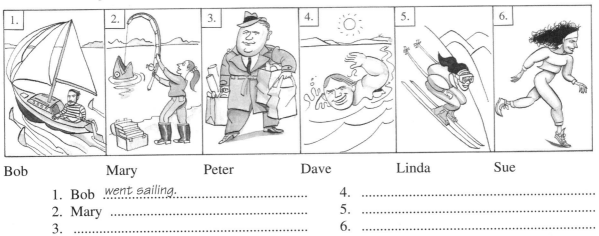

Bob Mary Peter Dave Linda Sue

1. Bob *went sailing.*..................................
2. Mary ....
3. ....
4. ....
5. ....
6. ....

51.3 Use the words in the list to finish these sentences. Use **to/on/for** if necessary.

home **shopping** **~~a swim~~** **Hawaii** **riding** **vacation** **the bank** **fishing** **a walk**

1. The water feels nice and warm. Let's go *for a swim.*..................................
2. Bob went .... and caught a lot of fish.
3. "Is Ann at home?" "No, she went .... to get some money."
4. He has three horses. He often goes ....
5. The weather is nice. Would you like to go .... in the park?
6. I'm going .... I have to buy a lot of food for the party.
7. It's late and I'm tired. I'm going .... Good night.
8. "Are you going .... soon?" "Yes, next month. We're going ...."

UNIT 52

I/me he/him they/them, etc.

A

people

subject:	**I**	**we**	**you**	**he**	**she**	**they**
object:	**me**	**us**	**you**	**him**	**her**	**them**

Subject			*Object*
I	**I** like Ann.	Ann likes **me**.	**me**
we	**We** like Ann.	Ann likes **us**.	**us**
you	**You** like Ann.	Ann likes **you**.	**you**
he	**He** likes Ann.	Ann likes **him**.	**him**
she	**She** likes Ann.	Ann likes **her**.	**her**
they	**They** like Ann.	Ann likes **them**.	**them**

Use **me/him/her**, etc. *(object)* after *prepositions* (**for/to/at/with**, etc.):

- This letter isn't **for you**. It's **for me**.
- Where's Tom? I want to talk **to him**.
- Who is that woman? Why are you looking **at her**?
- We're going to the movies. Do you want to come **with us**?
- They are going to the movies. Do you want to go **with them**?

B

things

subject:	**it**	**they**
object:	**it**	**them**

- I want **that book**. Please give **it** to me.
- I want **those books**. Please give **them** to me.
- Sue never drinks **milk**. She doesn't like **it**.
- I never go to **parties**. I don't like **them**.
- "Where's **the newspaper**?" "You're sitting **on it**."

Exercises

52.1 Finish the sentences with **him/her/them**.

1. I don't know those women. Do you know *them* ?
2. I don't know that man. Do you know .... ?
3. I don't know those people. Do you know .... ?
4. I don't know Fred's wife. Do you know .... ?
5. I don't know his friends. Do you know .... ?
6. I don't know the woman in the black coat. Do you know .... ?
7. I don't know Mr. Stevens. Do you know .... ?
8. I don't know those students. Do you know .... ?

52.2 Finish the sentences. Use **I/me/we/us/you/he/him/she/her/they/them**.

1. **I** want to see **her**, but *she* doesn't want to see *me*.
2. **I** want to see **him**, but .... doesn't want to see ....
3. **They** want to see **me**, but .... don't want to see ....
4. **We** want to see **them**, but .... don't want to see ....
5. **She** wants to see **him**, but .... doesn't want to see ....
6. **They** want to see **her**, but .... doesn't want to see ....
7. **I** want to see **them**, but .... don't want to see ....
8. **He** wants to see **us**, but .... don't want to see ....
9. **You** want to see **her**, but .... doesn't want to see ....

52.3 Finish the sentences. Use **me/us/him/her/it/them**.

1. Who is that woman? Why are you looking at *her* ?
2. "Do you know that man?" "Yes, I work with ...."
3. I'm talking to you. Please listen to ....
4. These photographs are nice. Do you want to look at .... ?
5. I like that camera. I'm going to buy ....
6. Where are the tickets? I can't find ....
7. We're going out. You can come with ....
8. I don't like dogs. I'm afraid of ....
9. Where is she? I want to talk to ....
10. Those apples are rotten. Don't eat ....

52.4 Put in **it/them** + **me/us/him/her/them**.

1. I want those books. Please give *them* to *me*.
2. He wants the key. Please give .... to ....
3. She wants the keys. Please give .... to ....
4. I want the letter. Please give .... to ....
5. They want the money. Please give .... to ....
6. We want the photographs. Please give .... to ....

UNIT 53

my/her/his/their, etc.

A

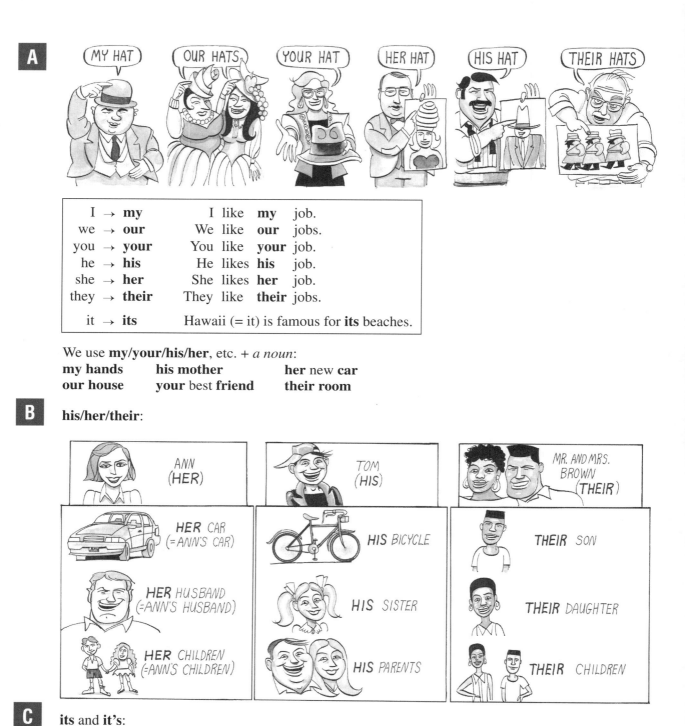

I	→	**my**	I	like	**my**	job.
we	→	**our**	We	like	**our**	jobs.
you	→	**your**	You	like	**your**	job.
he	→	**his**	He	likes	**his**	job.
she	→	**her**	She	likes	**her**	job.
they	→	**their**	They	like	**their**	jobs.
it	→	**its**	Hawaii (= it) is famous for **its** beaches.			

We use **my/your/his/her**, etc. + *a noun*:

my hands	**his mother**	**her** new **car**
our house	**your** best **friend**	**their room**

B

his/her/their:

C

its and **it's**:

its	Hawaii is famous for **its** beaches.
it's (= it **is**)	I like Hawaii. **It's** a beautiful place. (= It **is** beautiful.)

Exercises

53.1 Finish these sentences.

1. He *lives with his parents.* ....
2. They live with .... parents.
3. We .... parents.
4. Ann lives ....
5. I .... parents.
6. John ....
7. Do you live .... ?
8. Most children ....

53.2 Finish these sentences.

1. I *'m going to wash my hands.* ....
2. She's going to wash ....
3. We're going to ....
4. He's going to ....
5. They're going to ....
6. Are you going .... ?

53.3 Look at the family tree and finish the sentences.

1. I saw Liz with *her*.......... husband Tom.
2. I saw Ann and Ted with .... children.
3. I saw Ted with .... wife Ann.
4. I saw Sam with .... brother Bill.
5. I saw Ann with .... brother Bill.
6. I saw Liz and Tom with .... son Bill.
7. I saw Ann with .... parents.
8. I saw Sue and Robert with .... parents.

53.4 Put in **my/our/your/his/her/their/its**.

1. I like *my*.......... job.
2. Do you like .... job?
3. Does your father like .... job?
4. Ann is married. She works in a store and .... husband works in a bank.
5. I know Mr. Brown, but I don't know .... wife.
6. Put on .... coat when you go out. It's very cold.
7. .... favorite sport is tennis. I play a lot in the summer.
8. My sister plays tennis too, but .... favorite sport is golf.
9. We're staying at a very nice hotel. .... room is very comfortable.
10. Mr. and Mrs. Lee live in Taiwan, but .... son lives in Canada.
11. Thank you for .... letter. It was good to hear from you again.
12. We are going to invite all .... friends to the party.
13. John is a teacher, but .... sister is a nurse.
14. Do you think that most people are happy in .... jobs?
15. I gave the money to my mother, and she put it in .... purse.
16. I see that man a lot, but I don't know .... name.
17. They have two children, but I don't remember .... names.
18. The company has offices in many places, but .... head office is in Tokyo.

UNIT 54

"Whose is this?" "It's mine."

A

B

mine	ours	yours	his	hers	theirs

I	→	**my**	→	**mine**
we	→	**our**	→	**ours**
you	→	**your**	→	**yours**
he	→	**his**	→	**his**
she	→	**her**	→	**hers**
they	→	**their**	→	**theirs**

It's **my money**.	It's **mine**.
It's **our money**.	It's **ours**.
It's **your money**.	It's **yours**.
It's **his money**.	It's **his**.
It's **her money**.	It's **hers**.
It's **their money**.	It's **theirs**.

my/our/your/her/their + *a noun* (**my hands / your book**, etc.):

- **My hands** are cold.
- Is this **your book**?
- Ann gave me **her umbrella**.
- It's **their problem**, not **our problem**.

mine/ours/yours/hers/theirs *without a noun*:

- These books are **mine**, but this newspaper is **yours**. (= your newspaper)
- I didn't have an umbrella, so Ann gave me **hers**. (= her umbrella)
- It's their problem, not **ours**. (= our problem)
- "Is that their car?" "No, **theirs** is green." (= their car)

his *with or without a noun*:

- Is this **his camera**?
- It's a nice camera. Is it **his**?

C

We say: a friend **of mine** / a friend **of his** / some friends **of yours**, etc.:

- I went out to meet **a friend of mine**. (*not* "a friend of me")
- Are those people **friends of yours**? (*not* "friends of you")

D

Whose . . . ?

- **Whose book** is this? (= Is it your book? / his book? / my book?, etc.)

You can use **whose** with or without a noun:

- **Whose money** is this? / **Whose** is this? } It's mine.
- **Whose shoes** are these? / **Whose** are these? } They're John's.

Exercises

54.1 Finish the sentences with **mine/yours**, etc.

1. It's your money. It's *yours.*
2. It's my bag. It's ....
3. It's our car. It's ....
4. They're her shoes. They're ....
5. It's their house. ....
6. They're your books. ....
7. They're my glasses. ....
8. It's his coat. ....

54.2 Choose the right word.

1. Is this your/~~yours~~ book? (your is *right*)
2. It's their/~~theirs~~ problem, not ~~our~~/ours. (their and ours are *right*)
3. Are these your/yours shoes?
4. Is this camera your/yours?
5. That's not my/mine umbrella. My/Mine is yellow.
6. They know our/ours address, but we don't know their/theirs.
7. They have two children, but I don't know their/theirs names.
8. My/Mine room is bigger than her/hers, but her/hers is nicer.

54.3 Finish these sentences with **. . . friend(s) of mine/yours**, etc.

1. I went to the movies with a *friend of mine.*
2. They went on vacation with some *friends of theirs.*
3. She's going out with a friend ....
4. We had dinner with some ....
5. I played tennis with a ....
6. He's going to meet a ....
7. Do you know that man? Is he a .... ?

54.4 Look at the pictures. Write questions with **Whose . . . ?**

1. 2. 3. 4. 5. 6. 7. 8. 9. 10. 11. 12.

WAR AND PEACE

Gone with the wind

1. *Whose book is this?* ?
2. Whose .... ?
3. .... ?
4. .... ?
5. .... ?
6. .... ?
7. .... ?
8. .... ?
9. .... ?
10. .... ?
11. .... ?
12. .... ?

UNIT 55

I/me/my/mine

I, etc.	**me**, etc.	**my**, etc.	**mine**, etc.
I know Tom.	Tom knows **me**.	It's **my** car.	It's **mine**.
We know Tom.	Tom knows **us**.	It's **our** car.	It's **ours**.
You know Tom.	Tom knows **you**.	It's **your** car.	It's **yours**.
He knows Tom.	Tom knows **him**.	It's **his** car.	It's **his**.
She knows Tom.	Tom knows **her**.	It's **her** car.	It's **hers**.
They know Tom.	Tom knows **them**.	It's **their** car.	It's **theirs**.
See Unit 52.	See Unit 52.	See Unit 53.	See Unit 54.

- "Do **you** know that man?" "Yes, **I** know **him**, but I can't remember **his name**."
- She was very happy because **we** invited **her** to stay with **us** at **our house**.
- "Where are the children? Have **you** seen **them**?" "Yes, **they** are playing with **their friends** in the garden."
- That pen is **mine**. Can **you** give it to **me**, please?
- "Is this **your umbrella**?" "No, it's **yours**."
- **He** didn't have an umbrella, so **she** gave **him hers**. (= she gave her umbrella to him)
- **I** gave **him my address** and **he** gave **me his**. (= he gave his address to me)

Exercises

55.1 Finish the sentences in the same way.

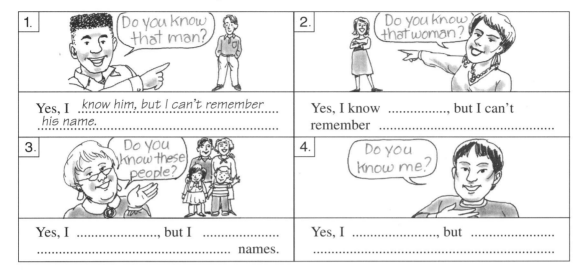

1. Do you know that man?	2. Do you know that woman?
Yes, I *know him, but I can't remember his name.*	Yes, I know ...., but I can't remember ....
3. Do you know these people?	**4.** Do you know me?
Yes, I ...., but I .... names.	Yes, I ...., but ....

55.2 Finish these sentences in the same way.

1. We invited her *to stay with us at our house.*
2. He invited us to stay with .... house.
3. They invited me to stay with .... house.
4. I invited her to stay ....
5. We invited them to ....
6. You invited him ....
7. She invited me ....

55.3 Finish the sentences.

1. It's hers. Give *it to her.*
2. They're mine. Give *them to me.*
3. It's his. Give it ....
4. They're hers. Give them ....
5. It's ours. Give ....
6. It's theirs. Give ....
7. They're his. Give ....
8. It's mine. Give ....

55.4 Finish the sentences in the same way.

Here's my address.
And here's mine.

1. I gave him *my address, and he gave me his.*
2. I have her .... address, and she gave me ....
3. He gave me .... address, and I gave ....
4. We gave her .... address, and she gave ....
5. I gave them .... address, and they ....
6. She gave us .... address, and ....
7. You gave him .... address, and ....
8. We gave them .... address, and ....
9. They gave you .... address, and ....
10. She gave him .... address, and ....

UNIT 56

myself/yourself/himself, etc.

A

I'm looking at myself.
I'm looking at him.
TOM
JACK

Jack is looking at Tom.
He is looking at **him**.

Tom is looking in the mirror.
He is looking at **himself**.

 **He** is looking at **him**.  **He** is looking at **himself**. 

different people — *the same person*

I	→ **me**	→	**myself**	**I**	looked at **myself**.	
he	→ **him**	→	**himself**	**He**	looked at **himself**.	
she	→ **her**	→	**herself**	**She**	looked at **herself**.	
you	→ **you**	→	**yourself**	**You**	looked at **yourself**.	*(one person)*
			yourselves	**You**	looked at **yourselves**.	*(two or more people)*
we	→ **us**	→	**ourselves**	**We**	looked at **ourselves**.	
they	→ **them**	→	**themselves**	**They**	looked at **themselves**.	

- **I cut myself** with a knife. (*not* "I cut me")
- She fell off her bicycle, but **she** didn't **hurt herself**.
- Do **you** sometimes **talk to yourself** when you are alone?
- If you want some more food, **help yourselves**.
- Did **they pay for themselves** or did you pay for them?
- "Did you all have a nice time?" "Yes, **we enjoyed ourselves**."

B

by myself/by yourself, etc. = alone

- **I** went on vacation **by myself**. (= I went on vacation alone.)
- She wasn't with her friends. **She** was **by herself**.

C

-selves and **each other**

- I looked at **myself** and Tom looked at **himself**.
  = We looked at **ourselves** *(in the mirror)*.
  but I looked at Tom and he looked at me.
  = We looked at **each other**.
- Sue and Ann are good friends. They know **each other** very well.
  (= Sue knows Ann and Ann knows Sue.)
- Bob and I live near **each other**.
  (= Bob lives near me and I live near him.)

We looked at ourselves.

We looked at each other.

Exercises

56.1 Finish the sentences with **myself/yourself**, etc.

1. He enjoyed himself.
2. I enjoyed ....
3. She enjoyed ....
4. We enjoyed ....
5. Did you enjoy .... ? *(one person)*
6. Did you and Bill enjoy .... ?
7. The children enjoyed ....
8. Jack didn't enjoy ....

56.2 Finish the sentences with **myself/yourself**, etc.

1. I cut myself with a knife.
2. Be careful! That plate is very hot. Don't burn ....
3. I'm not angry with *you*. I'm angry with ....
4. They never think about other people. They only think about ....
5. I got out of the shower and dried .... with a towel.
6. When people are alone, they often talk to ....
7. Don't pay for me. I want to pay for ....
8. He fell off the ladder, but he didn't hurt ....
9. I'd like to know more about you. Tell me about .... *(one person)*
10. Goodbye! Have a good trip and enjoy .... ! *(two people)*

56.3 Make sentences with **by myself / by yourself**, etc.

1. I went on vacation alone. I went on vacation by myself.
2. John lives alone. John lives ....
3. Do you live alone? Do you .... ?
4. She went to the movies alone. She ....
5. When I saw him, he was alone. When I saw him, ...
6. Don't go out alone. Don't ....
7. I had dinner alone. I ....

56.4 Finish the sentences. Use **each other**.

1. I looked at Bill and Bill looked at me. Bill and I looked at each other.
2. I know him and he knows me. We ....
3. She likes him and he likes her. They ....
4. You can help me and I can help you. We can ....
5. He understands her and she understands him.
   They ....
6. He gives her presents and she gives him presents.
   They ....
7. Tom didn't see Sue and Sue didn't see Tom.
   Tom and Sue ....
8. I didn't speak to her and she didn't speak to me.
   We ....
9. She often writes letters to him and he often writes letters to her.
   ....

UNIT 57

-'s (Ann's camera / my brother's car, etc.)

Ann**'s** camera (**her** camera) | my brother**'s** car (**his** car) | the manager**'s** office (**his** *or* **her** office)

A

We normally use **-'s** (*not* **of . . .**) for *people*:

- I stayed at **my sister's** house. (*not* "the house of my sister")
- Have you met **Mr. Kelly's** wife? (*not* "the wife of Mr. Kelly")
- Are you going to **James's** party?
- Ann is a **woman's** name.

You can use **-'s** without a noun:

- Mary's hair is longer than **Ann's**. (= Ann's hair)
- "Whose umbrella is this?" "It's **my mother's**." (= my mother's umbrella)
- "Where were you last night?" "At **John's**." (= John's house)

B

friend**'s** and friend**s'**

my friend**'s** house = *one friend* (= **her** house *or* **his** house)

my friend**s'** house = *two or more friends* (= **their** house)

We write **-'s** after **friend/student/mother**, etc. *(singular)*:
my mother**'s** car *(one mother)* my father**'s** car *(one father)*

We write **-'** after friend**s**/student**s**/parent**s**, etc. *(plural)*:
my parent**s'** car *(two parents)*

C

We use **of . . .** (*not usually* **-'s**) for *things*, *places*, etc.:

the roof **of the building** (*not* "the building's roof")
the beginning **of the movie** (*not* "the movie's beginning")
the time **of the next train** | the name **of this town**
the capital **of Spain** | the cause **of the problem**
the meaning **of this word** | the back **of the car**

Exercises

57.1 Look at the family tree and finish the sentences. Use **-'s**.

Liz and Tom are married.
They have two children, Sam and Ann.
Ann is married to Ted.
Ann and Ted have a son, Robert.

1. Tom is *Liz's* husband.
2. Liz is .... wife.
3. Sam is .... brother.
4. Sam is .... uncle.
5. Ann is .... wife.
6. Liz is .... grandmother.
7. Ann is .... sister.
8. Ted is .... husband.
9. Ted is .... father.
10. Robert is .... nephew.

57.2 Look at the big picture and then answer the questions.

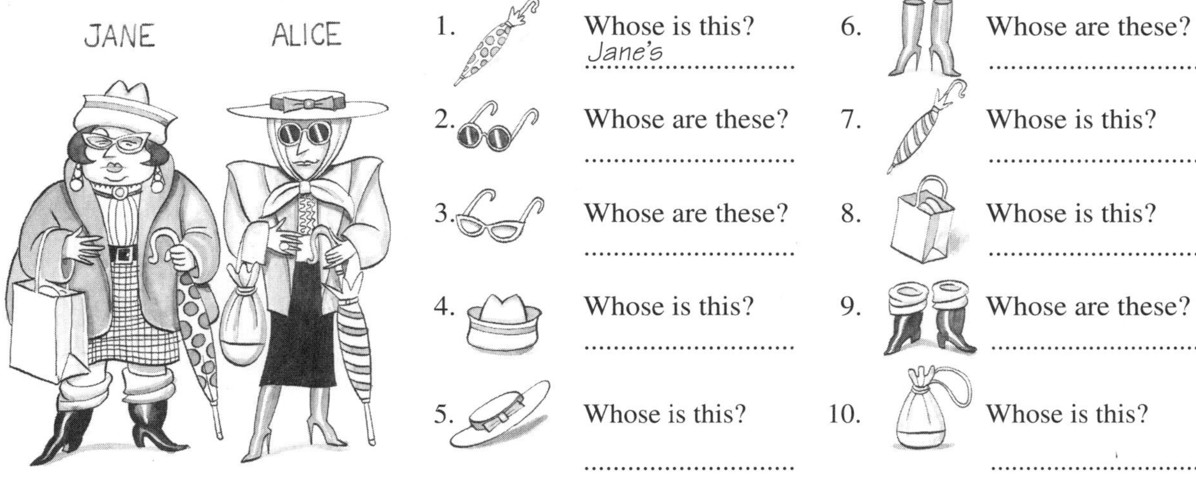

1. Whose is this? *Jane's*
2. Whose are these? ....
3. Whose are these? ....
4. Whose is this? ....
5. Whose is this? ....
6. Whose are these? ....
7. Whose is this? ....
8. Whose is this? ....
9. Whose are these? ....
10. Whose is this? ....

57.3 Complete the sentences. Sometimes you need **-'s**, sometimes **of . . .**

1. I like *Ann's camera.* (the camera / Ann)
2. What is *the name of this town* ? (the name / this town)
3. When is .... ? (the birthday / your sister)
4. Do you like .... ? (the color / this coat)
5. Write your name at .... (the top / the page)
6. What is .... ? (the address / Jane)
7. What was .... ? (the cause / the accident)
8. .... is near the city center. (the house / my parents)
9. .... is very good. (the English / Maria)
10. For me the morning is .... (the best part / the day)
11. .... is very interesting. (the job / my brother)
12. The car stopped at .... (the end / the street)
13. .... is blue. (the favorite color / Pat)
14. .... are very thin. (the walls / this house)

UNIT 58

a/an

He has **a** camera. She's waiting for **a** taxi. It's **a** nice day.

A

a = "one." Don't forget **a**:

- Do you want **a cup** of tea? (*not* "Do you want cup of tea?")
- Alice works in **a bank**. (*not* "in bank")
- I want to ask **a question**. (*not* "ask question")
- When I was **a child**, I liked reading stories.
- Bali is **a** large **island** in Indonesia.

B

an (*not* **a**) before **a/e/i/o/u**:

- They live in **an o**ld house. (*not* "a old house")
- **A m**ouse is **an a**nimal. It's **a s**mall animal.
- Can you give me **an e**xample, please?
- This is **an i**nteresting book.
- I brought **a h**at and **an u**mbrella.

also **an hour** (**h** is not pronounced)
but **a university** **a European** country
(these words sound like "yuniversity," "yuropean")

C

We use **a/an** for jobs, etc.:

- "What's your job?" **"I'm a dentist."** (*not* "I'm dentist.")
- "What does she do?" **"She's an engineer."**
- Would you like **to be a teacher**?
- Beethoven **was a composer**.
- Picasso **was a** famous **painter**.
- Are you **a student**?

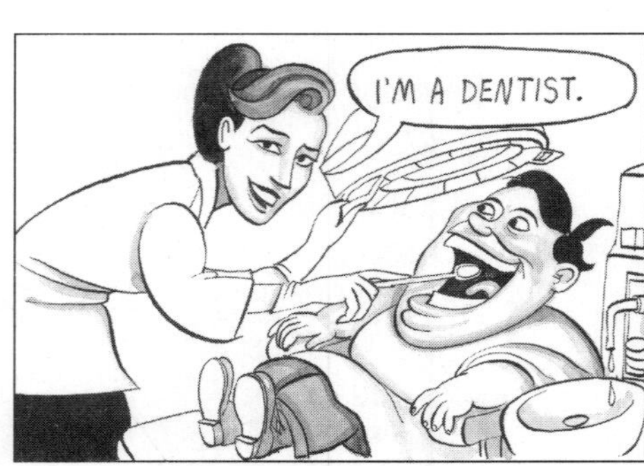

D

another (an + other) is one word (*not* "an other"):

- Can I have **another cup** of coffee?
- Open **another window**. It's very hot.

Exercises

58.1 Write **a** or **an**.

1. a book
2. an old book
3. .... window
4. .... horse
5. .... airport
6. .... university
7. .... organization
8. .... restaurant
9. .... Chinese restaurant
10. .... Indian restaurant
11. .... accident
12. .... bad accident
13. .... question
14. .... important question
15. .... hamburger
16. .... hour
17. .... economic problem
18. .... nice evening

58.2 What are these things? Choose your answer from the list and write a sentence.

animal ~~**bird**~~ **flower** **fruit** **musical instrument** **planet** **river** **tool** **game** **vegetable**

1. a duck? It 's a bird.
2. the Nile? It ....
3. a rabbit? It ....
4. tennis? It ....
5. a rose? It ....
6. a hammer? It ....
7. a carrot? It ....
8. Mars? It ....
9. a trumpet? It ....
10. a pear? It ....

58.3 What are their jobs? Look at the pictures and finish the sentences. The jobs are: **nurse** / **photographer** / **private detective** / ~~**dentist**~~ / **taxi driver** / **mechanic** / **sales clerk**.

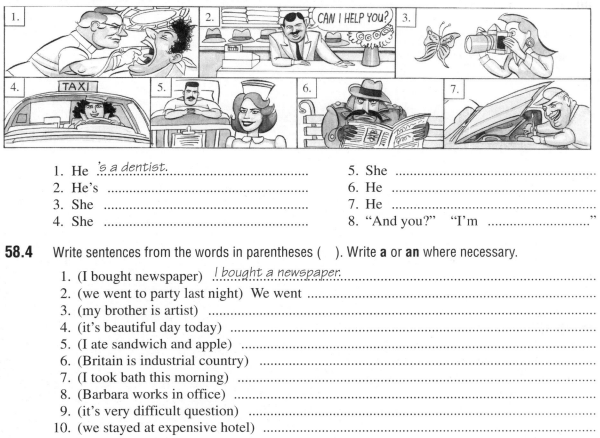

1. He 's a dentist.
2. He's ....
3. She ....
4. She ....
5. She ....
6. He ....
7. He ....
8. "And you?" "I'm ...."

58.4 Write sentences from the words in parentheses ( ). Write **a** or **an** where necessary.

1. (I bought newspaper) I bought a newspaper.
2. (we went to party last night) We went ....
3. (my brother is artist) ....
4. (it's beautiful day today) ....
5. (I ate sandwich and apple) ....
6. (Britain is industrial country) ....
7. (I took bath this morning) ....
8. (Barbara works in office) ....
9. (it's very difficult question) ....
10. (we stayed at expensive hotel) ....

UNIT 59

flower/flowers (singular and plural)

A

The plural of a noun is usually **-s**:

singular (= one)		*plural* (= two or more)
a flower	→	**some** flowers
a week	→	**six** weeks
a baby	→	**two** babies
a nice place	→	**many** nice places

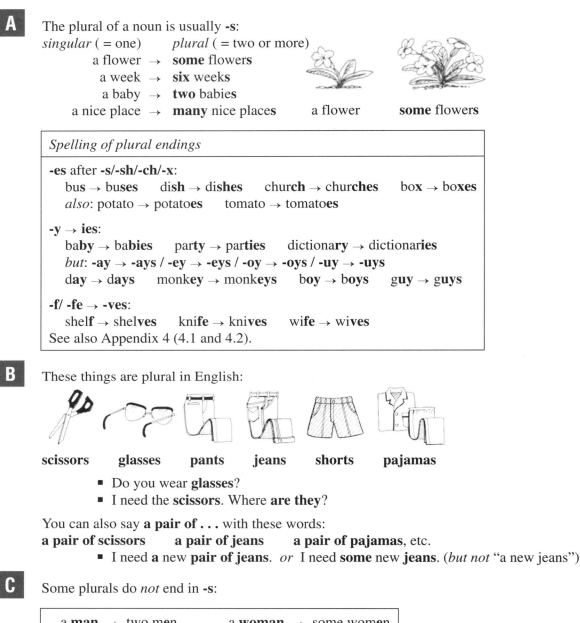

a flower **some** flowers

Spelling of plural endings
-es after **-s**/**-sh**/**-ch**/**-x**: bus → bus**es** dish → dish**es** church → church**es** box → box**es** *also*: potato → potato**es** tomato → tomato**es**
-y → **ies**: bab**y** → bab**ies** part**y** → part**ies** dictionar**y** → dictionar**ies** *but*: **-ay** → **-ays** / **-ey** → **-eys** / **-oy** → **-oys** / **-uy** → **-uys** d**ay** → d**ays** monk**ey** → monk**eys** b**oy** → b**oys** g**uy** → g**uys**
-f/ **-fe** → **-ves**: shel**f** → shel**ves** kni**fe** → kni**ves** wi**fe** → wi**ves** See also Appendix 4 (4.1 and 4.2).

B

These things are plural in English:

scissors

glasses

pants

jeans

shorts

pajamas

- Do you wear **glasses**?
- I need the **scissors**. Where **are they**?

You can also say **a pair of . . .** with these words:

a pair of scissors **a pair of jeans** **a pair of pajamas**, etc.

- I need **a** new **pair of jeans**. *or* I need **some** new **jeans**. (*but not* "a new jeans")

C

Some plurals do *not* end in **-s**:

a **man**	→	two m**e**n	a **woman**	→	some wom**e**n
a **child**	→	many child**ren**			
one **foot**	→	two f**ee**t	a **tooth**	→	all my t**ee**th
a **mouse**	→	some m**ice**			
a **sheep**	→	two **sheep**	a **fish**	→	many **fish**

also: a **person** → **two people / some people / many people**, etc.

- **She**'s **a** nice **person**. *but* **They** are nice **people**. (*not* "nice persons")
- **Some people are** very lazy. (*not* "Some people is")

Police is a plural word:

- **The police are** coming. (*not* "The police is coming.")

Exercises

59.1 Write the plural.

1. flower *flowers*
2. man *men*
3. boat ....
4. language ....
5. watch ....
6. country ....
7. knife ....
8. woman ....
9. address ....
10. sheep ....
11. tooth ....
12. leaf ....
13. child ....
14. foot ....
15. umbrella ....
16. person ....
17. family ....
18. holiday ....
19. sandwich ....
20. city ....
21. mouse ....

59.2 Put in **is** or **are**.

1. *Is* the store open?
2. *Are* the stores open?
3. My hands .... cold.
4. My nose .... cold.
5. My feet .... cold.
6. Where .... my camera?
7. Where .... my glasses?
8. Where .... the children?
9. Your coat .... dirty.
10. Your jeans .... dirty.
11. Who .... those men?
12. Who .... that woman?
13. Who .... those people?
14. Mice .... small animals.
15. Where .... the scissors?

59.3 Some of these sentences are right and some are wrong. Correct the sentences that are wrong. Write "okay" if the sentence is right.

1. She's a very nice person. *okay*
2. I need a new jeans. *I need a new pair of jeans.* (*or* *I need some new jeans.*)
3. I have two brother and four sister. ....
4. It's a great park with a lot of beautiful tree. ....
5. There are a lot of sheep in that field. ....
6. Do you make many mistake when you speak English? ....
7. She's married and she has three childs. ....
8. Most of my friend are students. ....
9. He put on his pajama and went to bed. ....
10. We went fishing but we didn't catch many fish. ....
11. There were three persons in the car, two women and a man. ....
12. I like your pant. Where did you get it? ....
13. The city center is usually full of tourist. ....
14. This scissor isn't very sharp. ....

59.4 Which is right? Complete the sentences.

1. It's a nice place. Many people *go* there for vacation. (**go** *or* **goes**?)
2. Some people .... always late. (**is** *or* **are**?)
3. The new taxes are not popular. People .... like them. (**don't** *or* **doesn't**?)
4. A lot of people .... television every day. (**watch** *or* **watches**?)
5. Three people .... hurt in the accident. (**was** *or* **were**?)
6. How many people .... in that house? (**live** *or* **lives**?)
7. .... the police carry guns in your country? (**Do** *or* **Does**?)
8. The police .... looking for the stolen car. (**is** *or* **are**?)
9. I need my glasses, but I can't find .... (**it** *or* **them**?)
10. I'm going to buy .... new pants today. (**a** *or* **some**?)

a car / some money (countable/uncountable 1)

A noun can be *countable* or *uncountable*.

A

Countable nouns For example:

(a) **car** (a) **hat** (a) **flower** (a) **man** (a) **house** (a) **party** (an) **idea**

You can use **one/two/three . . .** + *countable nouns* (you can *count* them):

one **car**

two **cars**

three **men**

four **houses**

Countable nouns can be *singular* (= one) or *plural* (= two or more):

singular:	**a car**	**my car**	**the car**, etc.		
plural:	**cars**	**two cars**	**the cars**	**some cars**	**many cars**, etc.

- I have **a car**.
- There aren't **many cars** in the parking lot.

Don't use the singular (**car/house**, etc.) alone. You need **a/an**:

- I don't have **a** car. (*not* "I don't have car.")

B

Uncountable nouns For example:

water **rain** **air** **rice** **salt** **oil** **plastic** **money** **music** **tennis**

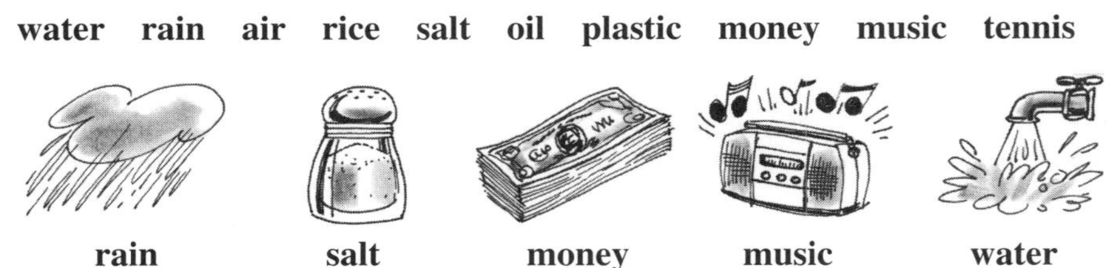

rain **salt** **money** **music** **water**

You *cannot* say **one/two/three . . .** + these things: ~~**one salt**~~ ~~**two moneys**~~

Uncountable nouns have only one form:

money **the money** **my money** **some money** **much money**, etc.

- I have **some money**.
- There isn't **much money** in the box.
- **Money** isn't everything.

Don't use **a/an** + *uncountable nouns*: ~~**a**~~ **money** ~~**a**~~ **music**

But you can say **a piece of . . . / a bottle of . . .**, etc. + *uncountable nouns*:

a piece of cheese	**a piece of** music	**a glass of** water
a bowl of rice	**a cup of** coffee	**a carton of** milk
a game of tennis	**a can of** oil	**a bar of** chocolate

For countable/uncountable nouns, see also Unit 61. For **a/an**, see Unit 58.

Exercises

60.1 What are these things? Some are countable and some are uncountable. Write **a/an** if necessary. The names of the things are:

bucket **cup** **sand** **tea** **toothpaste** **credit card** **money** **hat**
~~salt~~ **soap** **toothbrush** **~~umbrella~~**

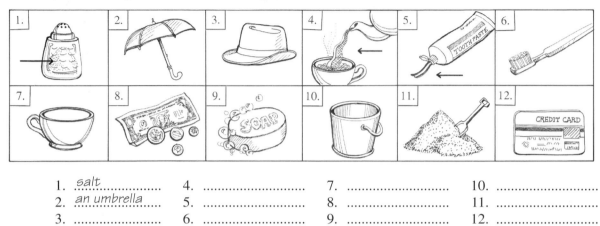

1. salt
2. an umbrella
3. ....
4. ....
5. ....
6. ....
7. ....
8. ....
9. ....
10. ....
11. ....
12. ....

60.2 Some of these sentences need **a/an**. Some of the sentences are right. Put in **a/an** where necessary.

1. I don't have car a car
2. Salt is not expensive. okay
3. Ann never wears hat. ....
4. Are you looking for job? ....
5. Mary doesn't eat meat. ....
6. I'm going to party tonight. ....
7. Do you like cheese? ....
8. Do you want cup of coffee? ....
9. I never drink milk. ....
10. Jamaica is island. ....
11. Jack made very bad mistake. ....
12. Everybody needs food. ....
13. Can you drive car? ....
14. I have great idea. ....

60.3 What are these things? Look at the pictures and write **a . . . of . . .** for each picture. Use the words in the boxes.

a	**bar**	**cup**	**loaf**	of	**bread**	**honey**	**soup**
	bowl	**glass**	**piece**		**chocolate**	**~~milk~~**	**water**
	~~carton~~	**jar**	**piece**		**coffee**	**paper**	**wood**

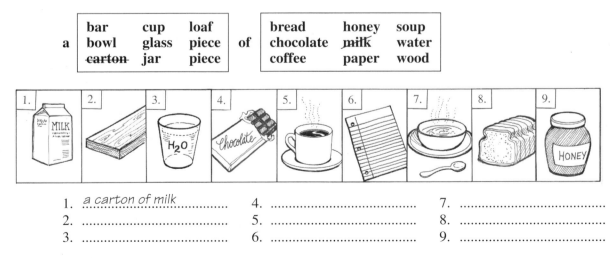

1. a carton of milk
2. ....
3. ....
4. ....
5. ....
6. ....
7. ....
8. ....
9. ....

UNIT 61

a car / some money (countable/uncountable 2)

A **a/an** and **some**

a/an + *singular countable nouns* (**car/apple/shoe**, etc.):
- I need **a** new **car**.
- Would you like **an apple**?

an apple

some + *plural countable nouns* (car**s**/apple**s**/shoe**s**, etc.):
- I need **some** new **shoes**.
- Would you like **some apples**?
  (= two or more apples)

some apples

some + *uncountable nouns* (**water/money/music**, etc.):
- I need **some money**.
- Would you like **some cheese**?
  (*or* Would you like **a piece of** cheese?)

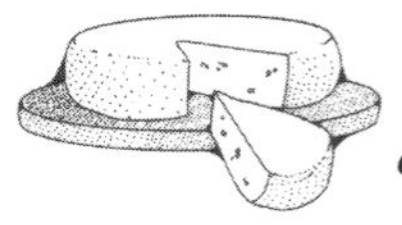
some cheese
or **a piece of** cheese

Compare **a/an** and **some**:
- She bought **a hat**, **some shoes**, and **some perfume**.
- I read **a newspaper**, wrote **some letters**, and listened to **some music**.

Many nouns are *sometimes countable* and *sometimes uncountable*. For example:

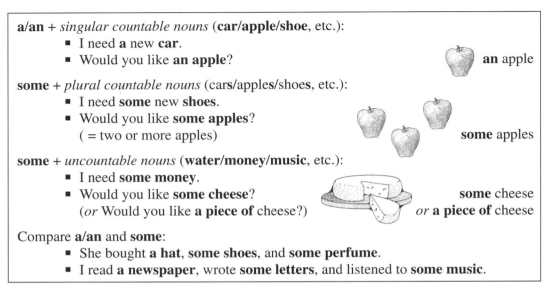

a cake | **some cupcakes** | **some cake** *or* **a piece of cake**
a chicken | **some chickens** | **some chicken** *or* **a piece of chicken**

B

Be careful with these words – they are usually uncountable in English:
bread **weather** **information** **advice** **hair** **furniture** **paper** **news**
- It's nice **weather** today. (*not* "It's a nice weather")
- I need **some information** about hotels in Prague.
- They have **some** very nice **furniture** in their house. (*not* "furnitures")
- She has long **hair**. (*not* "long hairs")
- I want to make a list. Can you give me **some paper** (*or* **a piece of** paper / **a sheet of** paper)? (*but*: "**a** paper" = **a newspaper**)
- I've just had **some** good **news** about my job. (*not* "a good news")
- I'm going to buy **some bread** (*or* **a loaf of** bread). (*not* "a bread")

For countable and uncountable nouns, see also Unit 60.
For **a/an**, see Unit 58.
For **some** and **any**, see Unit 69.

Exercises

61.1 What did you buy? Use the pictures to make sentences (**I bought . . .**).

1. *I bought a hat, some shoes, and some perfume.*
2. I bought ....
3. I ....
4. ....

61.2 Write sentences with **Would you like a/an . . . ?** or **Would you like some . . . ?**

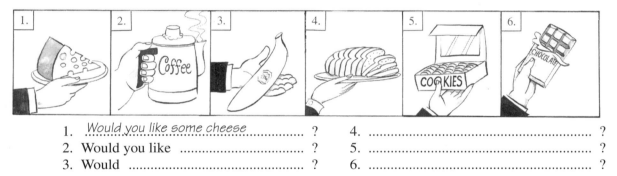

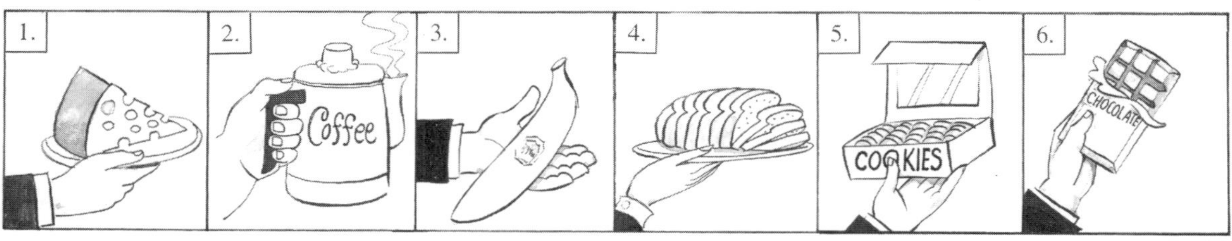

1. *Would you like some cheese* ?
2. Would you like .... ?
3. Would .... ?
4. .... ?
5. .... ?
6. .... ?

61.3 Put in **a/an** or **some**.

1. I read *a* newspaper, wrote *some* letters, and listened to *some* music.
2. I need .... money. I want to buy .... food.
3. We met .... interesting people at the party.
4. I'm going to open .... window to get .... fresh air.
5. She didn't eat much for lunch – only .... apple and .... bread.
6. We live in .... big house. There's .... nice garden with .... beautiful trees.
7. I'm going to make .... table. First, I need .... wood.
8. We talked to her and she gave us .... very good advice.
9. I want to write .... letter. I need .... pen and .... paper.
10. We had .... nice weather when we were on vacation.

61.4 Look at the underlined words in these sentences. Which is right?

1. I'm going to buy some new ~~shoe~~/shoes. (shoes is *right*)
2. They are going to buy some new chair/chairs.
3. They are going to buy some new furniture/furnitures.
4. He has big blue eye/eyes.
5. He has short black hair/hairs.
6. The tourist guide gave us some information/informations about the town.

a/an and the

A

a/an

(There are three windows here.
a window = *window* 1 *or* 2 *or* 3)

- They have **a car**. *(there are many cars and they have one)*
- I'm writing **a letter**. *(there are many letters, and I'm writing one)*
- When we were in Japan, we stayed at **a** small **inn**. *(there are many small inns in Japan)*
- Rome is **a** big **city** in Italy. *(there are many big cities in Italy, and Rome is one)*
- Borneo is **an island**. *(there are many islands, and Borneo is one)*

the

(There is only one window here, so we know which window.)

- I'm going to clean **the car** tomorrow. (= my car)
- I wrote to her but **the letter** never arrived. (= the letter that I wrote)
- We didn't enjoy our vacation. **The hotel** was awful. (= our hotel)
- Rome is **the capital** of Italy. *(there is only one capital of Italy)*
- What is **the** largest **island** in **the world**?

B

We say **the . . .** when it is clear which thing we mean. For example:

the door / the ceiling / the floor / the carpet, etc. *(of a room)*
the roof / the garden / the kitchen / the bathroom, etc. *(of a house)*
the center / the train station / the airport / the post office, etc. *(of a city)*

- "Where's Tom?" **"In the kitchen."** (= the kitchen of this house)
- I turned off **the light**, opened **the door**, and went out. (= the light and the door of the room)
- Do you live very far from **the city center**? (= the center of your city)
- I'd like to speak to **the manager**, please. (= the manager of this store)

Exercises

62.1 Put in **a/an** or **the**.

1. I wrote to her but *the*......... letter never arrived.
2. Tahiti is *an*......... island.
3. What is .... name of this town?
4. Jane is .... very nice person. You must meet her.
5. Montreal is .... large city in Canada.
6. What is .... largest city in Canada?
7. "What time is it?" "I don't know. I don't have .... watch."
8. When I went to Rome, I stayed with .... Italian friend of mine.
9. You look very tired. You need .... vacation.
10. Don't sit on .... floor. It's dirty.
11. "Let's go to .... restaurant this evening." "That's .... good idea. Which restaurant shall we go to?"
12. Can you turn on .... radio, please? I want to listen to some music.
13. Tom is in .... bathroom. He's taking .... shower.
14. This is a nice room, but I don't like .... color of .... carpet.
15. We live in .... old house near .... train station. It's two miles from .... city center.

62.2 Put in **a/an** or **the** where necessary in these sentences.

1. I turned off light, opened door, and went out. *the light* .... *the door* ....
2. Excuse me, can I ask question, please? ....
3. Tim is best player on our soccer team. ....
4. How far is it from here to airport? ....
5. Have a good vacation, and don't forget to send me postcard! ....
6. Do you have ticket for concert tomorrow night? ....
7. What is name of director of movie we saw last night? ....
8. Yesterday I bought jacket and shirt. Jacket was cheap, but shirt was expensive. ....
....
9. Peter and Mary have two children, boy and girl. Boy is seven years old and girl is three.
....

62.3 Complete the sentences. Use **a/an** or **the** + one of these:

bicycle **~~capital~~** **cigarette** **play** **difficult language** **kitchen** **nice day**
next train **roof** **~~small inn~~**

1. Rome is *the capital* .... of Italy.
2. When we were in Japan, we stayed at *a small inn.* ....
3. Can you ride .... ?
4. What's that man doing on .... of that house? Is he repairing something?
5. We went to the theater last night but .... wasn't very good.
6. Do you think English is .... for people to learn?
7. "Would you like .... ?" "No, thanks. I don't smoke."
8. "Where's Jack?" "He's in .... He's cooking something."
9. Excuse me, what time is .... to Toronto?
10. It's .... today. Let's go outside.

UNIT 63

the

A

the . . . = it is clear which thing or person we mean:

- Rome is **the capital of Italy**. *(there is only one capital)*
- What is **the name of this town**? *(the town has only one name)*
- Excuse me, where is **the nearest bank**?
- Who is **the President of the United States**?
- Can you tell me **the time**, please? (= the time now)
- My office is on **the first floor**. (= the first floor of the building)

Don't forget **the**:

- Do you live near **the city center**? (*not* "near city center")
- Which is **the best restaurant** in this town? (*not* "Which is best")

See also Unit 62.

B

the top of . . . / the end of . . ., etc.

- Write your name at **the top of the page**.
- **The beginning of the movie** was not very good.
- My house is at **the end of this street**.
- The table is in **the middle of the room**.
- Do you drive on **the left** or on **the right** in your country?

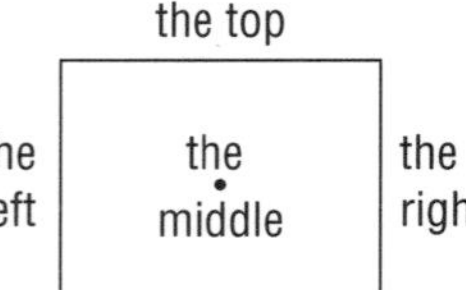

C

the same . . .

- We live on **the same street**. (*not* "on same street")
- These books are not different. They are **the same**. (*not* "They are same.")

Note that we say:

the — **the sun / the moon / the world / the sky / the ocean / the ground / the country**:

- **The sky** is blue and **the sun** is shining.
- I like swimming in **the ocean**.
- They live in a big city, but they want to live in **the country**.

the — **the police / the fire department / the army** (*of a city, country*, etc.):

- My brother is a soldier. He's in **the army**.
- Call **the police**! There's been a robbery!

the — **the piano / the guitar / the trumpet**, etc. *(musical instruments)*:

- Tom is learning to play **the piano**.

the / ~~the~~ — **the radio** *but* **television** (*without* **the**):

- I listen to **the radio** a lot.
- I like watching **television**. What's **on television** tonight?
  but Can you turn off **the television** (= the TV set)?

~~the~~ — **breakfast/lunch/dinner** (*without* **the**):

- I never **have breakfast**. (*not* "the breakfast")
- What are you going to have **for lunch**?
- **Dinner** is ready!

Exercises

63.1 Put in **the** where necessary. Write "okay" if the sentence is correct.

1. Sky is blue and sun is shining. *The sky the sun*
2. What are you going to have for lunch? *okay*
3. Our apartment is on third floor. ....
4. Help! Fire! Somebody call fire department. ....
5. Who was first person to walk on moon? ....
6. Which city is capital of your country? ....
7. What is largest city in world? ....
8. Would you like to be in army? ....
9. Do you live near ocean? ....
10. After dinner we watched television. ....
11. "Where is your dictionary?" "It's on top shelf on right." ....
12. We live in country, about five miles from nearest town. ....
13. Ann is coming to see us at end of May. ....
14. "Is this book cheaper than that one?" "No, they're same price." ....
15. Prime Minister is most important person in Canadian government. ....
16. I don't know everybody in this photograph. Who is man on left? ....
17. It was a very nice hotel, but I don't remember name. ....
18. I didn't like her first time I met her. ....
19. What do you usually have for breakfast? ....
20. "Do you have any milk?" "Yes, there's some in refrigerator." ....

63.2 Complete these sentences. Use **the same** + one of these words:

age **color** **day** **problem** ~~**street**~~ **time**

1. I live on Water Street and you live on Water Street. We live on *the same street.*
2. I arrived at 8:30 and you arrived at 8:30. We arrived at ....
3. I have no money and you have no money. We have ....
4. He's 25 and she's 25. They are ....
5. My shirt is dark blue and my jacket is dark blue. They are ....
6. I'm leaving on Monday and you're leaving on Monday. We're leaving on ....

63.3 Complete these sentences. Use the words in the list. Use **the** if necessary.

breakfast ~~**dinner**~~ **lunch** **police** **radio** **sky** **sun**
television ~~**time**~~ **trumpet**

1. "Can you tell me *the time* please?" "Yes, it's six thirty."
2. We had *dinner* at a restaurant last night.
3. .... is a star. It gives us light and warmth.
4. Did you see the movie on .... last night?
5. I was hungry this morning because I didn't have ....
6. .... stopped me because I was driving too fast.
7. "Can you play .... ?" "No, I can't play any musical instruments."
8. "What did you have for .... ?" "Just a salad."
9. When I'm working at home I like to listen to ....
10. .... is very clear tonight. You can see all the stars.

UNIT 64

go home / go to work / go to the movies

She's **at work**.

They're going **to school**.

He's **in bed**.

A

~~the~~ (*without* **the**)

go to work / get to work / be at work / start work / finish work, etc.
- What time do you **go to work** in the morning? (*not* "to the work")
- I **finish work** at 5 o'clock every day.

go to school / be at school / start school / graduate from school, etc.
- What did you **learn at school** today? (*not* "at the school")

go to college / be in college, etc.
- After she graduates from high school, she wants to **go to** college. (*not* "go to the college")
- "Do you go to high school?" "No, I'm **in college**."

go to prison/jail be in prison/jail
- I wouldn't like to **be in prison**. (*not* "in the prison")

go to bed / be in bed
- I'm tired. I'm **going to bed**. (*not* "to the bed")

go home / get home / arrive home / come home / walk home / leave home, etc.
- I'm tired. I'm **going home**. (*not* "to home")

be (at) home / stay (at) home (*with* or *without* **at**)
- Are you going out or are you **staying home**? (*or* "staying **at** home")

B

the (*with* **the**)

the movies	Do you **go to the movies** a lot?
the theater	We're **going to the theater** tonight.
the bank	I have to **go to the bank** today.
the post office	Are you **going to the post office**?
the hospital	Jack is very sick. He should **go to the hospital**.
the doctor	You're sick. You should **go to the doctor**.
the dentist	I'm **going to the dentist** tomorrow.

also **the station / the airport / the city center**, etc.
(See also Unit 62.)

Exercises

64.1 Where are these people? Look at the pictures and complete the sentences. Sometimes you need **the**.

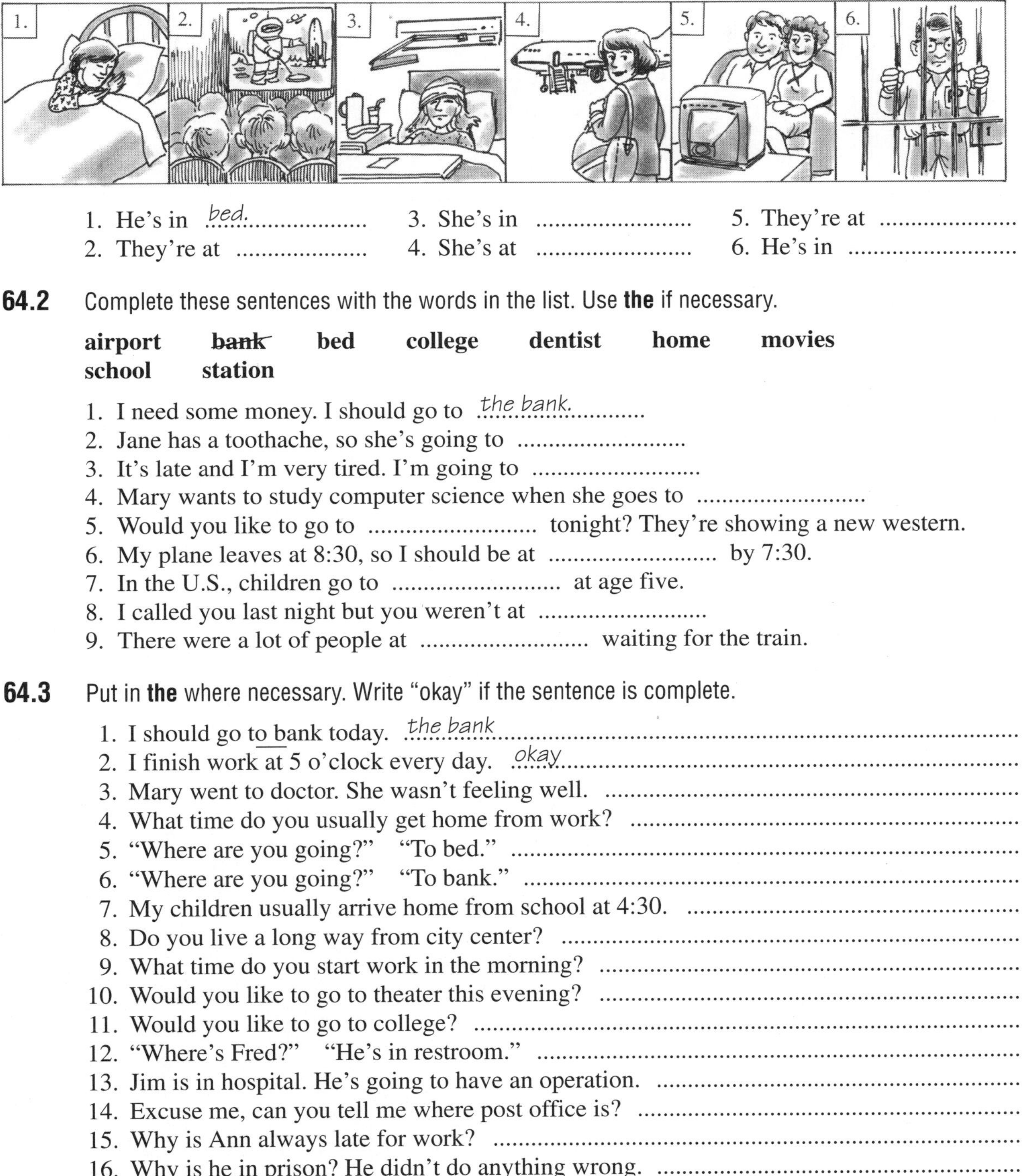

1. He's in bed. ....
2. They're at ....
3. She's in ....
4. She's at ....
5. They're at ....
6. He's in ....

64.2 Complete these sentences with the words in the list. Use **the** if necessary.

airport ~~**bank**~~ **bed** **college** **dentist** **home** **movies**
school **station**

1. I need some money. I should go to the bank. ....
2. Jane has a toothache, so she's going to ....
3. It's late and I'm very tired. I'm going to ....
4. Mary wants to study computer science when she goes to ....
5. Would you like to go to .... tonight? They're showing a new western.
6. My plane leaves at 8:30, so I should be at .... by 7:30.
7. In the U.S., children go to .... at age five.
8. I called you last night but you weren't at ....
9. There were a lot of people at .... waiting for the train.

64.3 Put in **the** where necessary. Write "okay" if the sentence is complete.

1. I should go to bank today. the bank ....
2. I finish work at 5 o'clock every day. okay ....
3. Mary went to doctor. She wasn't feeling well. ....
4. What time do you usually get home from work? ....
5. "Where are you going?" "To bed." ....
6. "Where are you going?" "To bank." ....
7. My children usually arrive home from school at 4:30. ....
8. Do you live a long way from city center? ....
9. What time do you start work in the morning? ....
10. Would you like to go to theater this evening? ....
11. Would you like to go to college? ....
12. "Where's Fred?" "He's in restroom." ....
13. Jim is in hospital. He's going to have an operation. ....
14. Excuse me, can you tell me where post office is? ....
15. Why is Ann always late for work? ....
16. Why is he in prison? He didn't do anything wrong. ....

UNIT 65

I like **music** I hate **exams**

(*not* "the music")

(*not* "the exams")

(*not* "the meat")

A ~~the~~

Do *not* say **the** for *general ideas*:

- I like **music**. (= music in general)
- I like **classical music**. (= classical music in general)
- We don't eat **meat** very often. (*not* "the meat")
- **Life** is not possible without **water**. (*not* "the life / the water")
- I hate **exams**. (= exams in general)
- Do they sell **foreign newspapers** in that store?
- I'm not very good at writing **letters**.

Do *not* say **the** for *games* and *sports*:

- My favorite sports are **tennis** and **skiing**. (*not* "the tennis / the skiing")

Do *not* say **the** for *languages* or *academic subjects* (**history/geography/biology/physics**, etc.):

- Do you think **English** is difficult? (*not* "the English")
- Tom's brother is studying **physics** and **chemistry**.

B **the** and ~~the~~

- **Flowers** are beautiful. (= flowers in general)
  but Your garden is very nice. **The flowers** are beautiful. (= the flowers in your garden)
- I don't like **cold weather**. (= cold weather in general)
  but **The weather** isn't very good today. (= the weather today)
- Are you interested in **history**?
  but Are you interested in **the history of your country**?
- We don't eat **steak** very often. (= steak in general)
  but Thank you for dinner. **The steak** was delicious!

Exercises

65.1 What do you think about these things? Begin your sentences with:

I love . . . / **I like . . .** / **I don't mind . . .** (= it's okay) / **I don't like . . .** / **I hate . . .**

1. (exams) *I hate exams.*
2. (dogs) ....
3. (hard work) ....
4. (Italian food) ....
5. (loud music) ....
6. (small children) ....
7. (meat) ....
8. (staying in hotels) ....
9. (jazz) ....
10. (big cities) ....

65.2 Are you interested in these things? Write sentences with:

I'm very interested in . . .	**I know a lot about . . .**
I'm interested in . . .	**I don't know much about . . .**
I'm not interested in . . .	**I don't know anything about . . .**

1. (history) *I'm very interested in history.*
2. (politics) ....
3. (sports) ....
4. (art) ....
5. (astronomy) ....
6. (economics) ....

65.3 Look at the underlined words in these sentences. Which is right (**the** or ~~**the**~~)?

1. Potatoes / ~~The potatoes~~ are not expensive. (Potatoes is *right.*)
2. This is a good meal. ~~Potatoes~~ / The potatoes are wonderful! (The potatoes is *right.*)
3. Everybody needs friends / the friends.
4. I never drink coffee / the coffee.
5. "Where's coffee / the coffee?" "It's on the shelf."
6. Jane doesn't go to parties / the parties very often.
7. Tennis / The tennis is a very popular sport.
8. We went for a swim in the river. Water / The water was very cold.
9. I don't like swimming in cold water / the cold water.
10. You should visit the museum. Paintings / The paintings are very beautiful.
11. Money / The money doesn't always bring happiness / the happiness.
12. English / The English is the language of international business.
13. Children / The children learn things / the things very quickly.
14. Excuse me, can you pass salt / the salt, please?
15. I enjoy eating in restaurants / the restaurants.
16. Do you like music / the music this band is playing?
17. I enjoy taking photographs / the photographs. It's my hobby.
18. Look at photographs / the photographs I took when I was on vacation.

UNIT 66 **the** (names of places)

A **Places** (continents/countries/provinces/states/islands/cities/towns, etc.)

Usually we do *not* say **the** + names of places:

~~the~~
- **France** is a very large country. (*not* "the France")
- **Cairo** is the capital of **Egypt**.
- **Nova Scotia** is a province of **Canada**.

But we say **the** + republic/states/kingdom/union, etc.:

the

- **the** People's **Republic** of China
- **the** United Arab **Emirates**
- **the** United **Kingdom** (**the** U.K.)
- **the** United **States** of America (**the** USA)

B **Places in towns** (streets/buildings, etc.)

Usually we do *not* say **the** + names of streets, roads, avenues, squares, etc.:

~~the~~
- Kevin lives on **Fifteenth Street**.
- Where is **Cherry Road**, please?
- **Union Square** is in downtown San Francisco.

Usually we do *not* say **the** + name of person/place + airport/station/university/park, etc.:

~~the~~

Kennedy Airport **Grand Central Station**
Golden Gate Park **Harvard University**

This is only a general rule. There are exceptions.

But we usually say **the** + names of hotels/restaurants/theaters/museums:

the

- **the Hilton (Hotel)**
- **the Science Museum**
- **the National Theater**
- **the Star of India** (restaurant)
- **the Roxy** (movie theater)
- **the Metropolitan Museum of Art**

C **Oceans/seas/rivers**, etc.

We say **the** + names of oceans/seas/rivers/canals:

the

- **the Atlantic (Ocean)**
- **the Amazon (River)**
- **the Mediterranean (Sea)**
- **the Suez Canal**

D **the . . . of . . .**

We say **the** + names with **. . . of . . .** :

the

- **the** Republic **of** Ireland
- **the** Great Wall **of** China
- **the** Gulf **of** Mexico
- **the** Museum **of** Modern Art
- **the** University **of** California

the north/south/east/west/middle (of . . .):

I've been to **the north of Italy** but not **to the south**.

E **the -s** *(plural names)*

We say **the** + *plural names* (**the -s**) of countries/islands/mountains:

the

the Netherlands **the** Canary Islands **the** Philippines **the** Andes

Exercises

66.1 These are geography questions. Choose your answer from the box. Sometimes you need to use "**The**."

Alps	**Amazon**	**Andes**	**Asia**	~~**Atlantic**~~	**Bahamas**	~~**Cairo**~~
Gulf of Mexico	**Jamaica**	**Ontario**	**Pacific**	**Switzerland**		
Thames	**Tokyo**	**United States**				

1. Cairo .... is the capital of Egypt.
2. The Atlantic .... is between Africa and America.
3. .... is a country in the middle of Europe.
4. .... is a river in South America.
5. .... is the largest continent in the world.
6. .... is the largest ocean.
7. .... is a river that flows through London.
8. .... is between Canada and Mexico.
9. .... is a province of Canada.
10. .... are mountains in South America.
11. .... is the capital of Japan.
12. .... is an island in the Caribbean.
13. .... are mountains in central Europe.
14. .... is between Texas and Cuba.
15. .... are a group of islands near Florida.

62.2 Put in **the** where necessary. If the sentence is correct, write "okay."

1. Kevin lives on Fifteenth Street. okay ....
2. Have you ever been to National Theater? the National Theater ....
3. "Where are you staying?" "At Park Hotel." ....
4. Seville is a large city in south of Spain. ....
5. Ottawa is the capital of Canada. ....
6. Manila is the capital of Philippines. ....
7. O'Hare Airport is in Chicago. ....
8. Most of the best stores are on Rodeo Drive. ....
9. Rocky Mountains are in North America. ....
10. In London, Houses of Parliament are beside River Thames. ....
11. Have you ever been to Metropolitan Museum? ....
12. Texas is famous for oil and cowboys. ....
13. Last night we saw a play at National Theater. ....
14. You must visit Museum of Folk Art. It's very interesting. ....
15. Bob studied chemistry at McGill University. ....
16. When I finish my studies, I'm going to United States for a year. ....
17. Panama Canal joins Atlantic Ocean and Pacific Ocean. ....
18. There are two movie theaters in our town – Regal and Plaza. ....
19. If you sail from Taiwan to Philippines, you cross South China Sea. ....
20. Mary comes from a small town in west of Ireland. ....
21. Europe is not a large continent but it has a large population. ....
22. Have you ever been to USA? ....

UNIT 67

this/that/these/those

A

this *(singular)*
this house/picture/man, etc.
Do you like this picture?
these *(plural)*
these houses/flowers/**men**, etc.
These flowers are for you.

that *(singular)*
that house/picture/man, etc.
Do you like that picture?
those *(plural)*
those houses/flowers/**people**, etc.
Who are those people?

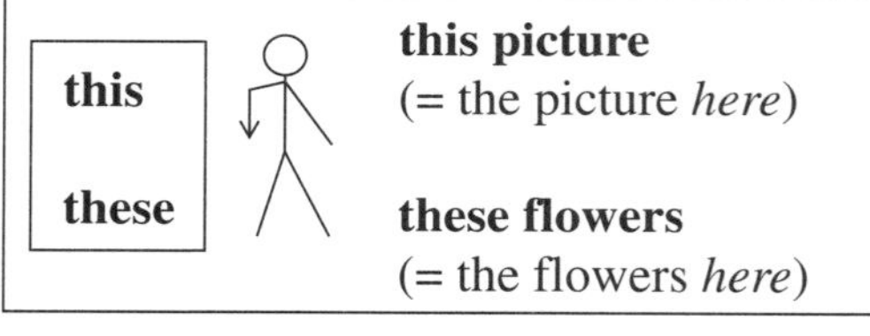

this
these
this picture
(= the picture *here*)
these flowers
(= the flowers *here*)

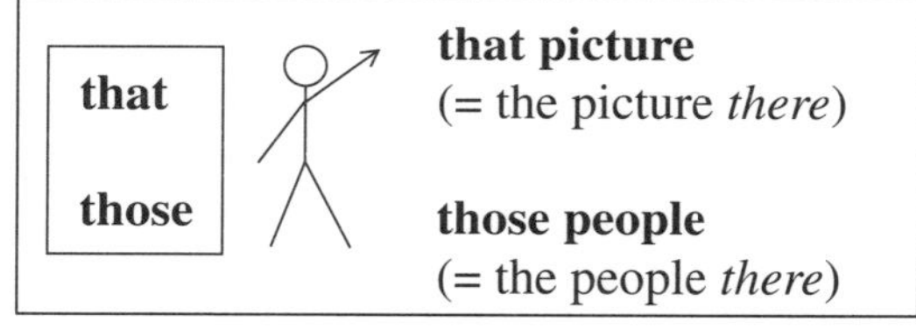

that
those
that picture
(= the picture *there*)
those people
(= the people *there*)

B

We use **this/that/these/those** *with a noun* (**this hotel / that woman**, etc.) *or without a noun* (**this/that**, etc.):

- **This hotel** is expensive, but it's very nice.
- "Who's **that woman**?" "I don't know."
- Do you like **these shoes**? I bought them last week.
- Don't eat **those apples**. They're rotten.

- **This** is a nice hotel, but it's very expensive.
- "Excuse me, is **this** your bag?" "Oh, yes. Thank you very much."
- "Who's **that**?" (= Who's that woman?) "I don't know. I've never seen her before."
- Which shoes do you like better? **These** or **those**?

For **this one / that one**, see Unit 68.

Exercises

67.1 Put in **this** or **these**.

1. *this* chair
2. *these* chairs
3. .... sandwich
4. .... things
5. .... children
6. .... place
7. .... houses
8. .... pants

Put in **that** or **those**.

9. .... picture
10. .... socks
11. .... men
12. .... tree
13. .... eggs
14. .... woman
15. .... room
16. .... people

67.2 Write questions: **Is this/that your . . . ?** or **Are these/those your . . . ?**

1. *Is this your bag?*
2.
3.
4.
5.
6.
7.
8.
9.
10.

67.3 Complete the sentences. Use **this/that/these/those** + these words:

birds **house** **plates** **postcards** **seat** ~~**shoes**~~

1. Do you like *these shoes*?
2. Who lives in ....?
3. Look at ....!
4. How much are ....?
5. Excuse me, is .... taken?
6. .... are dirty.
POST CARDS

UNIT 68

one/ones

A one (= a . . .)

Would you like **one** ?

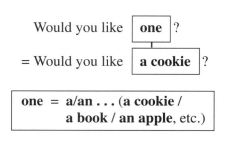

= Would you like **a cookie** ?

one = **a/an . . .** (**a cookie** / **a book** / **an apple**, etc.)

- I need **a pen**. Do you have **one**? (**one** = **a pen**)
- A: Is there **a bank** near here?
  B: Yes, there's **one** at the corner. (**one** = **a bank**)

B **one** and **ones**

one *(singular)*

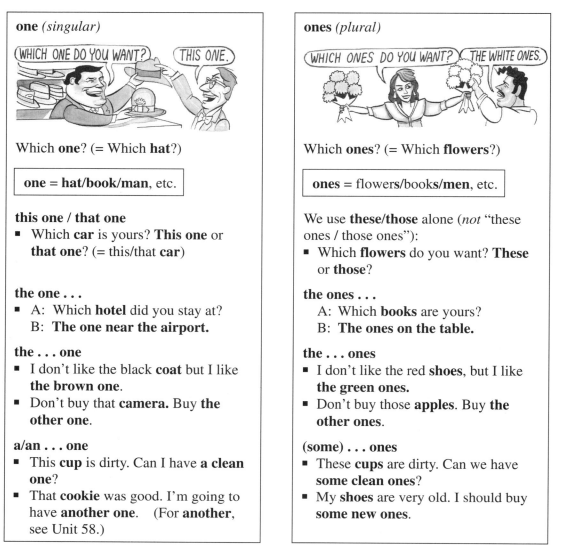

Which **one**? (= Which **hat**?)

one = **hat/book/man**, etc.

this one / that one
- Which **car** is yours? **This one** or **that one**? (= this/that **car**)

the one . . .
- A: Which **hotel** did you stay at?
  B: **The one near the airport.**

the . . . one
- I don't like the black **coat** but I like **the brown one**.
- Don't buy that **camera.** Buy **the other one**.

a/an . . . one
- This **cup** is dirty. Can I have **a clean one**?
- That **cookie** was good. I'm going to have **another one**. (For **another**, see Unit 58.)

ones *(plural)*

Which **ones**? (= Which **flowers**?)

ones = flower**s**/book**s**/**men**, etc.

We use **these/those** alone (*not* "these ones / those ones"):
- Which **flowers** do you want? **These** or **those**?

the ones . . .
A: Which **books** are yours?
B: **The ones on the table.**

the . . . ones
- I don't like the red **shoes**, but I like **the green ones.**
- Don't buy those **apples**. Buy **the other ones**.

(some) . . . ones
- These **cups** are dirty. Can we have **some clean ones**?
- My **shoes** are very old. I should buy **some new ones**.

Exercises

68.1 A asks B some questions. Use the information in the box to write B's answers. Use **one** (*not* "**a/ an...**") in the answers.

B doesn't need a car	B has just had a cup of coffee
there's a drugstore on First Street	B can't ride a bicycle
~~B doesn't have a pen~~	B doesn't have an umbrella

1. A: Can you lend me a pen? B: I'm sorry, *I don't have one.*
2. A: Would you like to have a car? B: No, I don't ....
3. A: Do you have a bicycle? B: No, I can't ....
4. A: Can you lend me an umbrella? B: I'm sorry, ...
5. A: Is there a drugstore near here? B: Yes, ...
6. A: Would you like a cup of coffee? B: No, thank you, ...

68.2 Complete the sentences. Use **a/an . . . one**. Use these words in your answers:

~~**clean**~~ **better** **bigger** **different** **new** **old**

1. This cup is dirty. Can I have *a clean one?*
2. I'm going to sell my car and then I'm going to buy ....
3. That's not a very good photograph. This is ....
4. This box is too small. I need ....
5. I want today's newspaper. This is ....
6. Why do we always go to the same restaurant? Let's go to ....

68.3 Use the information in the box to complete these conversations. Use **one/ones**.

the coat is black	the pictures are on the wall
the woman is tall with long hair	the books are on the top shelf
~~the hotel is near the station~~	the flowers are yellow
the house has a red door	~~the shoes are green~~
I took the photographs at the beach last week	the man has a moustache and glasses

1. A: We stayed at a hotel.
   B: *Which one* ?
   A: *The one near the station.*
2. A: Those shoes are nice.
   B: *Which ones.* ?
   A: *The green ones.*
3. A: That's a nice house.
   B: .... ?
   A: .... with ....
4. A: I like that coat.
   B: .... ?
   A: ....
5. A: I like those pictures.
   B: .... ?
   A: ....
6. A: Are those your books?
   B: .... ?
   A: ....
7. A: Do you know that woman?
   B: .... ?
   A: ....
8. A: Those flowers are beautiful.
   B: .... ?
   A: ....
9. A: Who's that man?
   B: .... ?
   A: ....
10. A: Have you seen my photographs?
    B: .... ?
    A: ....

UNIT 69

some any

A

some

Use **some** in *positive* sentences:

- I'm going to buy **some** eggs.
- There is **some** ice in the freezer.
- They made **some** mistakes.
- She said **something**.
- I saw **somebody** (*or* **someone**).

any

Use **any** in *negative* sentences:

- I'm **not** going to buy **any** eggs.
- There is**n't any** ice in the freezer.
- They did**n't** make **any** mistakes.
- She did**n't** say **anything**.
- I did**n't** see **anybody** (*or* **anyone**).

B

any and **some** in *questions*

In most questions (but not all) we use **any**:

- Is there **any** ice in the freezer?
- Did they make **any** mistakes?
- Are you doing **anything** this evening?
- I can't find Ann. Has **anybody** seen her?

We usually use **some** (*not* **any**) when we *offer* things (**Would you like some . . . ?**):

- A: Would you like **some** coffee?
  B: Yes, please.
- A: Would you like **something** to eat?
  B: No, thank you. I'm not hungry.

or ask for things (**Can I have some . . . ? / Can you lend me some . . . ?**, etc.):

- "Can I have **some** soup, please?" "Yes, of course. Help yourself."
- "Can you lend me **some** money?" "I'm sorry, I can't."

C

Compare **some** and **any**:

- We have **some** cheese, but we do**n't** have **any** bread.
- I did**n't** take **any** photographs, but Ann took **some**. (= some photographs)
- You can have **some** coffee, but I do**n't** want **any**. (= any coffee)
- I've just made **some** coffee. **Would you like some?** (= some coffee)
- I do**n't** have **any** money. **Can you lend me some?** (= some money)

For **something/somebody/anything/anybody**, see Unit 72.

Exercises

69.1 Put in **some** or **any**.

1. I'm going to buy ..some.... eggs.
2. They didn't make ..any.... mistakes.
3. I can pay. I have .... money.
4. There aren't .... stores in this part of the town.
5. Tom and Alice don't have .... children.
6. Do you have .... brothers or sisters?
7. There are .... beautiful flowers in the garden.
8. Is there .... mail for me this morning?
9. I don't have .... stamps, but Ann has ....
10. Do you know .... good hotels in Miami?
11. "Would you like .... tea?" "Yes, please."
12. Don't buy .... rice. We don't need ....
13. We don't have .... bread, so I'm going out to buy ....
14. When we were on vacation, we visited .... very interesting places.
15. I went out to buy .... milk, but they didn't have .... in the store.
16. I'm thirsty. Can I have .... water, please?

69.2 Complete the sentences. Use **some** or **any** + one of these words:

air **batteries** **chairs** **friends** **fruit** **languages** **milk** ~~**money**~~
pictures **problems** **shampoo** **stamps**

1. I can't buy you a cup of coffee. I don't have ..any money..................
2. I want to wash my hair. Is there .... ?
3. I'm going to the post office to get ....
4. Can you speak .... foreign .... ?
5. I don't have my camera, so I can't take ....
6. Sorry we're late. We had .... with the car.
7. Everybody was standing because there weren't .... in the room.
8. It's hot in this office. I'm going out for .... fresh ....
9. Why isn't the radio working? Are there .... in it?
10. Can I have .... in my coffee, please?
11. Last night I went to a restaurant with .... of mine.
12. "Would you like .... ?" "No, thank you. I've had enough to eat."

69.3 Put in **somebody** (or **someone**) / **something** / **anybody** (or **anyone**) / **anything**.

1. She said ..something.........., but I didn't understand it.
2. "What's wrong?" "There's .... in my eye."
3. Do you know .... about politics?
4. I went shopping, but I didn't buy ....
5. .... has broken the window. I don't know who.
6. There isn't .... in the box. It's empty.
7. I'm looking for my keys. Has .... seen them?
8. Would you like .... to drink?
9. I didn't eat .... because I wasn't hungry.
10. I can do this job alone. I don't need .... to help me.

UNIT 70

not + any no none

He **doesn't have any** money.

He has no money.

A: How much money does he have?
B: **None.**

A

not (**n't**) + **any**

- I'm **not** going to do **any** work this evening.
- There are**n't any** good hotels in this city.
- Ann took some photographs, but I did**n't** take **any**. (= any photographs)

B

no + *noun* (**no money / no job**, etc.)
No . . . = **not** + **any** *or* **not** + **a**. We use **no . . .** especially after **have/has** and **there is/are**:

- He has **no** money. (= He does**n't have any** money.)
- There are **no** buses after 11:30. (= There are**n't any** buses after 11:30.)
- It's a nice house but there's **no** garage. (= It's a nice house but there is**n't a** garage.)

C

Remember: *negative verb* + **any** *positive verb* + **no**

- I **don't have any** friends. *or* I **have no** friends.
  (*but not* "I don't have no friends.")
- There **aren't any** good hotels in this city. *or* There **are no** good hotels in this city.

D

no and **none**

Use **no** + *noun* (**no money / no friends / no sugar**, etc.):

- I can't wait. I have **no time**.
- There is **no sugar** in your coffee.

Use **none** *alone (without a noun)*:

- "How much time do we have?" "**None** (= no time). We should go now."
- "How many mistakes did you make?" **"None."** (= no mistakes)

E

none and **no one**

none = **0** (zero). **None** is an answer for **How much? / How many?** *(things or people)*:

- "**How much** money do you have?" **"None."** (= no money)
- "**How many** people did you meet?" **"None."** (= no people)

no one = **nobody. No one** is an answer for **Who?**:

- "**Who** did you meet?" **"No one."** (= nobody)

For **no one / nobody**, see Unit 71.

Exercises

70.1 Write these sentences again with **no**.

1. He doesn't have any money. *He has no money.*
2. There aren't any pictures on the walls. There are ....
3. Carol doesn't have any free time. Carol ....
4. There isn't a restaurant in this hotel. ....

Write these sentences again with **any**.

5. He has no money. *He doesn't have any money.*
6. There's no gas in the car. There ....
7. I have no stamps. I ....
8. Tom has no brothers or sisters. ....

70.2 Put in **no** or **any**.

1. There aren't *any* good hotels here.
2. There are *no* buses today.
3. I didn't write .... letters last night.
4. There are .... restaurants in this part of town.
5. She can't speak .... foreign languages.
6. Don't buy .... food. We don't need ....
7. My brother is married, but he has .... children.
8. I'm afraid there's .... coffee. Would you like some tea?
9. "Look at those birds!" "Birds? Where? I can't see .... birds."
10. The man asked me for advice, but I couldn't give him ....

70.3 Complete the sentences. Use **any** or **no** + one of these words:

difference film friends furniture money photographs questions sugar swimming pool ~~**work**~~

1. I'm not going to do *any work* this evening.
2. I didn't put .... in my coffee this morning.
3. They want to take a vacation, but they have ....
4. It's a nice hotel, but there's ....
5. I'm not going to answer ....
6. He's always alone. He has ....
7. There is .... between these two machines. They are the same.
8. I can't take .... There's .... in the camera.
9. There wasn't .... in the room. It was completely empty.

70.4 Give short answers (one or two words) to these questions. Use **none** where necessary.

1. How many letters have you written today? *Two / A lot / None.*
2. How many sisters do you have? ....
3. How much coffee did you drink yesterday? ....
4. How many photographs have you taken today? ....
5. How many legs does a snake have? ....

UNIT 71

not + anybody/anyone/anything nobody / no one / nothing

A

not + anybody/anyone
nobody / no one
(for people)

There **isn't anybody** in the room.
There **is nobody** in the room.
A: **Who** is in the room?
B: **Nobody.**

not + anything
nothing
(for things)

There **isn't anything** in the bag.
There **is nothing** in the bag.
A: **What**'s in the bag?
B: **Nothing.**

any**body** = any**one**   no**body** = no **one** (**-body** and **-one** are the same):

- I don't know **anybody** (*or* **anyone**).
- There is **no one** (*or* **nobody**) here.

not (**n't**) + **anybody/anyone/anything**

- Please do**n't** tell **anybody** (*or* **anyone**).
- Jack has a bad memory. He ca**n't** remember **anything**.

nobody = not + anybody	**nothing = not + anything**
no one = not + anyone	

- I'm lonely. I have **nobody** to talk to. (= I do**n't** have **anybody**)
- The house is empty. There is **no one** in it. (= there is**n't anyone**)
- She said **nothing**. (= She did**n't** say **anything**.)

You can use **nobody / no one / nothing** at the beginning of a sentence or alone (without other words):

- The house is empty. **Nobody** lives there. (*not* "Anybody lives there.")
- **Nobody** is perfect.
- "Who did you speak to?" **"No one."**
- "What did you say?" **"Nothing."** (*not* "Anything.")

B

Remember: *negative verb* + **anybody/anyone/anything**
positive verb + **nobody / no one / nothing**

- He does**n't** understand **anything**. (*not* "He doesn't understand nothing.")
- Do**n't** tell **anybody**. (*not* "Don't tell nobody.")
- There **is nothing** to do in this town. (*not* "There isn't nothing to do.")

Exercises

71.1 Write these sentences again with **nobody / no one / nothing**.

1. There isn't anything in the bag. *There's nothing in the bag.*
2. There isn't anybody in the office There's ....
3. I don't have anything to do. I ....
4. There isn't anything on TV tonight. ....
5. Jack doesn't have anyone to help him. ....
6. We didn't find anything. ....

71.2 Write these sentences again with **anybody/anyone/anything**.

1. There is nothing in the bag. *There isn't anything in the bag.*
2. I have nothing to read. I don't have ....
3. There's nobody in the bathroom. ....
4. We have nothing to eat. ....
5. There was no one on the bus. ....
6. She heard nothing. ....

71.3 Answer these questions with **nobody / no one / nothing**.

1a. What did you say? *Nothing.*
2a. Who saw you? *Nobody. / No one.*
3a. What do you want? ....
4a. Who did you meet? ....
5a. Who knows the answer? ....
6a. What did you buy? ....
7a. What happened? ....
8a. Who was late? ....

Now answer the same questions with full sentences. Use **nobody / no one / nothing** or **anybody/anyone/anything**.

1b. *I didn't say anything.*
2b. *Nobody saw me. / No one saw me.*
3b. I don't ....
4b. I didn't ....
5b. .... the answer.
6b. I ....
7b. ....
8b. ....

71.4 Complete the sentences with **nobody / no one / nothing / anybody / anyone / anything**.

1. I went out of the house. *Nobody / No one* saw me.
2. Jack has a bad memory. He can't remember *anything.*
3. Be quiet! Don't say ....
4. I didn't know about the meeting. .... told me.
5. "What did you have to eat?" ".......... . I wasn't hungry."
6. "What did you say?" "I didn't say ...."
7. Dan has gone somewhere. .... knows where he is. He didn't tell .... where he was going.
8. "What are you doing tonight?" ".......... . Why?"
9. I don't know .... about car engines.
10. "How much does it cost to visit the museum?" ".......... . It's free."
11. She was sitting alone. She wasn't with ....
12. I heard a knock on the door, but when I opened it there was .... there.

some-/any-/no- + -body/-one/-thing/-where

Somebody (*or* **Someone**) broke the window.

somebody/someone = *a person, but we don't know who*

There is **something** in her mouth.

something = *a thing, but we don't know what*

Tom lives **somewhere** near Toronto.

somewhere = *in a place, but we don't know where*

	people (**-body** *or* **-one***)	*things* (**-thing**)	places (**-where**)
some-	**somebody** *or* **someone**	**something**	**somewhere**
any-	**anybody** *or* **anyone**	**anything**	**anywhere**
no-	**nobody** *or* **no one**	**nothing**	**nowhere**

* **-body** and **-one** are the same: **somebody** = **someone**, **nobody** = **no one**, etc.

somebody
someone
something
somewhere

- There is **somebody** (*or* **someone**) at the door.
- She said **something**, but I didn't understand her.
- They live **somewhere** in the south of France.

anybody
anyone
anything
anywhere

in questions
- Is there **anybody** (*or* **anyone**) at home?
- Are you doing **anything** tonight?
- Did you go **anywhere** interesting for your vacation?

See Unit 69.

in negatives (**not** + **any-**)
- There is**n't anybody** (*or* **anyone**) at the door.
- It's dark. I can't see **anything**.
- I'm staying here. I'm **not** going **anywhere**.

See Units 69 and 71.

nobody
no one
nothing
nowhere

- There is **nobody** (*or* **no one**) at the door.
- "What did you say?" **"Nothing."**
- I don't like this town. There is **nowhere** to go.

You can use **something/anybody/nowhere**, etc. + **to . . .** :
- I'm hungry. I want **something to eat**. (= something that I can eat)
- He doesn't have **anybody to talk** to. (= anybody that he can talk to)
- There's **nowhere to go** in this town. (= nowhere that people can go)

Exercises

72.1 Put in **somebody** (or **someone**) / **something** / **somewhere**.

1. She said *something.* .... — What did she say?
2. I lost .... — What did you lose?
3. They went .... — Where did they go?
4. I'm going to call .... — Who are you going to call?

Put in **nobody** (or **no one**) / **nothing** / **nowhere**.

5a. What did you say? — *Nothing.* ....
6a. Where are you going? — ....
7a. What do you want? — ....
8a. Who are you looking for? — ....

Now answer the same questions with full sentences. Use **not** + **anybody** (or **anyone**) / **anything** / **anywhere**.

5b. *I didn't say anything.* ....
6b. I'm not going ....
7b. I ....
8b. I ....

72.2 Put in **somebody/nothing/anywhere**, etc.

1. It's dark. I can't see *anything.* ....
2. Tom lives *somewhere* .... near Toronto.
3. Do you know .... about computers?
4. "Listen!" "What? I can't hear ...."
5. "What are you doing here?" "I'm waiting for ...."
6. "What's wrong?" "I have .... in my eye."
7. "Did .... see you?" "No, ..."
8. They weren't hungry, so they didn't eat ....
9. "What is going to happen?" "I don't know. .... knows."
10. "Do you know .... in Tokyo?" "Yes, I have a few friends there."
11. "What's in that suitcase?" "........................ . It's empty."
12. I'm looking for my glasses. I can't find them ....

72.3 Complete the sentences. Use a word from the first box + **to** + a word from the second box. (You can use a word more than once.)

something	**anything**	**nothing**	**to**	**do**	**drink**	**eat**	**~~go~~**
somewhere	**anywhere**	**nowhere**		**play**	**read**	**sit**	**stay**

1. We don't go out very much because there's *nowhere to go.* ....
2. There isn't any food in the house. We don't have ....
3. I'm bored. I have ....
4. "Why are you standing?" "Because there isn't ...."
5. "Would you like .... ?" "Yes, please – a glass of orange juice."
6. Children need ....
7. I want .... I'm going to buy a magazine.
8. All the hotels were full. There was ....

UNIT 73

every everybody/everything, etc.

A every

Every house on the street is the same.

(**every house** on the street = **all the houses** on the street)

Use **every** + *singular noun* (**every house / every country / every time**, etc.):

- Sue has been to **every country** in Europe. (*not* "every countries")
- **Every summer** we take a vacation at the beach.
- She looks different **every time** I see her.

Use a *singular verb* (**is/was/has**, etc.) after **every . . .** :

- **Every house** on the street **is** the same. (*not* "Every house . . . are")
- **Every country has** a national flag. (*not* "Every country have")

Compare **every** and **all**:

- **Every student** in the class passed the examination.
  All the students in the class passed the examination.
- **Every country has** a national flag.
  All countries have a national flag.

B

every } **all** } **day/morning/evening/night/summer**, etc.

every day = on all days:

- A: How often do you read a newspaper?
  B: **Every day**.
- Bill watches TV **every night**.
  (= on all nights of the week)

all day = the complete day from beginning to end:

- The weather was bad yesterday. It rained **all day**.
- I was tired after work yesterday, so I watched TV **all evening**. (= the complete evening)

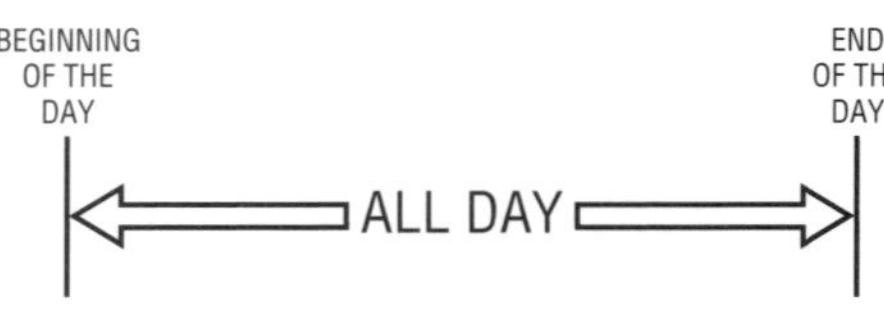

C everybody (*or* everyone) / everything / everywhere

everybody/everyone *(people)* **everything** *(things)* **everywhere** *(places)*

- **Everybody** (*or* **Everyone**) needs friends. (= all people need friends)
- Do you have **everything** you need? (= all the things you need)
- I lost my watch. I've looked for it **everywhere**. (= I've looked in all places)

Use a *singular verb* after **everybody/everyone/everything**:

- **Everybody has** problems. (*not* "Everybody have")

Exercises

73.1 Complete the sentences. Use **every** + one of these words:

day **room** **~~student~~** **time** **word**

1. *Every student* in the class passed the examination.
2. My job is very boring. .... is the same.
3. .... in the hotel has two telephones.
4. Pat is a good tennis player. When we play, she wins ....
5. "Did you understand what she said?" "Yes, ..."

73.2 Put in **every** or **all**.

1. Yesterday it rained *all* day.
2. Bill watches TV *every* evening.
3. Barbara gets up at 6:30 .... morning.
4. I was sick yesterday, so I stayed in bed .... day.
5. I buy a newspaper .... day, but I don't always read it.
6. "How often do you go skiing?" "............. year, usually in March."
7. "Were you home at 10 o'clock yesterday?" "Yes, I was home .... morning. I went out after lunch."
8. The weather was nice last Sunday, so we worked in the garden .... afternoon.
9. We didn't have a very good vacation. We went to the beach for ten days and it rained .... day.
10. My sister loves cars. She buys a new one .... year.
11. I saw Jack at the party, but he wasn't very friendly. He didn't speak to me .... evening.
12. They go away on vacation for two or three weeks .... summer.

73.3 Put in **everybody** (or **everyone**) / **everything** / **everywhere**.

1. *Everybody* needs friends.
2. Sue knows .... about computers.
3. I like the people here. .... is very friendly.
4. It's a nice hotel. It's comfortable and .... is clean.
5. Ken never uses his car. He goes .... by motorcycle.
6. Let's have dinner. .... is hungry.
7. Their house is full of books. There are books ....
8. You're right. .... you say is true.

73.4 Complete the answers to these questions. Use **everybody**.

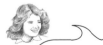

1.	Do you know Bob?	Yes, *everybody knows* Bob.
2.	Are you tired today?	Yes, ... today.
3.	Do you like Mary?	Yes, ...
4.	Are you going to the party?	Yes, ...
5.	Have you see the movie?	Yes, ...
6.	Were you surprised?	Yes, ...

UNIT 74

all most some no/none any

all

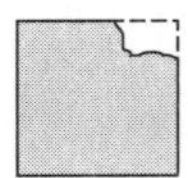
most

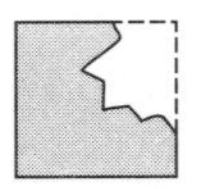
some

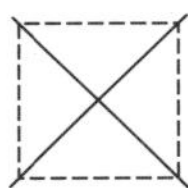
no/none/not + any

any

A

all/most/some/no/any + *noun* (**all cities / most people**, etc.)

all **most** **some** **no** **any**	~~**of**~~	**cities** **people** **music** **buses**

- **All** big **cities** have the same problems.
- **Most people** like Jack.
- I like **some classical music**, but not all.
- There are **no buses** on Sundays.
  or There are**n't any buses** on Sundays.

Don't use **of** in these sentences:

- **Most children** like playing. (*not* "Most of children")
- **Some birds** cannot fly. (*not* "Some of birds")

B

most of the . . . / some of my . . . / none of these . . ., etc.

most **some** **none** **any**	**of**	**the . . .** **this/that . . .** **these/those . . .** **my/your . . .**, etc.

- **Most of my friends** live nearby.
- **Some of this money** is yours.
- Have you read **any of these books**?
- **None of the students** passed the exam.
- I do**n't** know **any of those people**.

C

Remember: **most children** *but* **most of the** children
some people *but* **some of these** people
no friends *but* **none of my** friends

Compare:

- **Most children** like playing. (= most children in general)
  but **Most of the children** at this school are under 11 years old.

D

You can use **all (of) the . . . / all (of) my . . .**, etc. *with* or *without* **of**:

- **All (of) the students** failed the exam.
- She has lived in Paris **all (of) her life**.

E

all of it / most of them / some of us, etc.

all **most** **some** **none** **any**	**of**	**it** **them** **us** **you**

- You can have **some of this cake**, but not **all of it**.
- A: Do you know those people?
  B: **Most of them**, but not **all of them**.
- **Some of us** are going out tonight. Would you like to come with us?
- He has a lot of books, but he has**n't** read **any of them**.

For **some/any**, see Unit 69.
For **no/none**, see Unit 70.

Exercises

74.1 Complete the sentences. Use the word in parentheses (**some/most**, etc.). Sometimes you need **of** (**some of** / **most of**, etc.).

1. *Most* people like Jack. (most)
2. *Some of* this money is yours. (some)
3. .... people are very rude. (some)
4. .... the stores in the city center close at 6:00. (most)
5. You can change money in .... banks. (most)
6. I don't like .... the pictures in the living room. (any)
7. .... countries have a capital city. (all)
8. .... my friends went on vacation last year. (none)
9. Do you know .... the people in this photograph? (any)
10. .... birds can fly. (most)
11. I enjoyed .... the movie, but I didn't like the ending. (most)
12. .... sports are very dangerous. (some)
13. We can't find anywhere to stay. .... the hotels are full. (all)
14. Try .... this cheese. It's delicious. (some)
15. The weather was bad when we were on vacation. It rained .... the time. (most)

74.2 Look at the pictures and answer the questions. Use **all/most/some/none of them**.

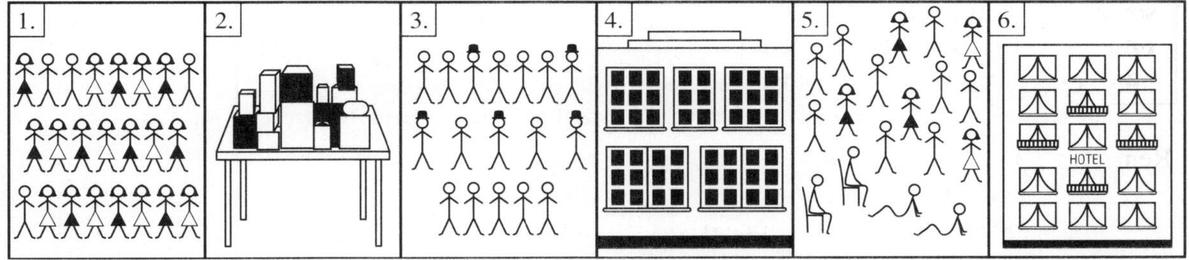

1. How many of the people are women? *Most of them.*
2. How many of the boxes are on the table? ....
3. How many of the men are wearing hats? ....
4. How many of the windows are open? ....
5. How many of the people are standing? ....
6. How many of the hotel rooms have a balcony? ....

74.3 Answer these questions. Use the word in parentheses (**all/most/some/none**) + **of it** / **of them**.

1. How much of that book did you read? (some) *Some of it.*
2. Are your friends going to the party? (most) *Yes, most of them.*
3. How many of those books have you read? (all) ....
4. How much of this money do you want? (all) ....
5. Were the questions on the test easy? (most) ....
6. Are the stores open tomorrow? (some) ....
7. How many of those people do you know? (none) ....
8. Did you understand the conversation? (most) ....
9. Have you seen these photographs? (some) ....

UNIT 75 both either neither

A We use **both/either/neither** to talk about *two* things or people:

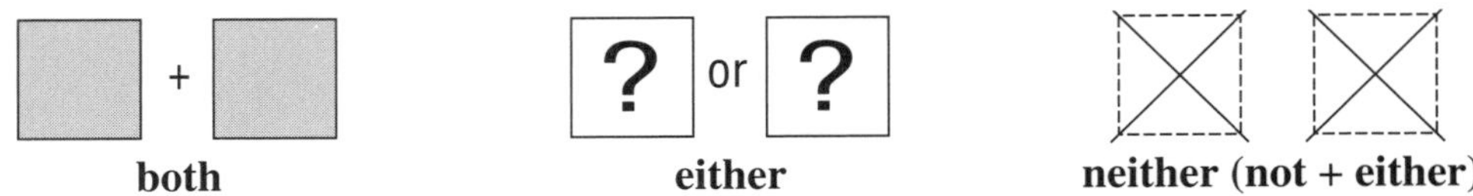

- Rosa has two children. **Both** are married. (= both children)
- A: Do you like classical music or pop music?
  B: **Both.** (= classical *and* pop)
- Would you like tea or coffee? You can have **either**. (= tea *or* coffee)
- A: Do you want to go to the movies or a concert?
  B: **Neither.** I want to stay home. (**neither** = *not* the movies *or* a concert)

B **both/either/neither** + *noun*:

both + *plural*	**both windows/books/children**, etc.
either **neither** + *singular*	**either window/book/child**, etc. **neither window/book/child**, etc.

- Ann has two sisters and a brother. **Both sisters are** married.
- Last year I went to Miami and Atlanta. I liked **both cities** very much.
- I read two books, but **neither book was** very interesting.
- There are two ways from here to the station. You can go **either way**.

C **both/either/neither of . . .** :

both* **either** **neither**	**of**	**the . . .** **those/these . . .** **my/your/Tom's**, etc. **. . .**

- I like **both of those pictures**.*
- **Both of Ann's sisters are** married.*
- I have**n't** read **either of these books**.
- **Neither of my parents is** Mexican.

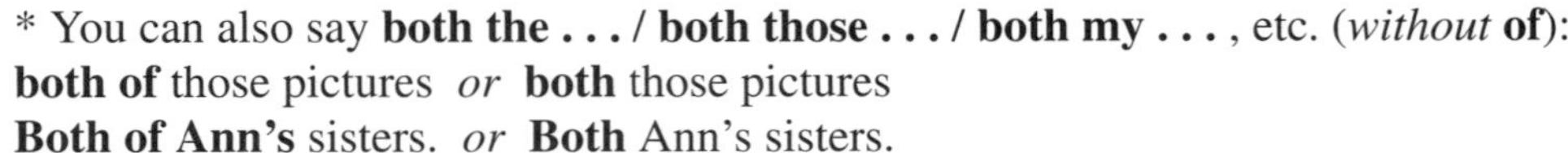

* You can also say **both the . . . / both those . . . / both my . . .**, etc. (*without* **of**):
both of those pictures *or* **both** those pictures
Both of Ann's sisters. *or* **Both** Ann's sisters.

D **both of them / neither of us**, etc.

both **either** **neither**	**of**	**them** **us** **you**

- Ann has two sisters. **Both of them are** married.
- Tom and I didn't eat anything. **Neither of us was** hungry.
- Who are those two men? I don't know **either of them**.

Exercises

75.1 Put in **both/either/neither**.

1. Ann has two sisters and a brother. *Both* sisters are married.
2. There were two pictures on the wall. I didn't like *either* of them.
3. It was a very good tennis match. .... players played well.
4. It wasn't a good tennis match. .... player played well.
5. "Is your friend Canadian or American?" "............. . She's Australian."
6. We went away for two days, but the weather wasn't very good. It rained .... days.
7. "I bought two newspapers. Which one do you want?" "............. . It doesn't matter which one."
8. I invited Jack and Linda to my party, but .... of them came.
9. "Do you go to work by car or by bus?" "............. . I always walk."
10. "Which jacket do you prefer, this one or that one?" "I don't like .... of them."
11. "Do you work or are you a student?" "............. . I have a job, but I study too."
12. Ann and I didn't know the time because .... of us had a watch.

75.2 Write sentences for the pictures. Use **Both . . .** and **Neither . . .**

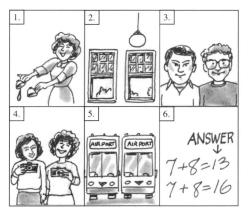

1. *Both cups are empty.*
2. .... are open.
3. .... wearing a hat.
4. .... cameras.
5. .... to the airport.
6. .... is right.

75.3 A man and a woman answered some questions. Their answers to all the questions were the same.
Write sentences with **Both/Neither of them . . .**

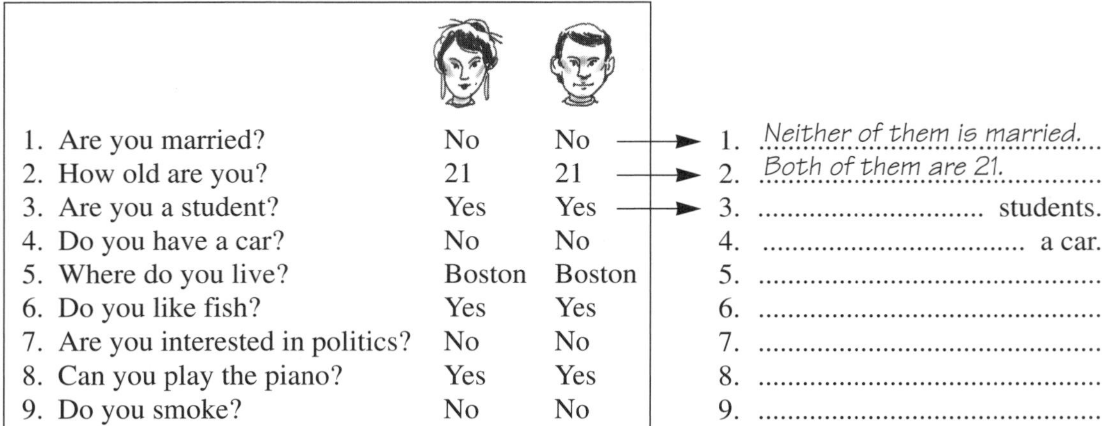

1. Are you married?	No	No	1. *Neither of them is married.*
2. How old are you?	21	21	2. *Both of them are 21.*
3. Are you a student?	Yes	Yes	3. .... students.
4. Do you have a car?	No	No	4. .... a car.
5. Where do you live?	Boston	Boston	5. ....
6. Do you like fish?	Yes	Yes	6. ....
7. Are you interested in politics?	No	No	7. ....
8. Can you play the piano?	Yes	Yes	8. ....
9. Do you smoke?	No	No	9. ....

UNIT 76

a lot much many

a lot of money / much money

a lot of books / many books

A

We use **much** + *uncountable noun*:

much money **much food**
much time **much coffee**

- Do you drink **much coffee**?
- **How much money** do you have?
- She doesn't have **much time**.
- A: Do you have any **money**?
  B: I have some but not **much**.
- Sue spoke to me but she didn't say **much**.

We use **many** + *plural noun*:

many books **many** stores
many people **many** questions

- Do you know **many people**?
- How **many** photographs did you take?
- He doesn't have **many** friends.
- A: Did you take any photographs?
  B: I took some but not **many**.
- I've been to Paris **many** times.

We use **a lot of** + *uncountable or plural noun*:

a lot of money **a lot of coffee** **a lot of people** **a lot of** questions

- I drink **a lot of coffee**.
- We spent **a lot of money**.
- She doesn't have **a lot of** free **time**.
- I know **a lot of people**.
- We took **a lot of** photographs.
- Did they ask you **a lot of** questions?

B

We use **much** in questions and negative sentences. We do not normally use **much** in positive sentences:

- Do you drink **much coffee / a lot of coffee**?
- I don't drink **much coffee / a lot of coffee**.
  but I drink **a lot of coffee**. (*not* "I drink much coffee.")

We use **many** and **a lot** (**of**) in all kinds of sentences:

- Do you know **many people / a lot of people**?
- I don't know **many people / a lot of people**.
- I know **many people / a lot of people**.

C

We use **a lot of** + *noun*. Compare **a lot** and **a lot of**:

- He eats **a lot**. (*not* "a lot of")
  but He eats **a lot of food**. (**a lot of** + *noun*)

Note that we say:

- There **is** a lot of **food/money/coffee**, etc. *(singular verb)*
  but There **are** a lot of trees/stores/**people**, etc. *(plural verb)*
  A lot of **people speak** English. *(not* "A lot of people speaks")

D

Sometimes **much** or **a lot** = **often**:

- "Do you watch TV **much**?" "No, **not much**." (= not often)
- I don't like to stay home, so I go out **a lot**.

For countable and uncountable nouns, see Unit 60.

Exercises

76.1 Answer the questions with **I have . . .**

1. Do you have any money? — *I have some but not much.*
2. Do you have any coffee? — I have some but ....
3. Do you have any books? — ....
4. Do you have any stamps? — ....
5. Do you have any cheese? — ....

76.2 Write questions with **How much . . . ?** or **How many . . . ?**

1. I took some photographs. — *How many photographs did you take* ?
2. I lost some money. — .... ?
3. I drank some water. — .... ?
4. I made some mistakes. — .... ?
5. I wrote some letters. — .... ?
6. I bought some food. — .... ?

76.3 In some of these sentences it is more natural to use **a lot (of)**. Change the sentences where necessary. Write "okay" if the sentence is correct.

1. Do you drink much tea? *okay*
2. Tom drinks ~~much tea~~. *a lot of tea*
3. It was a cold winter. We had much snow. ....
4. Did you have much snow last winter? ....
5. It costs much money to travel around the world. ....
6. We went on a cheap vacation. It didn't cost much. ....
7. Dan knows much about economics. ....
8. "Do you know anything about computers?" "Not much." ....

76.4 Complete the sentences with **a lot of** + one of the following:

accidents ~~**books**~~ **fun** **interesting things** **mistakes** **traffic**

1. I like reading. I have *a lot of books.*
2. I don't speak French very well. I make ....
3. We enjoyed our visit to the museum. We saw ....
4. We enjoyed our vacation. We had ....
5. This road is very dangerous. There are ....
6. It takes me a long time to drive to work. There is always ....

76.5 Write the questions and answers. Use **much** and **a lot**.

1. (go to the movies) — *Do you go to the movies much* ? — No, *not much.*
2. (watch TV) — *Do you watch TV much* ? — Yes, *a lot.*
3. (go swimming) — .... go swimming .... ? — No, ...
4. (play tennis) — Do .... ? — Yes, ...
5. (travel) — .... ? — Yes, ...

UNIT 77

(a) little (a) few

a little water

a few books

A

(a) little + *uncountable noun*:

(a) little water **(a) little money**
(a) little time **(a) little soup**

(a) few + *plural noun*:

(a) few books **(a) few** questions
(a) few people **(a) few** days

B

a little = some but not much:

- She didn't eat anything, but she drank **a little water**.
- I speak **a little Spanish**. (= some Spanish but not much)
- A: Can you speak **Spanish**?
  B: **A little.**

a few = some but not many:

- Last night I wrote **a few letters**.
- We're going away for **a few days**.
- I speak **a few words** of Spanish.
- A: Do you have any **stamps**?
  B: **A few.** Do you want one?

C

~~a~~ **little** (*without* **a**) = nearly no . . . *or* nearly nothing:

- There was **little food** in the refrigerator. It was nearly empty.

You can say **very little**:

- She's very thin because she eats **very little**. (= nearly nothing)

~~a~~ **few** (*without* **a**) = nearly no . . . :

- There were **few** people in the park. It was nearly empty.

You can say **very few**:

- Her English is very good. She makes **very few mistakes**.

D

little and **a little**:

a little is a *positive* idea:

- They have **a little money**, so they're not poor. (= some but not much money)

~~a~~ **little** is a *negative* idea:

- They have **little money**. They are very poor. (= nearly no money)

few and **a few**:

a few is a *positive* idea:

- I have **a few friends**, so I'm not lonely. (= some but not many friends)

~~a~~ **few** is a *negative* idea:

- I'm sad and lonely. I have **few friends**. (= nearly no friends)

Exercises

77.1 Answer the questions with **a little** or **a few**.

1. Do you have any time? *A little.*
2. Do you have any envelopes? ....
3. Do you have any sugar? ....
4. Did he ask any questions? ....
5. Do we have any gas? ....
6. Does he speak English? ....
7. Do you know many people? ....
8. Would you like some soup? ....

77.2 Put in **a little** or **a few** + one of these words:

air chairs days friends houses ~~letters~~ milk Russian times

1. Last evening I wrote *a few letters* to my family and friends.
2. Can I have .... in my coffee, please?
3. "When did John go away?" ".................................... ago."
4. "Do you speak any foreign languages?" "Yes, Italian and ...."
5. "Are you going out alone?" "No, I'm going with ...."
6. "Have you ever been to Taiwan?" "Oh, yes. ...."
7. I live in a very small town. There is a store, a post office, and .... – that's all.
8. I'm going out for a walk. I need .... fresh ....
9. There wasn't much furniture in the room – just a table and ....

77.3 Complete the sentences. Use **very little / very few** + one of these words:

coffee hotels ~~mistakes~~ rain time

1. Her English is very good. She makes *very few mistakes.*
2. I drink .... I don't like it much.
3. In summer the weather is very dry. There is ....
4. It's hard to find a place to stay in this town. There are ....
5. We have to hurry. We have ....

77.4 Put in **little** or **a little / few** or **a few**.

1. There was *little* food in the refrigerator. It was nearly empty.
2. "When did you see Kim?" ".. days ago."
3. He's very lazy. He does .... work.
4. They're not rich, but they have .... money – enough to live.
5. Last night I went to a restaurant with .... friends.
6. The TV stations aren't very good. There are .... good programs.
7. I can't decide now – I need .... time to think about it.
8. Nearly everybody has a job. There is .... unemployment in this town.
9. He's not well known. .... people have heard of him.

UNIT 78

big/tired/beautiful, etc. (adjectives)

A

adjective + *noun* (**nice day / brown eyes**, etc.):

adjective	+ *noun*
It's a **nice**	**day** today.
Ann has **brown**	**eyes**.
There's a very **old**	**church** in this town.
Do you like **Chinese**	**food**?
I don't speak any **foreign**	**languages**.
There are some **beautiful yellow**	**flowers** in the garden.

The adjective is *before* the noun:

- They live in a **modern house**. (*not* "a house modern")

The endings of adjectives do not change:

a different place **different** places (*not* "differents")

B

be (am/is/are/was/were, etc.) + *adjective*:

- The weather **is nice** today.
- Those flowers **are** very **beautiful**.
- A: Can you close the window, please?
  B: Why? **Are** you **cold**?
- The movie **wasn't** very **good**. It **was boring**.
- Please **be quiet**. I'm reading.

For **get** + *adjective*, see Unit 50.

C

look/feel/smell/taste/sound + *adjective*:

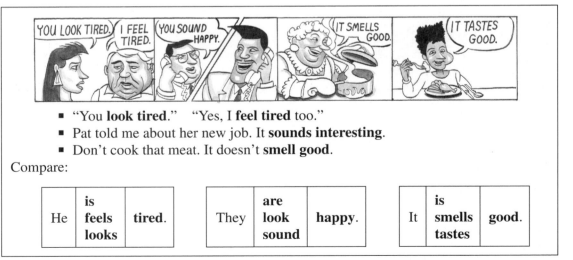

- "You **look tired**." "Yes, I **feel tired** too."
- Pat told me about her new job. It **sounds interesting**.
- Don't cook that meat. It doesn't **smell good**.

Compare:

He	**is** **feels** **looks**	**tired**.

They	**are** **look** **sound**	**happy**.

It	**is** **smells** **tastes**	**good**.

Exercises

78.1 The following words are adjectives (**black/foreign**, etc.) or nouns (**air/job**, etc.). Use an adjective and a noun to complete each sentence.

air	**black**	**clouds**	**dangerous**	**expensive**	**~~foreign~~**	**fresh**
hotels	**interesting**	**job**	**knife**	**~~languages~~**	**long**	**old**
person	**photograph**	**problem**	**serious**	**sharp**	**vacation**	

1. Jack doesn't speak any *foreign languages.*
2. Look at those .... in the sky! It's going to rain.
3. She works very hard and she's very tired. She needs a ....
4. I enjoy talking to her. She's an ....
5. Fire fighting is a ....
6. Can you open the window? We need some ....
7. This is an .... of Tom – he looks very different now.
8. I have a .... I hope you can help me.
9. I need a .... to cut these onions.
10. They have a lot of money – they always stay at ....

78.2 Write sentences for the pictures. Use:

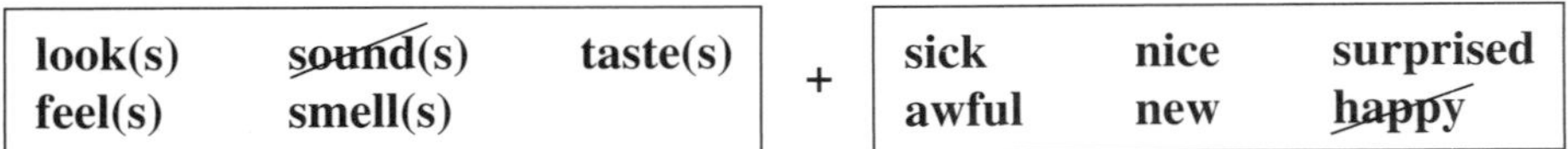

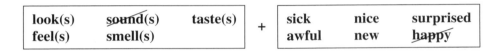

			+			
look(s)	**~~sound~~(s)**	**taste(s)**		**sick**	**nice**	**surprised**
feel(s)	**smell(s)**			**awful**	**new**	**~~happy~~**

1. You *sound happy.*
2. It ....
3. I ....
4. You ....
5. They ....
6. It ....

78.3 In these conversations you don't agree with Tom. Use the word in parentheses ( ).

	Tom	You		
1.	You sound happy.	Really?	(feel)	*I don't feel happy.*
2.	He's American.	Really?	(sound)	He doesn't ....
3.	She's very rich.	Really?	(look)	She ....
4.	You look cold.	Really?	(feel)	I ....
5.	They are very friendly.	Really?	(look)	They ....
6.	That hamburger looks good.	Really?	(taste)	It ....

UNIT 79

quickly/badly/suddenly, etc. (adverbs)

She ate her dinner very **quickly**.

Suddenly the shelf fell down.

A

Quickly and **suddenly** are *adverbs*.

adjective + **-ly** → *adverb*					
adjective:	quick	bad	sudden	careful	heavy
adverb:	quick**ly**	bad**ly**	sudden**ly**	careful**ly**	heav**ily**, etc.
Spelling:	easy → eas**ily** heavy → heav**ily** See Appendix 4 (4.2).				

Adverbs tell you how something happens or how somebody does something:

- The train **stopped suddenly**.
- I **opened** the door **slowly**.
- Please **listen carefully**.
- I **understand** you **perfectly**.

B

Compare adjectives and adverbs.

Adjective	*Adverb*
▪ Sue **is** very **quiet**.	▪ Sue **speaks** very **quietly**. (*not* "speaks very quiet")
▪ **Be careful!**	▪ **Listen carefully!** (*not* "listen careful")
▪ It was **a bad game**.	▪ Our team **played badly**.

These words are adjectives *and* adverbs:

fast hard late early

▪ Ben is **a fast runner**.	Ben can **run fast**. (*not* "fastly")
▪ Her job **is** very **hard**.	She **works** very **hard**. (*not* "hardly")
▪ The bus **was late/early**.	I **went** to bed **late/early**.

good *(adjective)* → **well** *(adverb)*:

▪ Her English **is** very **good**.	She **speaks** English very **well**. (*not* "speaks English very good")
▪ It was **a good game**.	Our team **played well**.

But **well** is also an *adjective* (= not sick; in good health):

- "How are you?" "**I'm** very **well**, thank you. And you?"

Exercises

79.1 Look at the pictures and complete the sentences with one of these adverbs:

badly ~~**carefully**~~ **dangerously** **fast** **angrily** **quietly**

1. FRAGILE

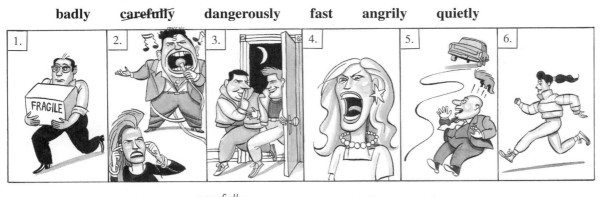

1. He carried the box *carefully*.
2. He sings very ....
3. They came in ....
4. She shouted at me ....
5. He was driving ....
6. She can run very ....

79.2 Choose a verb + adverb from the boxes to complete these sentences.

come	**explain**	**know**	~~**listen**~~
sleep	**think**	**win**	**work**

\+

~~**carefully**~~	**clearly**	**easily**	**well**
carefully	**quickly**	**hard**	**well**

1. I'm going to say something very important, so please *listen* to me *carefully*.
2. John! I need your help. .... !
3. I've met him but I don't .... him very ....
4. They .... At the end of the day they're always tired.
5. I'm tired this morning. I didn't .... last night.
6. You're a much better tennis player than me. When we play, you always ....
7. .... before you answer the question.
8. Our teacher isn't very good. He doesn't .... things very ....

79.3 Choose the right word.

1. I opened the door ~~slow~~/slowly. (slowly is *right*)
2. Why are you angry/angrily? I haven't done anything.
3. Bill is a careful/carefully driver. He drives careful/carefully.
4. Can you please repeat that slow/slowly?
5. Come on, Dan! Why are you always so slow/slowly?
6. The party was very good/well. I enjoyed it very much.
7. Tom didn't do very good/well on his exam.
8. Jane is studying hard/hardly for her exams.
9. "Where's Mary?" "She was here, but she left sudden/suddenly."
10. I met them a long time ago, so I don't remember them very good/well.
11. My brother isn't very good/well at the moment.
12. Don't eat your dinner so quick/quickly. It's not good for you.
13. Those oranges look nice/nicely. Can I have one?
14. I don't want to work for that company. They pay their workers very bad/badly.
15. Please be quiet/quietly. I'm reading.

UNIT 80

old/older expensive / more expensive

old **older** heavy **heavier** expensive **more expensive**

Older / heavier / more expensive are *comparative* forms.
The comparative form is **-er** (**older**) *or* **more . . .** (**more expensive**).

A

Short adjectives (1 syllable) **old/cheap/nice**, etc. → **-er**

old → old**er** **slow** → slow**er** **cheap** → cheap**er**
nice → nic**er** **late** → lat**er** **big** → bigg**er**

Spelling: big → bigg**er** ho**t** → ho**tt**er thi**n** → thi**nn**er [See Appendix 4 (4.4).]

- Rome is **old** but Athens is **older**. (*not* "more old")
- Is it **cheaper** to go by car or by train? (*not* "more cheap")
- Sue wants to buy a **bigger** car.
- This coat is okay but I think the other one is **nicer**.

but **good/well** → **better** **bad** → **worse** **far** → **farther**

- The weather wasn't very **good** yesterday, but it's **better** today.
- Which is **worse** – a headache or toothache?
- "Do you feel **better** today?" "No, I feel **worse**."
- "How **far** is the station? A mile?" "No, **farther**. About two miles."

B

-y *adjectives* (2 syllables) **easy/heavy**, etc. → **-ier**

eas**y** → eas**ier** heav**y** → heav**ier** earl**y** → earl**ier**

- Don't send a letter. It's **easier** to call me. (*not* "more easy")
- The bag is **heavy** but the suitcase is **heavier**.

C

Long adjectives (2/3/4 syllables) **modern** (= MOD-ERN) / **expensive** (= EX-PEN-SIVE), etc. → **more . . .**

modern → **more modern** **polite** → **more polite** **tired** → **more tired**
expensive → **more expensive** **interesting** → **more interesting**

- I don't like this house. I prefer **more modern** houses. (*not* "moderner")
- Don't talk about your job. Let's talk about something **more interesting**.
- Is it **more expensive** to go by car or by train?

For **older than . . .** , **more expensive . . .** , see Unit 81.

Exercises

80.1 Look at the pictures and write the comparative (**older** / **more modern**, etc.).

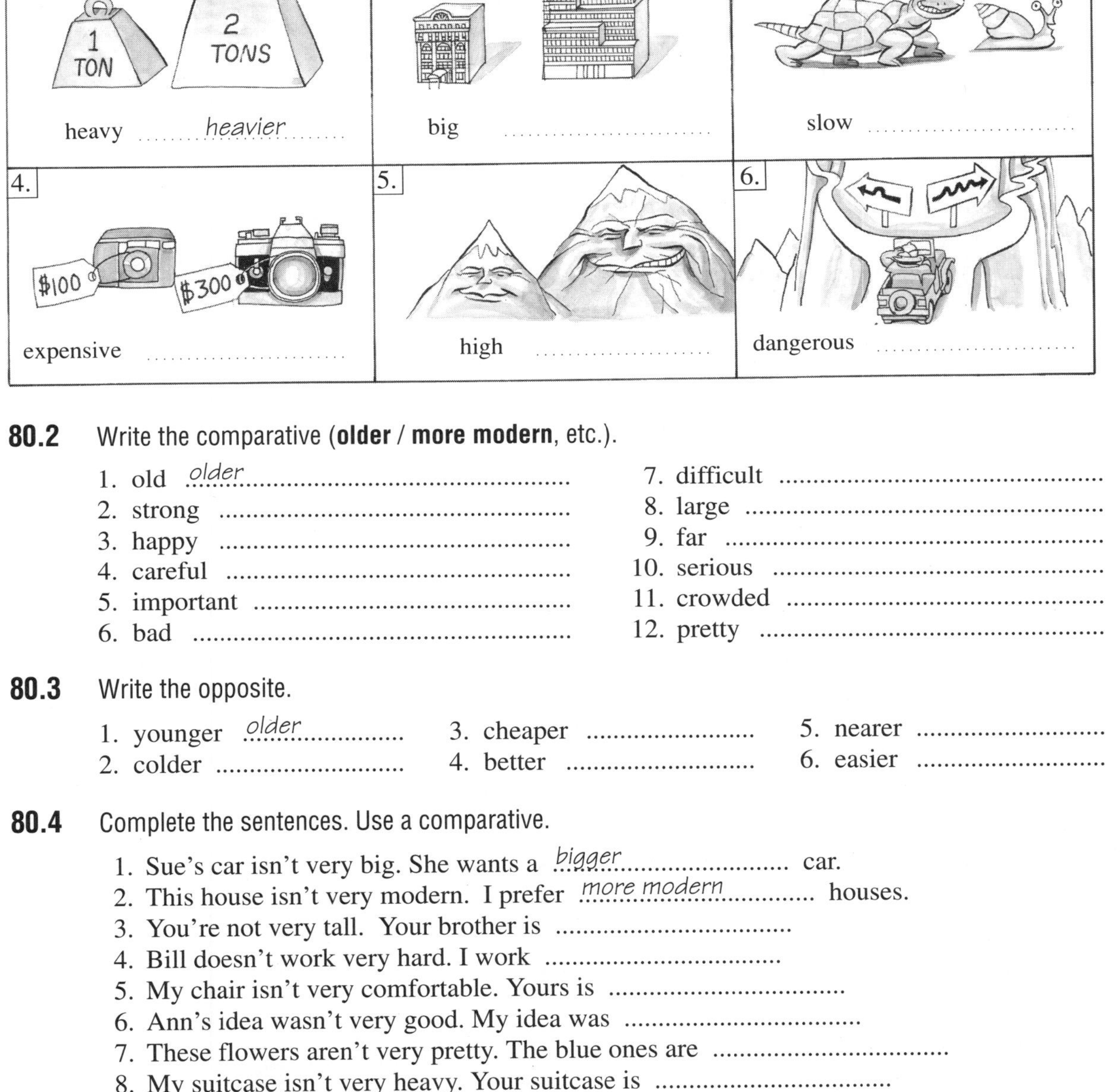

1. heavy *heavier*
2. big ....
3. slow ....
4. expensive ....
5. high ....
6. dangerous ....

80.2 Write the comparative (**older** / **more modern**, etc.).

1. old *older*
2. strong ....
3. happy ....
4. careful ....
5. important ....
6. bad ....
7. difficult ....
8. large ....
9. far ....
10. serious ....
11. crowded ....
12. pretty ....

80.3 Write the opposite.

1. younger *older*
2. colder ....
3. cheaper ....
4. better ....
5. nearer ....
6. easier ....

80.4 Complete the sentences. Use a comparative.

1. Sue's car isn't very big. She wants a *bigger* car.
2. This house isn't very modern. I prefer *more modern* houses.
3. You're not very tall. Your brother is ....
4. Bill doesn't work very hard. I work ....
5. My chair isn't very comfortable. Yours is ....
6. Ann's idea wasn't very good. My idea was ....
7. These flowers aren't very pretty. The blue ones are ....
8. My suitcase isn't very heavy. Your suitcase is ....
9. I'm not very interested in art. I'm .... in history.
10. It isn't very warm today. It was .... yesterday.
11. These tomatoes don't taste very good. The other ones tasted ....
12. Rhode Island isn't very big. New Jersey is ....
13. This city isn't very beautiful. Paris is ....
14. This knife isn't very sharp. Do you have a .... one?
15. People today aren't very polite. In the past they were ....

UNIT 81

older than . . . more expensive than . . .

She's **taller than** him.

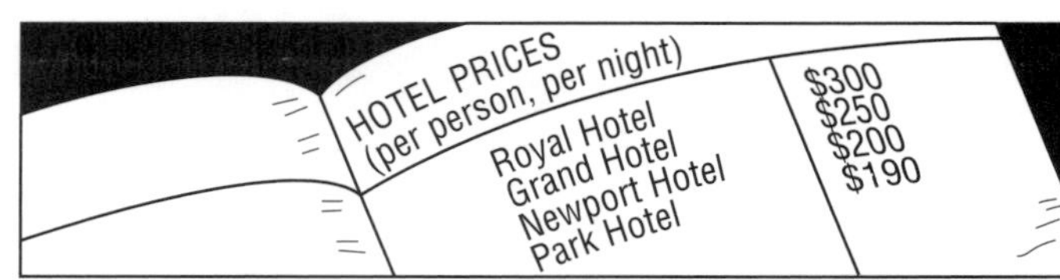

The Royal Hotel is **more expensive than** the Grand.

A

We use **than** after *comparatives* (**older than . . . / more expensive than . . .**, etc.):

- Athens is **older than** Rome.
- Are oranges **more expensive than** apples?
- It's **easier** to call **than** to write a letter.
- "How are you today?" "Not bad. **Better than** yesterday."
- Last night the restaurant was **more crowded than** usual.

B

We say . . . than **me** / than **him** / than **her** / than **us** / than **them**:

- I can run faster **than him**. *or* I can run faster **than he can**.
- You are a better singer **than me**. *or* You are a better singer **than I am**.
- I got up earlier **than her**. *or* I got up earlier **than she did**.

C

more/less than . . .

- A: How much did your shoes cost? Twenty dollars?
  B: No, **more than** that. (= **more than** $20)
- The movie was very short – **less than** an hour.
- They have **more money than they need**.
- You go out **more than me**. (= more often than me)

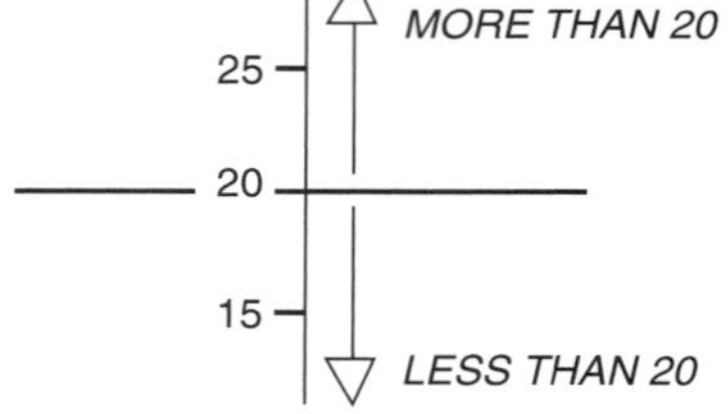

D

a little /a little bit / much + older / more expensive, etc.

Box A is **a little bit bigger** than Box B.

Box C is **much bigger** than Box D.

a little **a little bit** **much**	bigger older better more difficult more expensive	than . . .

- Canada is **much bigger** than Japan.
- Ann is **a little bit older** than Dan – she's 25 and he's 24½.
- A car is **much more expensive** than a motorcycle.

For **old/older**, **expensive / more expensive**, see also Unit 80.

Exercises

81.1 Write sentences about Liz and Ben. Use **than**.

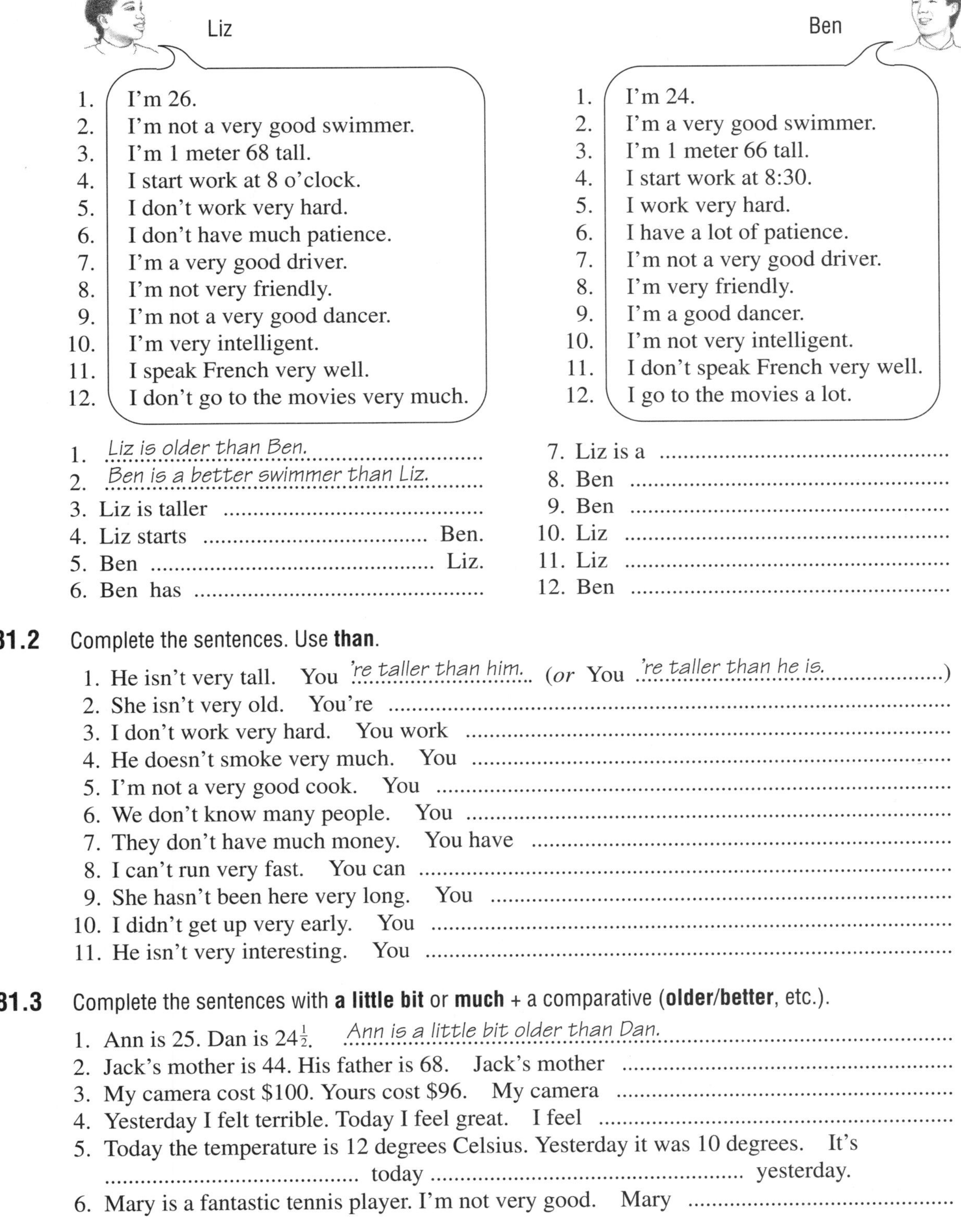

Liz

1. I'm 26.
2. I'm not a very good swimmer.
3. I'm 1 meter 68 tall.
4. I start work at 8 o'clock.
5. I don't work very hard.
6. I don't have much patience.
7. I'm a very good driver.
8. I'm not very friendly.
9. I'm not a very good dancer.
10. I'm very intelligent.
11. I speak French very well.
12. I don't go to the movies very much.

Ben

1. I'm 24.
2. I'm a very good swimmer.
3. I'm 1 meter 66 tall.
4. I start work at 8:30.
5. I work very hard.
6. I have a lot of patience.
7. I'm not a very good driver.
8. I'm very friendly.
9. I'm a good dancer.
10. I'm not very intelligent.
11. I don't speak French very well.
12. I go to the movies a lot.

1. *Liz is older than Ben.*
2. *Ben is a better swimmer than Liz.*
3. Liz is taller ....
4. Liz starts .... Ben.
5. Ben .... Liz.
6. Ben has ....
7. Liz is a ....
8. Ben ....
9. Ben ....
10. Liz ....
11. Liz ....
12. Ben ....

81.2 Complete the sentences. Use **than**.

1. He isn't very tall. You *'re taller than him.* (*or* You *'re taller than he is.*)
2. She isn't very old. You're ....
3. I don't work very hard. You work ....
4. He doesn't smoke very much. You ....
5. I'm not a very good cook. You ....
6. We don't know many people. You ....
7. They don't have much money. You have ....
8. I can't run very fast. You can ....
9. She hasn't been here very long. You ....
10. I didn't get up very early. You ....
11. He isn't very interesting. You ....

81.3 Complete the sentences with **a little bit** or **much** + a comparative (**older/better**, etc.).

1. Ann is 25. Dan is $24\frac{1}{2}$. *Ann is a little bit older than Dan.*
2. Jack's mother is 44. His father is 68. Jack's mother ....
3. My camera cost $100. Yours cost $96. My camera ....
4. Yesterday I felt terrible. Today I feel great. I feel ....
5. Today the temperature is 12 degrees Celsius. Yesterday it was 10 degrees. It's .... today .... yesterday.
6. Mary is a fantastic tennis player. I'm not very good. Mary ....

UNIT 82

not as . . . as

She's old, but she's **not as old as** he is.

Box A is**n't as big as** Box B.

A

not as . . . as . . . :

- Rome is **not as old as** Athens. (= Athens is **older**)
- The Grand Hotel is**n't as expensive as** the Royal. (= the Royal is **more expensive**)
- I do**n't** play tennis **as often as** you. (= you play **more often**)
- The weather is better than yesterday. It is**n't as cold**. (= as cold **as yesterday**)

B

not as much as . . . / not as many as . . . :

- I do**n't** have **as much money as** you. (= you have **more money**)
- I do**n't** know **as many people as** you. (= you know **more people**)
- I do**n't** go out **as much as** you. (= you go out **more**)

Compare **not as . . . as** and **than**:

- Rome is **not as old as** Athens.
  Athens is **older than** Rome. (*not* "older as Rome")
- Tennis is**n't as popular as** soccer.
  Soccer is **more popular than** tennis.
- I do**n't** go out **as much as** you.
  You go out **more than** me.

For **much/many**, see Unit 76.

C

We say . . . as **me** / as **him** / as **her**, etc.:

- She's not as old **as him**. *or* She's not as old **as he is**.
- You don't have as much patience **as me**. *or* You don't have as much patience **as I have**.

D

Note that we say **the same as . . .** :

- My hair is **the same color as** yours. (*not* "the same like")
- I arrived at **the same time as** Tom.

Exercises

82.1 Look at the pictures and write sentences about A, B, and C.

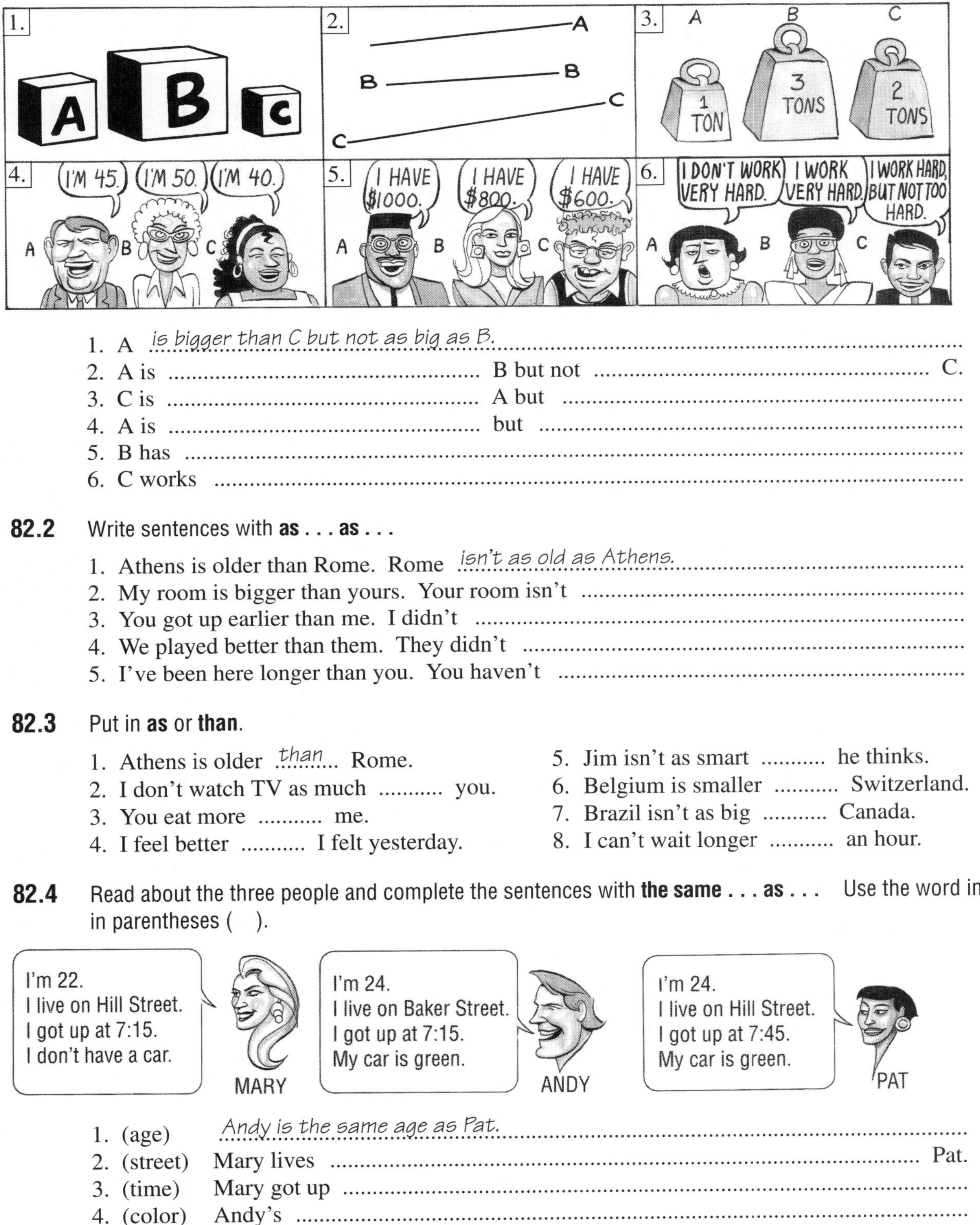

1. A *is bigger than C but not as big as B.*
2. A is .... B but not .... C.
3. C is .... A but ....
4. A is .... but ....
5. B has ....
6. C works ....

82.2 Write sentences with **as . . . as . . .**

1. Athens is older than Rome. Rome *isn't as old as Athens.*
2. My room is bigger than yours. Your room isn't ....
3. You got up earlier than me. I didn't ....
4. We played better than them. They didn't ....
5. I've been here longer than you. You haven't ....

82.3 Put in **as** or **than**.

1. Athens is older *than* Rome.
2. I don't watch TV as much .... you.
3. You eat more .... me.
4. I feel better .... I felt yesterday.
5. Jim isn't as smart .... he thinks.
6. Belgium is smaller .... Switzerland.
7. Brazil isn't as big .... Canada.
8. I can't wait longer .... an hour.

82.4 Read about the three people and complete the sentences with **the same . . . as . . .** Use the word in in parentheses ( ).

I'm 22.
I live on Hill Street.
I got up at 7:15.
I don't have a car.
MARY
I'm 24.
I live on Baker Street.
I got up at 7:15.
My car is green.
ANDY
I'm 24.
I live on Hill Street.
I got up at 7:45.
My car is green.
PAT

1. (age) *Andy is the same age as Pat.*
2. (street) Mary lives .... Pat.
3. (time) Mary got up ....
4. (color) Andy's ....

UNIT 83

the oldest the most expensive

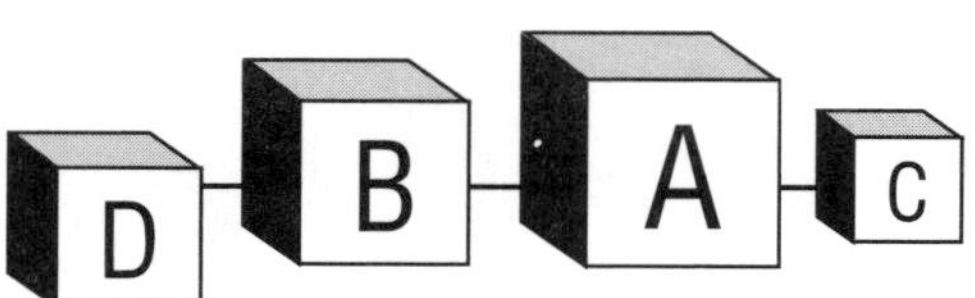

HOTEL PRICES
(per person, per night)

Royal Hotel	$300	Sunset	$150
Grand Hotel	$250	Willows	$140
Newport	$200	Carlton	$130
Park	$190	Star	$120
Palace	$190	Station	$100

Box A is **bigger than** box B.
Box A is **bigger than** all the other boxes.
Box A is **the biggest** box.

The Royal Hotel is **more expensive than** the Grand.
The Royal Hotel is **more expensive than** all the other hotels in the town.
The Royal Hotel is **the most expensive** hotel in the town.

Bigg**er** / old**er** / **more** expensive, etc. are *comparative* forms. (See Unit 81.)
Bigg**est** / old**est** / **most** expensive, etc. are *superlative* forms.

A

The superlative form is **-est** (**oldest**) *or* **most . . .** (**most expensive**):

Short adjectives (**old/cheap/nice**, etc.) → **the -est**:

old → **the** old**est** **cheap** → **the** cheap**est** **nice** → **the** nic**est**
but **good** → **the best** **bad** → **the worst**

Spelling: big → the bi**gg**est hot → the ho**tt**est [See Appendix 4 (4.4).]

-y *adjectives* (**easy/heavy**, etc.) → **the -iest**:

eas**y** → **the** eas**iest** heav**y** → **the** heav**iest** prett**y** → **the** prett**iest**

Long adjectives (**modern/expensive/interesting**, etc.) → **the most . . .**

modern → **the most modern** **interesting** → **the most interesting**

B

Don't forget **the**. We say **the** oldest . . . / **the** most expensive . . . , etc.:

- The church is very old. It's **the oldest** building in the town. (= it is old**er than** all the other buildings)
- What is **the longest** river in the world?
- Money is important, but it isn't **the most important** thing in life.
- Excuse me, where is **the nearest** bank?

C

You can use **the oldest / the best / the most expensive**, etc. *without* a noun:

- Ken is a good tennis player. He is **the best** in our school. (**the best** = the best player)

D

You can use the superlative + **I've ever . . . / you've ever . . .** :

- It was a very bad movie – **the worst** movie **I've ever** seen.
- What is **the most unusual** thing **you've ever done**?

For **I've ever . . . / you've ever** (present perfect), see Unit 15.

Exercises

83.1 Write sentences with comparatives (**older**, etc.) and superlatives (**the oldest**, etc.).

1. **(big/small)**
   (A/D) *A is bigger than D.* ....
   (A) *A is the biggest.* ....
   (B) *B is the smallest.* ....
2. **(long/short)**
   (C/A) C is .... A.
   (D) D is ....
   (B) B ....
3. **(young/old)**
   (D/C) D ....
   (B) B ....
   (C) ....
4. **(expensive/cheap)**
   (D/A) ....
   (C) ....
   (A) ....
5. **(good/bad)**
   (A/C) ....
   (A) ....
   (D) ....

83.2 Write sentences with a superlative (**the longest**, etc.).

~~Sydney~~	Brazil
Everest	Jupiter
Alaska	the Nile

large
long
high

country	planet
~~city~~	state
river	mountain

the USA	the solar system
Africa	South America
the world	~~Australia~~

1. *Sydney is the largest city in Australia.* ....
2. Everest ....
3. ....
4. ....
5. ....
6. ....

83.3 Complete the sentences. Use a superlative (**the oldest**, etc.).

1. This building is very old. It's *the oldest building* .... in the town.
2. It was a very happy day. It was .... of my life.
3. It's a very good movie. It's .... I've ever seen.
4. She's a very popular singer. She's .... in our country.
5. It was a very bad mistake. It was .... I've ever made.
6. It's a very pretty town. It's .... I've ever seen.
7. It was a very cold day. It was .... of the year.
8. He's a very interesting person. He's .... I've ever met.

UNIT 84 enough

Sue wants to buy a sandwich.

A sandwich is two dollars.
Sue has only one dollar.

So she can't buy a sandwich because she doesn't have **enough** money.

A (**not**) **enough** + *noun* (**enough money / enough houses**, etc.):

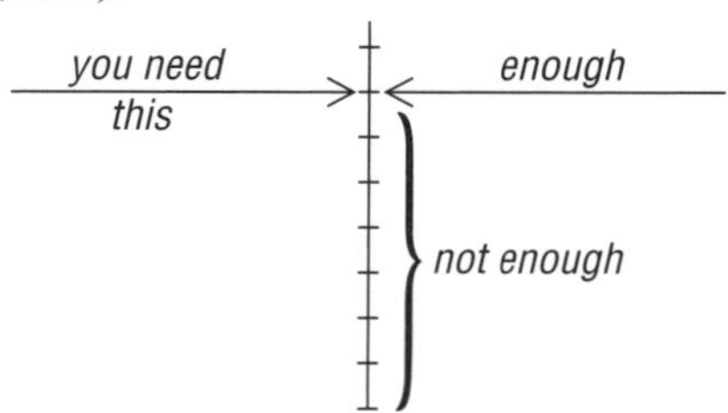

- A: Is there **enough sugar** in your coffee?
  B: Yes, thank you.
- We wanted to play soccer, but we didn't have **enough players**.
- Why don't you buy a car? You have **enough money**. (*not* "money enough")

B (**not**) **enough** *without a noun*:

- I have some money, but **not enough** to buy a car. (= I need more money to buy a car.)
- "Would you like something else to eat?" "No, thanks, I've had **enough**."
- You always stay home. You don't go out **enough**.

C *adjective* + **enough** (**good enough / warm enough**, etc.):

- A: Do you want to go swimming?
  B: No, it isn't **warm enough**. (*not* "enough warm").
- Can you hear the radio? Is it **loud enough** for you?
- Don't buy that coat. It's nice, but it isn't **long enough**. (= it's too short)

He isn't **tall enough** (to reach the shelf).

Remember:

enough + *noun*:	**enough** money	**enough** time	**enough** people
but *adjective* + **enough**:	good **enough**	old **enough**	loud **enough**

D We say

enough	**for** somebody/something	**to do** something

- This shirt isn't big **enough for me**.
- I don't have **enough** money **for a car**.

but
- I don't have **enough** money **to buy** a car. (*not* "for buy a car")
- Is your English good **enough to have** a conversation?
- There weren't **enough chairs for everybody to sit** down.

Exercises

84.1 Look at the pictures and complete the sentences. Use **enough** + one of these words:

big **chairs** **long** **~~money~~** **paint** **strong** **~~tall~~** **wind**

1. *She doesn't have enough money.*
2. *He isn't tall enough.*
3. She doesn't have ....
4. The car isn't ....
5. His legs aren't ....
6. There aren't ....
7. There isn't ....
8. He isn't ....

84.2 Complete the sentences. Use **enough** + one of these words:

big **clothes** **eat** **fruit** **~~loud~~** **old** **practice** **~~sugar~~** **time** **tired**

1. "Is there *enough sugar* in your coffee?" "Yes, thank you."
2. Can you hear the radio? Is it *loud enough* for you?
3. He can get married if he wants to – he's ....
4. Did you have .... to answer all the questions on the exam?
5. This house isn't .... for a large family.
6. He's very thin. He doesn't ....
7. You don't eat .... You should eat more – it's good for you.
8. It's late, but I don't want to go to bed now. I'm not ....
9. He has .... He doesn't need any new ones.
10. She's not a very good tennis player because she doesn't ....

84.3 Complete the sentences. Use **enough** + one of these words + **to . . .** :

bread **money** **old** **~~time~~** **warm** **well**

1. I didn't have breakfast this morning. I didn't have *enough time to have breakfast.*
2. They're not getting married. They're not .... married.
3. Don't sit outside. It isn't .... outside.
4. We can't make sandwiches. We don't have ....
5. They didn't go on vacation. They didn't have ....
6. Don't go to work today. You aren't ....

UNIT 85 too

There is **too much sugar** in it.

The shoes are **too big** for him.

A

too much / too many = more than you want, more than is good:

- I don't like the weather here. There is **too much rain**. (= more rain than is good)
- Let's go to another restaurant. There are **too many people** here.
- She studies all the time. I think she studies **too much**.

For **much/many**, see Unit 76.

B

too + *adjective* (**too big / too loud**, etc.):

- Please turn the radio down. It's **too loud**. (= louder than I want)
- I can't work. I'm **too tired**.

C

too and **not enough**

- There's **too much sugar** in my coffee. (= more sugar than I want)
- I don't feel very well. I **ate too much**.
- The radio is **too loud**. Can you turn it down, please?
- The hat is **too big** for her.

- There's **not enough sugar** in my coffee. (= I want more sugar)
- That child is very thin. He **doesn't eat enough**.
- The radio is**n't loud enough**. Can you turn it up, please?
- The hat is**n't big enough** for her. (= it's **too small** for her)

For **enough**, see Unit 84.

C

We say **too . . . for** somebody/something **to do** something:

- These shoes are **too** big **for me**.
- It's a small house – **too** small **for a large family**.

but
- It's **too** cold **to go** out. (*not* "for go out")
- I'm **too** tired **to work**.
- She speaks **too** fast **for me to understand** her.

Exercises

85.1 Look at the pictures and complete the sentences. Use **too** + one of these words:

big crowded fast high hot ~~loud~~

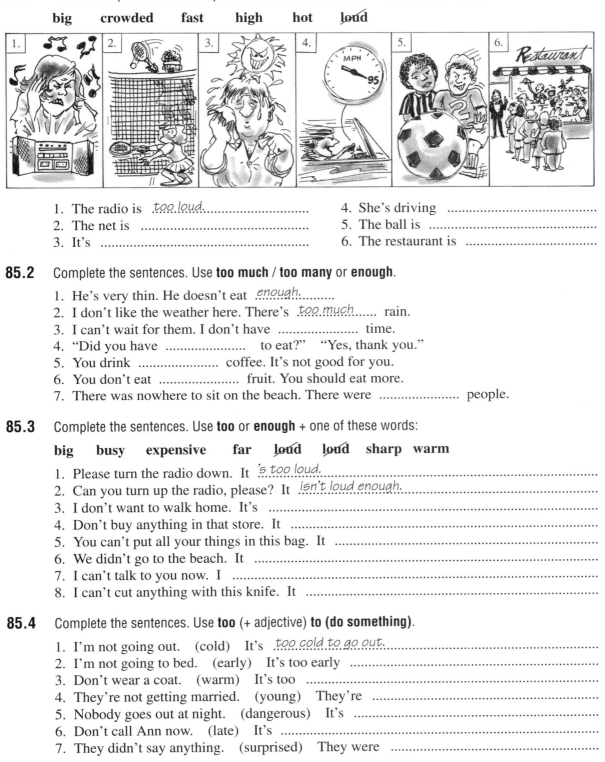

1. The radio is *too loud*.
2. The net is ....
3. It's ....
4. She's driving ....
5. The ball is ....
6. The restaurant is ....

85.2 Complete the sentences. Use **too much / too many** or **enough**.

1. He's very thin. He doesn't eat *enough*.
2. I don't like the weather here. There's *too much* rain.
3. I can't wait for them. I don't have .... time.
4. "Did you have .... to eat?" "Yes, thank you."
5. You drink .... coffee. It's not good for you.
6. You don't eat .... fruit. You should eat more.
7. There was nowhere to sit on the beach. There were .... people.

85.3 Complete the sentences. Use **too** or **enough** + one of these words:

big busy expensive far ~~loud~~ ~~loud~~ sharp warm

1. Please turn the radio down. It *'s too loud*.
2. Can you turn up the radio, please? It *isn't loud enough*.
3. I don't want to walk home. It's ....
4. Don't buy anything in that store. It ....
5. You can't put all your things in this bag. It ....
6. We didn't go to the beach. It ....
7. I can't talk to you now. I ....
8. I can't cut anything with this knife. It ....

85.4 Complete the sentences. Use **too** (+ adjective) **to (do something)**.

1. I'm not going out. (cold) It's *too cold to go out*.
2. I'm not going to bed. (early) It's too early ....
3. Don't wear a coat. (warm) It's too ....
4. They're not getting married. (young) They're ....
5. Nobody goes out at night. (dangerous) It's ....
6. Don't call Ann now. (late) It's ....
7. They didn't say anything. (surprised) They were ....

UNIT 86

still yet

A

still

An hour ago it was raining.

It is **still** raining now.

still = something is the same as before:

- A: Does your daughter work?
  B: No, she's **still** in school. (= she was in school before and she's in school now)
  (For **at school** and **in school**, see Unit 93.)
- I had a lot to eat, but I'm **still** hungry.
- "Did you sell your car?" "No, I **still** have it."
- "Do you **still** live in Berlin?" "No, I live in Frankfurt now."

B

yet

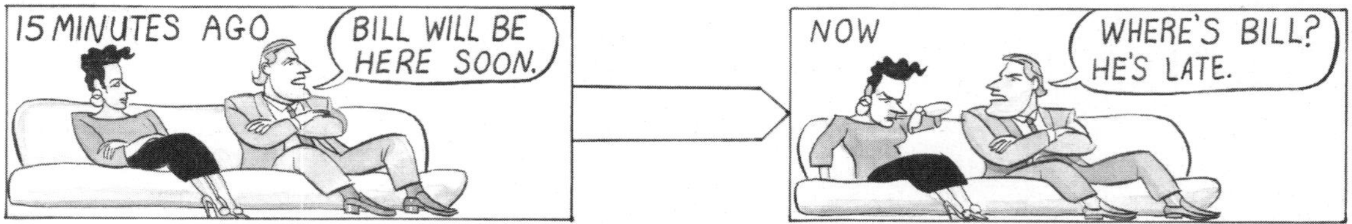

Fifteen minutes ago they were waiting for Bill to come.

They are **still** waiting for Bill. He hasn't come **yet**.

Yet = until now.
We use **yet** in *negative sentences* (**He hasn't come yet.**) and in *questions* (**Has he come yet?**).
Yet is usually at the end of a sentence:

- "Where's Tom?" "He **isn't** here **yet**." (= He will be here, but until now he hasn't come.)
- "What are you doing tonight?" "I **don't** know **yet**." (= I will know later, but I don't know at the moment.)
- "Are you ready to go **yet**?" "**Not yet.** In a minute." (= I will be ready, but I'm not ready at the moment.)

We often use the *present perfect* (**I have done) + yet**:

- "What's in the newspaper today?" "I don't know. I **haven't read** it **yet**." (= I'm going to read it, but I haven't read it until now.)
- "**Has** it **stopped** raining **yet**?" "No, it's still raining."

For the present perfect, see Units 14 and 15.

C

Compare **yet** and **still**:

- She hasn't gone **yet**. = She's **still** here. (*not* "She is yet here.")
- I haven't finished eating **yet**. = I'm **still** eating.

Exercises

86.1 You meet Carol. The last time you saw her was two years ago. Ask her some questions with **still**.

Carol – two years ago.

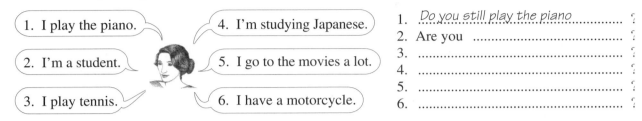

1. I play the piano.
2. I'm a student.
3. I play tennis.
4. I'm studying Japanese.
5. I go to the movies a lot.
6. I have a motorcycle.

1. *Do you still play the piano* .... ?
2. Are you .... ?
3. .... ?
4. .... ?
5. .... ?
6. .... ?

86.2 Write questions with **yet**.

1. It was raining ten minutes ago. Perhaps it has stopped now.
   You ask: *Has it stopped raining yet* .... ?
2. You are waiting for Ann to arrive. She wasn't here half an hour ago. Perhaps she is here now. *You ask*: .... Ann .... ?
3. You are waiting for me to finish reading the newspaper. Perhaps I have finished now.
   You ask: .... you .... ?
4. We are going out together. You are waiting for me to get ready. Perhaps I am ready now.
   You ask: .... ?
5. Tom can't decide where to go on vacation. Perhaps he has decided now.
   You ask: .... ?

86.3 Write three sentences for each situation. Look at the example carefully.

before *now*

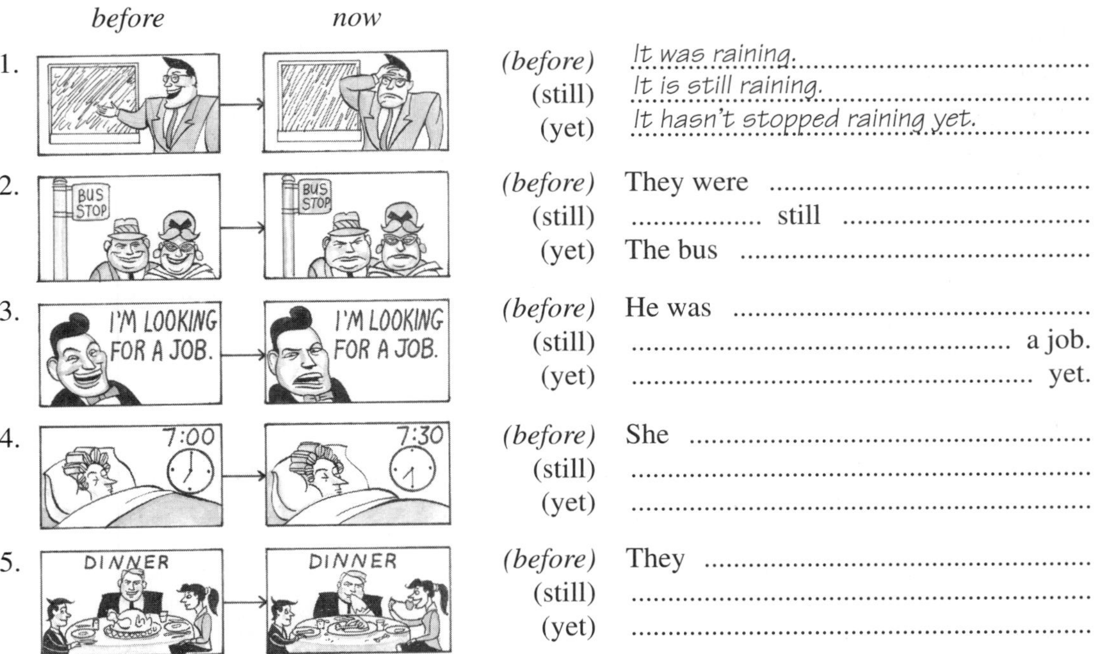

1. *(before)* *It was raining.* ....
   (still) *It is still raining.* ....
   (yet) *It hasn't stopped raining yet.* ....
2. *(before)* They were ....
   (still) .... still ....
   (yet) The bus ....
3. *(before)* He was ....
   (still) .... a job.
   (yet) .... yet.
4. *(before)* She ....
   (still) ....
   (yet) ....
5. *(before)* They ....
   (still) ....
   (yet) ....

UNIT 87

Word order (1)

A

verb + object

Sue	**reads**	**a newspaper**	every day.
subject	*verb*	*object*	

The *verb* (**reads**) and the *object* (**a newspaper**) are usually together:

- Sue **reads a newspaper** every day.

  (not "Sue **reads** every day a **newspaper**.")

subject	*verb*	*+ object*	
You	**speak**	**English**	very well.
I	**watched**	**television**	all night.
We	**invited**	**a lot of people**	to the party.
My brother	**called**	**the police**	immediately.

- I **like Italian food** very much. (*not* "I like very much Italian food.")
- Ann **borrowed some money** from the bank. (*not* "Ann borrowed from the bank some money.")
- I **opened the door** very quietly. (*not* "I opened very quietly the door.")
- Bill usually **wears a black hat**. (*not* "Bill wears usually a black hat.")
- Why do you always **make the same mistake**? (*not* "Why do you make always the same mistake?")

B

place and *time*

	place (where?)	*time (when? how long? how often?)*
Bill walks	**to work**	**every morning**.
We arrived	**at the airport**	**at 7 o'clock**.
Are you going	**to the party**	**tonight**?
They' ve lived	**in the same house**	**for 20 years**.
I usually go	**to bed**	**early**.

place is usually before *time*:

- They go **to school every day**. (*not* "They go every day to school.")
- I went **to the bank yesterday afternoon**. (*not* "I went yesterday afternoon to the bank.")
- Jack's brother has been **in the hospital since June**. (*not* ". . . since June in the hospital.")

Exercises

87.1 Put the words in the right order.

1. (a newspaper / reads / every day / Sue) *Sue reads a newspaper every day.*
2. (soccer / don't like / very much / I) I ....
3. (lost / I / my watch / last week) ....
4. (Tom / the letter / slowly / read) ....
5. (Mary / do you know / very well?) .... ?
6. (ate / we / very quickly / our dinner) ....
7. (did you buy / in Taiwan / that jacket?) .... ?
8. (I / very well / French / don't speak) ....
9. (crossed / the street / they / carefully) ....
10. (from my brother / borrowed / $50 / I) ....
11. (we / enjoyed / very much / the party) ....
12. (passed / Ann / easily / the exam) ....
13. (every day / do / the same thing / we) ....
14. (I / this picture / don't like / very much) ....
15. (in her wallet / the money / put / the woman) ....
16. (did you watch / on television / the news?) .... ?
17. (my plan / carefully / I / explained) ....
18. (she / drinks / everyday / two cups of coffee) ....
19. (a lot of housework / did /I / yesterday) ....
20. (we / at the concert / some friends / met) ....
21. (he / the same clothes / wears / every day) ....
22. (I / want to speak / fluently / English) ....

87.2 Put the words in the right order.

1. (to work / every morning / walks / Bill) *Bill walks to work every morning.*
2. (at the party / we / early / arrived) We ....
3. (didn't go / yesterday / I / to work) I ....
4. (to work / tomorrow / are you going?) .... ?
5. (they / since 1989 / here / have lived) ....
6. (will you be / this evening / home?) .... ?
7. (next week / they / to Buenos Aires / are going) ....
8. (to the movies / last night / did you go?) .... ?
9. (on Monday / here / will they be?) .... ?
10. (goes / every year / to Italy / Kim) ....
11. (in Canada / Liz / in 1976 / was born) ....
12. (I / in bed / this morning / my breakfast / had) ....
13. (next year / Barbara / to college / is going) ....
14. (many times / my parents / have been / to the United States) ....
15. (a beautiful bird / this morning / I / in the park / saw) ....
16. (my umbrella / last night / I think I left / in the restaurant) ....

UNIT 88

Word order (2)

A

always	**usually**	**often**	**sometimes**	**rarely/seldom**	**never**	**ever**
also	**just**	**still**	**already**	**both**	**all**	

These words **(always/usually**, etc.) are often with the verb in the middle of a sentence:

- My brother **never speaks** to me.
- She**'s always** late.
- Do you **often eat** in restaurants?
- I **sometimes eat** too much. (*or* **Sometimes** I eat too much.)
- I don't want to go to the movies. **I've already seen** that film.
- I have three sisters. They**'re all** married.
- A: Where's Linda?
  B: She **just went** out.

B

always/never, etc. go *before* the verb:

	Verb
always	**go**
often +	**play**
never	**feel**
etc.	etc.

- I **always go** to work by car. (*not* "I go always")
- Ann **often plays** tennis.
- I **sometimes feel** sad.
- They **usually have** dinner at 7 o'clock.
- We **rarely** (*or* **seldom**) **watch** television.
- Tom is a good golfer. He **also plays** tennis and volleyball. (*not* "He plays also tennis . . . ")
- I have three sisters. They **all live** in the same city.

C

but **always/never**, etc. go *after* **am/is/are/was/were**:

am	**always**
is	**often**
are +	**never**
was	etc.
were	

- I **am never** sick. (*not* "I never am sick.")
- They **are usually** home in the evenings.
- In the winter it **is often** very cold here.
- When I was a child, I **was always** late for school.
- "Where's Bob?" "He**'s still** in bed."
- I have two brothers. They**'re both** doctors.

D

always/never, etc. go *between* two verbs (**have . . . been / can . . . find**, etc.):

Verb 1		*Verb 2*
will		**go**
can	**always**	**find**
do	**often**	**remember**
etc.	**never**	etc.
have	etc.	**gone**
has		**been**
		etc.

- I **will always remember** you.
- It **doesn't often rain** here.
- **Do** you **usually go** home by car?
- I **can never find** my keys.
- **Have** you **ever been** to Turkey?
- A: Where are your friends?
  B: They**'ve all gone** to the movies.

For **all**, see Unit 74. For **both**, see Unit 75. For **still**, see Unit 86.

Exercises

88.1 Look at Ben's answers to the questions and write sentences with **often/never**, etc.

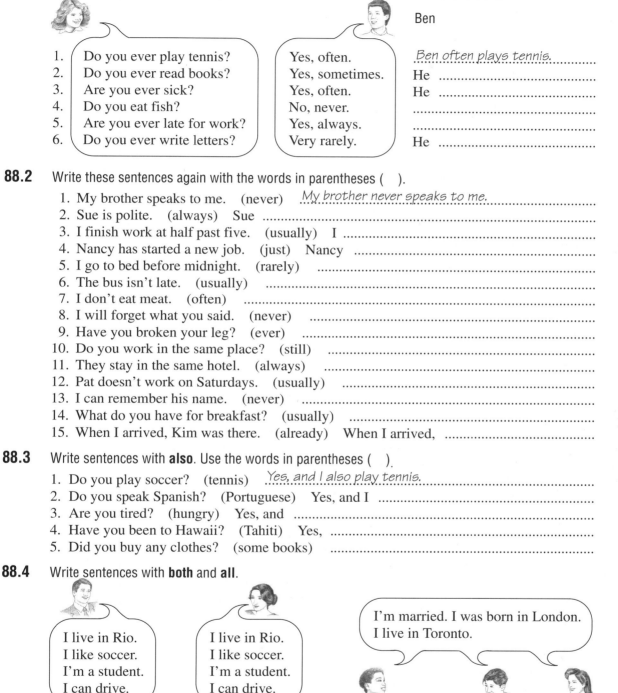

	Question	Ben	
1.	Do you ever play tennis?	Yes, often.	*Ben often plays tennis.*
2.	Do you ever read books?	Yes, sometimes.	He ....
3.	Are you ever sick?	Yes, often.	He ....
4.	Do you eat fish?	No, never.	....
5.	Are you ever late for work?	Yes, always.	....
6.	Do you ever write letters?	Very rarely.	He ....

88.2 Write these sentences again with the words in parentheses ( ).

1. My brother speaks to me. (never) *My brother never speaks to me.*
2. Sue is polite. (always) Sue ....
3. I finish work at half past five. (usually) I ....
4. Nancy has started a new job. (just) Nancy ....
5. I go to bed before midnight. (rarely) ....
6. The bus isn't late. (usually) ....
7. I don't eat meat. (often) ....
8. I will forget what you said. (never) ....
9. Have you broken your leg? (ever) ....
10. Do you work in the same place? (still) ....
11. They stay in the same hotel. (always) ....
12. Pat doesn't work on Saturdays. (usually) ....
13. I can remember his name. (never) ....
14. What do you have for breakfast? (usually) ....
15. When I arrived, Kim was there. (already) When I arrived, ...

88.3 Write sentences with **also**. Use the words in parentheses ( ).

1. Do you play soccer? (tennis) *Yes, and I also play tennis.*
2. Do you speak Spanish? (Portuguese) Yes, and I ....
3. Are you tired? (hungry) Yes, and ....
4. Have you been to Hawaii? (Tahiti) Yes, ...
5. Did you buy any clothes? (some books) ....

88.4 Write sentences with **both** and **all**.

I live in Rio.
I like soccer.
I'm a student.
I can drive.
I live in Rio.
I like soccer.
I'm a student.
I can drive.
I'm married. I was born in London.
I live in Toronto.

1. *They both live in Rio.*
2. They .... soccer.
3. .... students.
4. ....
5. They .... married.
6. They .... London.
7. ....

UNIT 89

Give me that book! Give it to me!

A

give	lend	pass	send	show

After these verbs (**give**, **lend**, etc.) there are two possible structures:

(give) something to somebody

- I gave **the money to Jack**.

or **(give) somebody something**

- I gave **Jack the money**.

B

(give) something to somebody:

- That book is mine. **Give it to me!**
- This is your father's key. Can you **give it to him**?
- I **lent my car to a friend of mine**.
- "Have you seen these photographs?" "Yes, you **showed them to us**."

		(**something**)	to (**somebody**)
Can you	**give**	this key	**to** your father?
Can you	**give**	it	**to** him?
I	**lent**	my car	**to** a friend of mine.
You	**showed**	them	**to** us.

C

(give) somebody something:

- Give **me that book**! It's mine. (*not* "Give to me that book!")
- Tom gave **his mother some flowers**. (*not* "Tom gave to his mother some flowers.")

		(**somebody**)	(**something**)
Tom	**gave**	his mother	some flowers.
Don't forget to	**send**	Lee	a birthday card.
Can you	**pass**	me	the salt, please?
If you see Jack, can you	**give**	him	this letter?
How much money did you	**lend**	them?	

D

Compare:

- I gave **the book to Pat**.

but I gave **Pat the book**. (*not* "I gave to Pat the book.")

We prefer the first structure (**give something to somebody**) when the *thing* is **it** or **them**:

- I gave **it to her**. (*not usually* "I gave her it.")
- Give **them to your father**. (*not usually* "Give your father them.")

Exercises

89.1 Mark had some things that he didn't want – an armchair, a TV set, some books, some cassettes, a radio, and a lamp. He gave these things to different people. Look at the pictures and write a sentence for each thing.

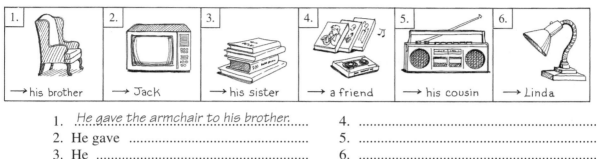

1.	2.	3.	4.	5.	6.
→ his brother	→ Jack	→ his sister	→ a friend	→ his cousin	→ Linda

1. *He gave the armchair to his brother.*
2. He gave ....
3. He ....
4. ....
5. ....
6. ....

89.2 You wanted to give presents to your friends. You thought about it and you decided to give them the things in the pictures. Write a sentence for each person.

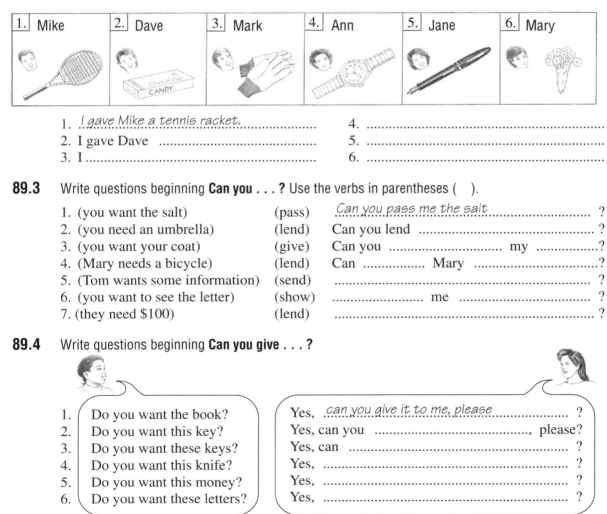

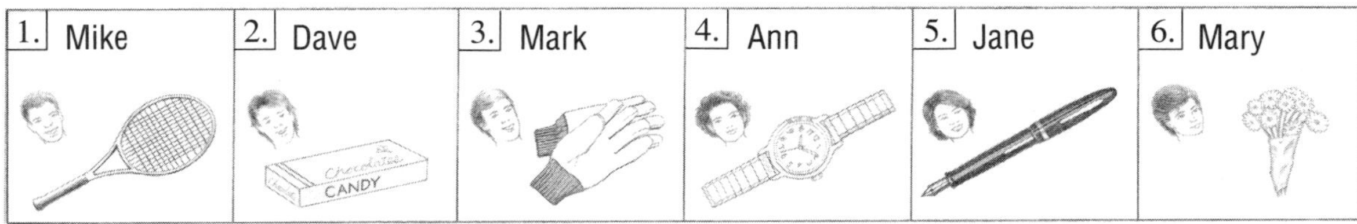

1. *I gave Mike a tennis racket.*
2. I gave Dave ....
3. I ....
4. ....
5. ....
6. ....

89.3 Write questions beginning **Can you . . . ?** Use the verbs in parentheses ( ).

1. (you want the salt) (pass) *Can you pass me the salt* ?
2. (you need an umbrella) (lend) Can you lend .... ?
3. (you want your coat) (give) Can you .... my ....?
4. (Mary needs a bicycle) (lend) Can .... Mary ....?
5. (Tom wants some information) (send) .... ?
6. (you want to see the letter) (show) .... me .... ?
7. (they need $100) (lend) .... ?

89.4 Write questions beginning **Can you give . . . ?**

1. Do you want the book? — Yes, *can you give it to me, please* ?
2. Do you want this key? — Yes, can you ...., please?
3. Do you want these keys? — Yes, can .... ?
4. Do you want this knife? — Yes, ... ?
5. Do you want this money? — Yes, ... ?
6. Do you want these letters? — Yes, ... ?

UNIT 90

at 10:30 on Monday in April

A

at

at	8 o'clock 10:30 midnight, etc.

- I start work **at 8 o'clock**.
- The stores close **at 5:30 p.m.**

on

on	Sunday(s)/Monday(s), etc. April 25/June 6, etc. New Year's Day, etc.

- Goodbye! See you **on Friday**.
- I don't work **on Sundays**.
- The concert is **on November 22**.

in

in	April/June, etc. 1985/1750, etc. (the) summer/spring, etc.

- I'm going on vacation **in October**.
- Ann graduated from college **in 1990**.
- The park is lovely **in the spring**.

also

at night	▪ I can't sleep **at night**.
at the end/beginning of . . .	▪ I'm going on vacation **at the end of October**.
at the moment	▪ Are you busy **at the moment**?

in the morning / in the afternoon / in the evening
- I always feel good **in the morning**.
- Do you often go out **in the evening**?

but

on Monday morning / on Tuesday afternoon / on Friday evening / on Saturday night, etc.
- I'm meeting Sue **on Monday morning**.
- Are you doing anything **on Friday night**?

on the weekend / on weekends
- What are you doing **on the weekend**?

B

in five minutes / in a few days / in six weeks / in two years, etc.

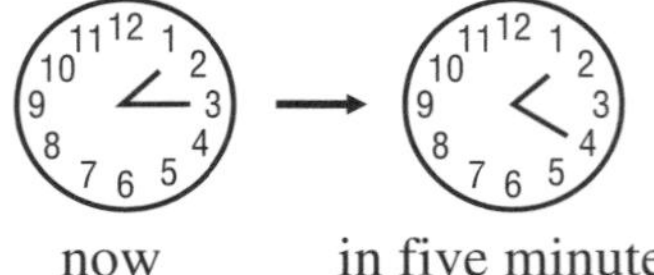

- Hurry! The train leaves **in five minutes**. (= it leaves five minutes from now)
- Goodbye. I'll see you **in a few days**. (= a few days from now)

C

~~at~~ ~~on~~ ~~in~~ We do *not* use **at/on/in** before:

this . . . (**this morning / this week**, etc.) **last . . .** (**last August / last week**, etc.)
every . . . (**every day / every week**, etc.) **next . . .** (**next Monday / next week**, etc.)

- They're going on vacation **next Monday**. (*not* "on next Monday")
- **Last summer** we went to Europe. (*not* "In last summer")

Exercises

90.1 Write **at/on/in**.

1. *on*...... June 6
2. *at*...... 8 o'clock
3. .... Wednesday
4. .... 12:30 a.m.
5. 1776
6. .... September
7. .... September 24
8. .... Friday
9. 1984
10. .... midnight
11. .... New Year's Day
12. .... the winter
13. *in*...... the evening
14. .... the morning
15. .... Monday morning
16. .... Saturday night
17. .... night
18. .... the moment
19. .... the weekend
20. .... Tuesday afternoon
21. .... the end of my vacation

90.2 Write **at/on/in**.

1. Goodbye! See you *on*...... Friday.
2. Where were you .... February 28?
3. I got up .... 8 o'clock this morning.
4. I like getting up early .... the morning.
5. My sister got married .... May.
6. Sue and I first met .... 1991.
7. Did you go out .... Friday?
8. Did you go out .... Friday evening?
9. Do you often go out .... the evening?
10. Let's meet .... 7:30 tomorrow evening.
11. I'm starting my new job .... June 3.
12. We often go to the beach .... the summer.
13. Tom isn't here .... the moment.
14. Ann's birthday is .... January.
15. Do you work .... Saturdays?
16. I will send you the money .... the end of this month.
17. .... the autumn, the leaves fall from the trees.
18. The company started .... 1970.
19. I often go away .... the weekend.
20. I like looking at the stars in the sky .... night.

90.3 Write sentences with **in . . .**

now

1. 5:25 → 5:30 — It's 5:25 now. The train leaves at 5:30.
   The train leaves in five minutes.
2. MONDAY → THURSDAY — It's Monday today. I'll call you on Thursday.
   I'll .... days.
3. JUNE 14 → JUNE 28 — Today is June 14. My exam is on June 28.
   My ....
4.  →  — It's 3 o'clock now. Tom will be here at 3:30.
   Tom ....

90.4 Write **at/on/in** if necessary. (Sometimes there is no preposition.)

1. I'm leaving *on*...... Saturday.
2. I'm leaving *—*...... next Saturday.
3. I always feel tired .... the evening.
4. Will you be home .... this evening?
5. We went to Mexico .... last summer.
6. What do you do .... the weekend?
7. She calls me .... every Sunday.
8. Can you play tennis .... next Sunday?
9. I'm afraid I can't come to the party .... Sunday.
10. We went to bed late .... last night.
11. I don't like going out alone .... night.
12. I won't be out very long. I'll be back .... ten minutes.

UNIT 91

from . . . to until since for

A

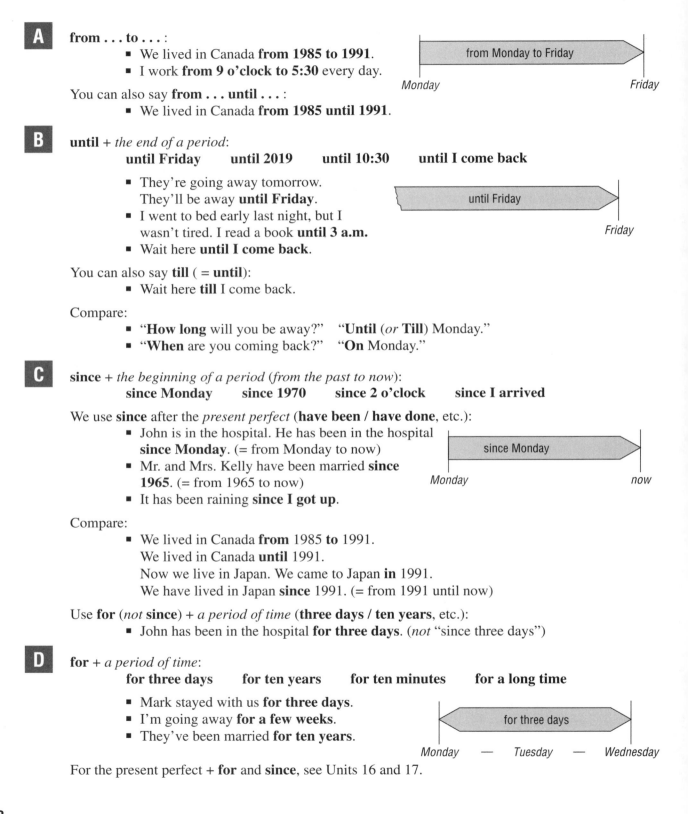

from . . . to . . . :

- We lived in Canada **from 1985 to 1991**.
- I work **from 9 o'clock to 5:30** every day.

You can also say **from . . . until . . .** :

- We lived in Canada **from 1985 until 1991**.

B

until + *the end of a period*:

until Friday **until 2019** **until 10:30** **until I come back**

- They're going away tomorrow. They'll be away **until Friday**.
- I went to bed early last night, but I wasn't tired. I read a book **until 3 a.m.**
- Wait here **until I come back**.

You can also say **till** (= **until**):

- Wait here **till** I come back.

Compare:

- "**How long** will you be away?" "**Until** (*or* **Till**) Monday."
- "**When** are you coming back?" "**On** Monday."

C

since + *the beginning of a period* (*from the past to now*):

since Monday **since 1970** **since 2 o'clock** **since I arrived**

We use **since** after the *present perfect* (**have been / have done**, etc.):

- John is in the hospital. He has been in the hospital **since Monday**. (= from Monday to now)
- Mr. and Mrs. Kelly have been married **since 1965**. (= from 1965 to now)
- It has been raining **since I got up**.

Compare:

- We lived in Canada **from** 1985 **to** 1991.
  We lived in Canada **until** 1991.
  Now we live in Japan. We came to Japan **in** 1991.
  We have lived in Japan **since** 1991. (= from 1991 until now)

Use **for** (*not* **since**) + *a period of time* (**three days / ten years**, etc.):

- John has been in the hospital **for three days**. (*not* "since three days")

D

for + *a period of time*:

for three days **for ten years** **for ten minutes** **for a long time**

- Mark stayed with us **for three days**.
- I'm going away **for a few weeks**.
- They've been married **for ten years**.

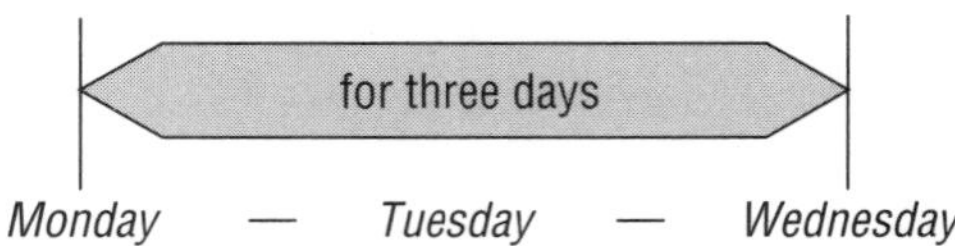

For the present perfect + **for** and **since**, see Units 16 and 17.

Exercises

91.1 Read the information about these people and complete the sentences. Use **from . . . to / until / since**.

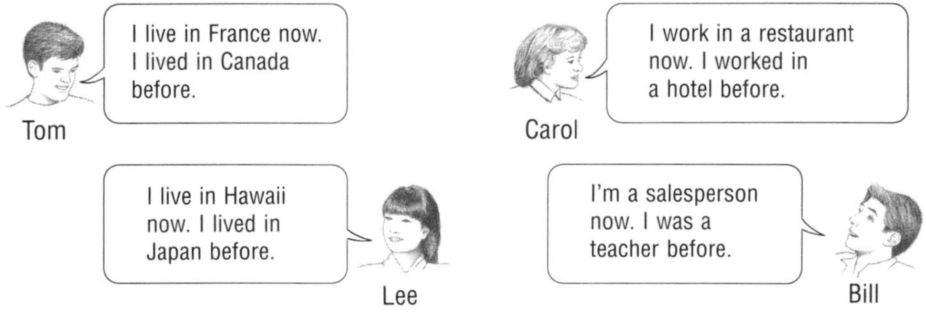

I live in France now. I lived in Canada before.
Tom
I work in a restaurant now. I worked in a hotel before.
Carol
I live in Hawaii now. I lived in Japan before.
Lee
I'm a salesperson now. I was a teacher before.
Bill

1. (Tom / Canada / 1985–91) *Tom lived in Canada from 1985 to 1991.*
2. (Tom / Canada / → 1991) Tom lived in Canada .... 1991.
3. (Tom / France / 1991 →) Tom has lived in France .... 1991.
4. (Lee / Japan / → 1985) Lee lived in ....
5. (Lee / Hawaii / 1985 →) Lee has lived in ....
6. (Carol / a hotel / 1987–90) Carol worked .... 1987 ....
7. (Carol / a restaurant / 1990 →) Carol has worked ....
8. (Bill / a teacher / 1986–92) Bill was a ....
9. (Bill / a salesperson / 1992 →) Bill has been ....

Now write sentences with **for**.

10. (Tom / Canada) *Tom lived in Canada for six years.*
11. (Tom / France) Tom has lived in France ....
12. (Lee / Hawaii) Lee has lived ....
13. (Carol / a hotel) Carol worked in ....
14. (Carol / a restaurant) Carol has worked ....
15. (Bill / a teacher) Bill was ....
16. (Bill / a salesperson) Bill has been ....

91.2 Put in **until/since/for**.

1. Mr. and Mrs. Kelly have been married *since* 1965.
2. I was tired this morning. I stayed in bed .... 10 o'clock.
3. We waited .... half an hour, but they didn't come.
4. "How long have you been here?" ".............. half past eight."
5. "How long did you stay at the party last night?" ".............. midnight."
6. John and I are good friends. We have known each other .... ten years.
7. I'm tired. I'm going to lie down .... a few minutes.
8. Don't open the door of the train .... it stops.
9. I've lived in this house .... I was seven years old.
10. Jack is out of town. He'll be away .... next Wednesday.
11. Next week I'm going to Los Angeles .... four days.
12. I usually finish work at 5:30, but sometimes I work .... 6 o'clock.
13. "How long have you known Ann?" ".............. we were in school together."
14. Where have you been? I've been waiting for you .... 20 minutes.

UNIT 92

before after during while

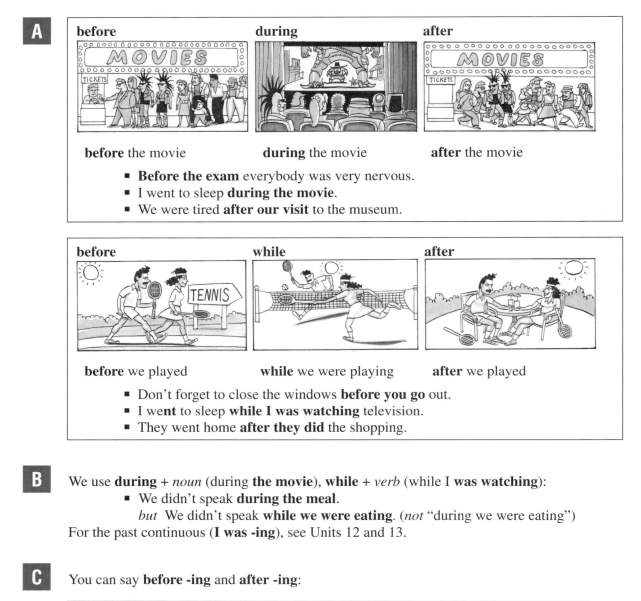

A

before the movie | **during** the movie | **after** the movie

- **Before the exam** everybody was very nervous.
- I went to sleep **during the movie**.
- We were tired **after our visit** to the museum.

before we played | **while** we were playing | **after** we played

- Don't forget to close the windows **before you go** out.
- I went to sleep **while I was watching** television.
- They went home **after they did** the shopping.

B

We use **during** + *noun* (during **the movie**), **while** + *verb* (while I **was watching**):

- We didn't speak **during the meal**.
  but We didn't speak **while we were eating**. (*not* "during we were eating")

For the past continuous (**I was -ing**), see Units 12 and 13.

C

You can say **before -ing** and **after -ing**:

before -ing

- I always have breakfast **before** go**ing** to work.
  (= before I go to work)
- **Before** eat**ing** the apple, she washed it.
  (= before she ate the apple)

after -ing

- I started work **after** read**ing** the newspaper.
  (= after I read the newspaper)
- **After** do**ing** the shopping, they went home.
  (= after they did the shopping)

Exercises

92.1

Complete the sentences. Use **before/during/after** + the best ending from the box.

before **during** **after**	+	**the concert** **the course** **the end**	~~**the exam**~~ **lunch** **the night**	**they moved to Australia** **you cross the street**

1. Everybody was nervous *before the exam.* ....
2. I usually have lunch at 1:30, and .... I go back to work.
3. The movie was very boring. We left ....
4. Ann went to evening classes to learn Spanish. She learned a lot ....
5. My aunt and uncle lived in Japan ....
6. Somebody broke a window .... Did you hear anything?
7. A: Are you going home .... ?
   B: No, we're going to a restaurant.
8. Always look both ways ....

92.2

Put in **during** or **while**.

1. We didn't speak *while*.......... we were eating.
2. We didn't speak *during*.......... the meal.
3. Bob called .... you were out.
4. She wrote a lot of letters .... she was on vacation.
5. The students looked very bored .... class.
6. I read the newspaper .... I was waiting for Jack.
7. I don't eat much .... the day, but I always have a big meal in the evening.
8. I fell out of bed .... I was asleep.

92.3

Complete these sentences with **before -ing . . .**

1. She washed the apple. Then she ate it.
   She washed the apple before eating it. .... *or* *Before eating the apple, she washed it.*
2. Think carefully. Then answer the question.
   Think carefully before ....
3. Mary put on her glasses. Then she read the letter.
   Mary put on her glasses ....
4. The man took off his coat. Then he got into the car.
   Before .... his coat.

Write sentences with **after -ing . . .**

5. We walked for three hours. We were very tired.
   We were very tired after ....
6. I ate too much ice cream. I felt sick.
   I felt ....
7. I read the book a second time. I understood it better.
   ....
8. John graduated from school. Then he worked in a department store for two years.
   ....

UNIT 93

in at (places)

A

in

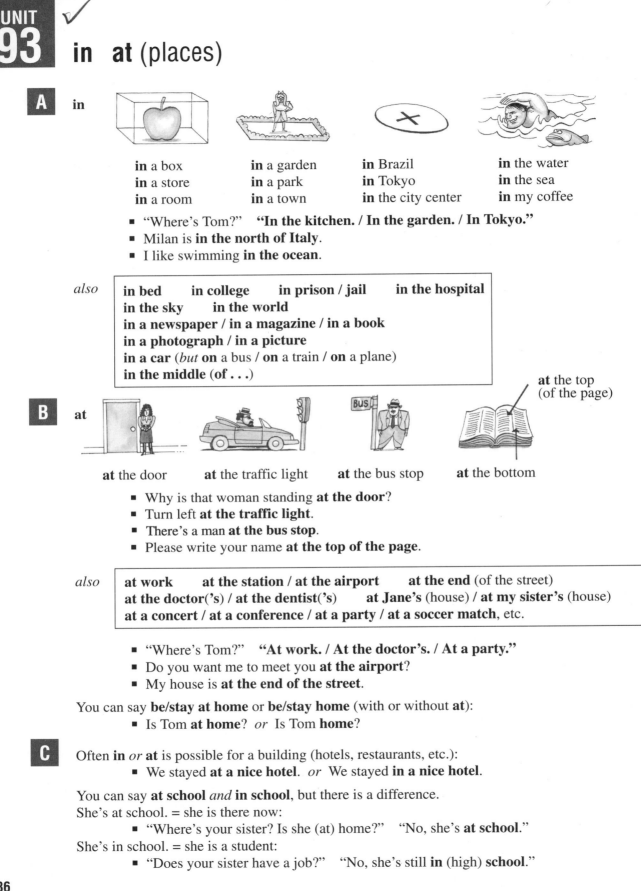

in a box	**in** a garden	**in** Brazil	**in** the water
in a store	**in** a park	**in** Tokyo	**in** the sea
in a room	**in** a town	**in** the city center	**in** my coffee

- "Where's Tom?" **"In the kitchen. / In the garden. / In Tokyo."**
- Milan is **in the north of Italy**.
- I like swimming **in the ocean**.

also

in bed **in college** **in prison / jail** **in the hospital**
in the sky **in the world**
in a newspaper / in a magazine / in a book
in a photograph / in a picture
in a car (*but* **on** a bus / **on** a train / **on** a plane)
in the middle (of . . .)

B

at

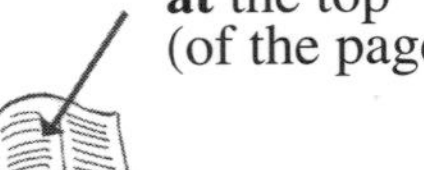

at the top (of the page)

at the door **at** the traffic light **at** the bus stop **at** the bottom

- Why is that woman standing **at the door**?
- Turn left **at the traffic light**.
- There's a man **at the bus stop**.
- Please write your name **at the top of the page**.

also

at work **at the station / at the airport** **at the end** (of the street)
at the doctor('s) / at the dentist('s) **at Jane's** (house) **/ at my sister's** (house)
at a concert / at a conference / at a party / at a soccer match, etc.

- "Where's Tom?" **"At work. / At the doctor's. / At a party."**
- Do you want me to meet you **at the airport**?
- My house is **at the end of the street**.

You can say **be/stay at home** or **be/stay home** (with or without **at**):

- Is Tom **at home**? *or* Is Tom **home**?

C

Often **in** *or* **at** is possible for a building (hotels, restaurants, etc.):

- We stayed **at a nice hotel**. *or* We stayed **in a nice hotel**.

You can say **at school** *and* **in school**, but there is a difference.
She's at school. = she is there now:

- "Where's your sister? Is she (at) home?" "No, she's **at school**."

She's in school. = she is a student:

- "Does your sister have a job?" "No, she's still **in** (high) **school**."

Exercises

93.1 Complete the sentences for the pictures. Use **in** or **at** + one of these:

the airport **bed** **a box** **the end of the street** ~~**the kitchen**~~ **the hospital** **a party** **the sky**

in the kitchen.
ıoes are ....
....
....

5. The store is ....
6. The stars are ....
7. She's ....
8. They're ....

the sentences. Use **in** + one of these:

ₖ **that field** ~~**the kitchen**~~ **this photograph** **the river** **my tea**

s *in the kitchen.* He's making dinner.
at those beautiful horses ....
swim .... The water is very dirty.
's too much sugar .... I can't drink it.
nany pages are there .... ?
s the man .... ? Do you know him?

r **at**.

ere's Sue?" "She's *at* ...... work."
didn't the bus driver stop .... the bus stop?
traight .... the traffic light and turn right .... the gas station.
e was a big table .... the middle of the room.
t is the longest river .... the world?
there many people .... the concert on Friday?
ırother is studying math .... Concordia College.
ere does your sister live?" "......... Brussels."
ʏou read about the accident .... the newspaper?
you be .... home tomorrow afternoon?
lied for a year .... Munich, a lovely city .... Germany.
1ary home yet?" "No, she's still .... school."
is coming by train. I'm going to meet him .... the station.
lie is .... the hospital. He's going to have an operation tomorrow.
ked at the list of names. My name was .... the bottom of the list.
ally do my shopping .... the city center.

UNIT 94

to in at (places)

A

to

go/come/return/walk, etc. **to . . .**

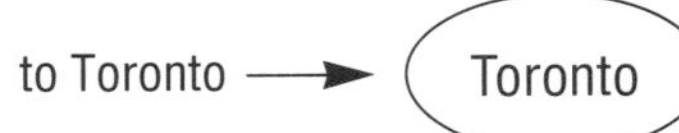

We're **going to Toronto** next week.

- I want to **go to Mexico**.
- We **walked** from my house **to the city center**.
- What time do you **go to bed**?
- Do you want to **go to college**?

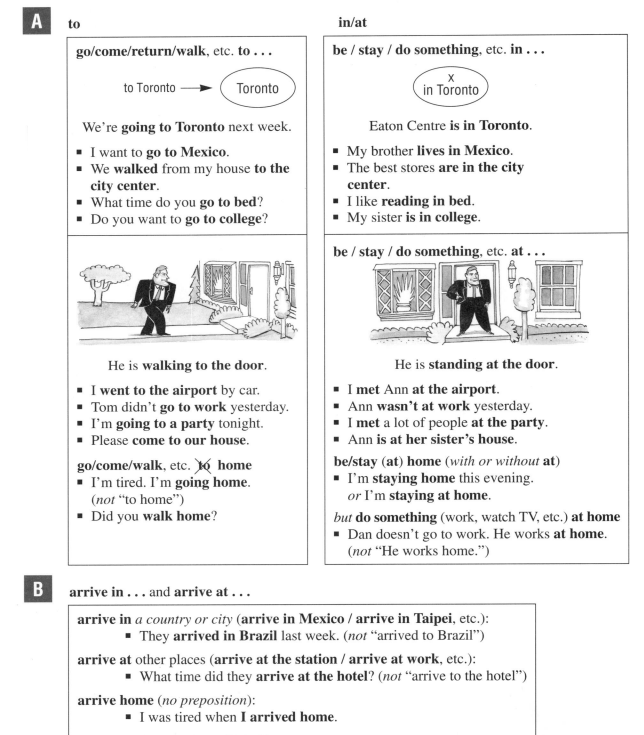

He is **walking to the door**.

- I **went to the airport** by car.
- Tom didn't **go to work** yesterday.
- I'm **going to a party** tonight.
- Please **come to our house**.

go/come/walk, etc. ~~to~~ **home**

- I'm tired. I'm **going home**. (*not* "to home")
- Did you **walk home**?

in/at

be / stay / do something, etc. **in . . .**

Eaton Centre **is in Toronto**.

- My brother **lives in Mexico**.
- The best stores **are in the city center**.
- I like **reading in bed**.
- My sister **is in college**.

be / stay / do something, etc. **at . . .**

He is **standing at the door**.

- I **met** Ann **at the airport**.
- Ann **wasn't at work** yesterday.
- I **met** a lot of people **at the party**.
- Ann **is at her sister's house**.

be/stay (**at**) **home** (*with or without* **at**)

- I'm **staying home** this evening. *or* I'm **staying at home**.

but **do something** (work, watch TV, etc.) **at home**

- Dan doesn't go to work. He works **at home**. (*not* "He works home.")

B

arrive in . . . and **arrive at . . .**

arrive in *a country or city* (**arrive in Mexico / arrive in Taipei**, etc.):

- They **arrived in Brazil** last week. (*not* "arrived to Brazil")

arrive at other places (**arrive at the station / arrive at work**, etc.):

- What time did they **arrive at the hotel**? (*not* "arrive to the hotel")

arrive home (*no preposition*):

- I was tired when **I arrived home**.

For **get to** (= arrive), see Unit 50.

For **in** an **at**, see Unit 93.

Exercises

94.1 Complete these sentences. Use **to** + one of these:

the bank **bed** **the movies** **a concert** **Italy** **the hospital** ~~**work**~~

1. Pat was sick yesterday, so she didn't go *to work.*
2. It's late and I'm tired. I think I'll go ....
3. We have to go .... today. We don't have any money.
4. "Are you going out tonight?" "Yes, I'm going ...."
5. I'd like to go .... I've never been there before.
6. We don't go .... very often, but we rent a lot of videos.
7. After the accident three people were taken ....

94.2 Write **to** or **in**.

1. "Where's Jack?" "*In* bed."
2. I'm going .... the store to buy some milk.
3. Tom went .... the kitchen to make some coffee.
4. "Where's Tom?" "He's .... the kitchen making some coffee."
5. Would you like to go .... the theater this evening?
6. I got a postcard from Sue this morning. She's on vacation .... Puerto Rico.
7. John lives .... a small village .... Japan.
8. What time do you usually go .... bed?
9. Bill's sister is very sick. She's .... the hospital.
10. After graduating from high school, Bill went .... college.
11. The train left Brussels at 7 o'clock and arrived .... Paris at 9:30.
12. I was tired this morning. I stayed .... bed until 10 o'clock.
13. Next year we hope to go .... Canada to visit some friends.
14. Would you like to live .... another country?

94.3 Write **to** or **at** if necessary. (Sometimes there is no preposition.)

1. Pat didn't go *to* work yesterday.
2. Ann is sick. She went .... the doctor.
3. Are you going .... the party on Saturday night?
4. I talked to some nice people .... the party.
5. "Where were you this morning?" "I was .... work."
6. "Do you usually walk .... work?" "No, I go by bicycle."
7. We had a good meal .... a restaurant, and then we went back .... the hotel.
8. What time are you going .... home?
9. I went .... Mary's house, but she wasn't .... home.
10. There were no taxis, so we walked .... home.
11. How often do you go .... the dentist?
12. What time do you usually arrive .... work in the morning?
13. It was very late when we arrived .... home.
14. The boy jumped into the river and swam .... the other side.
15. There were 20,000 people .... the soccer game.
16. "Are your children here?" "No, they're .... school."

UNIT 95 on under behind, etc. (prepositions)

A on

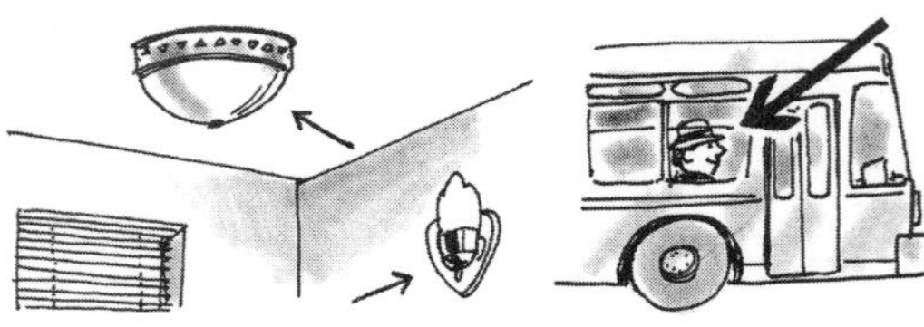

on a table
on a plate
on the floor, etc.

on a wall
on a door
on the ceiling, etc.

on a bus
on a train
on a plane, etc.

on the f
on the s

- There are some books **on the shelf** and some pictures **on the wall**.
- I met Sue **on the bus**.
- The office is **on the first floor**. (*not* "in the first floor")
- There are a lot of apples **on the tree**.

also **on a horse / on a bicycle / on a motorcycle**

B under

under the table

under a tree

- The cat is **under** the table.
- The woman is standing **under** a tree.
- I'm wearing a jacket **under** my coat.

C next to (*or* beside) / between / in front of / in back of / behind

A is **next to** B. *or* A is **beside** B.
B is **between** A and C.
D is **in front of** B.
E is **in back of** B. *or* E is **behind** B.

also
A is **on the left**.
C is **on the right**.
B is **in the middle** (of the group).

D across from

The supermarket is **across from** the theate

E above and below

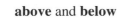

A is **above** the line.
B is **below** the line.

The pictures are **a**
The shelves are **be**

ises

:he sentences. Use **on** + one of these:

ı **a bicycle** **his finger** **this plant** **the door** ~~**the wall**~~

ctures *on the wall* .... look very nice.
the weather is nice in the summer, I like lying ....
aves .... are a beautiful color.
ıuse is number 45 – the number is ....
s wearing a silver ring ....
:d to carry a lot of things ....

ɜ pictures and complete the sentences with a preposition (**on**/**under**, etc.).

t is *under* .... the table.
is a tree .... the house.
artment is .... a store.
standing .... the piano.
me is .... the door.
6. The town hall is .... the bus station.
7. The calendar is .... the clock.
8. The cupboard is .... the sink.
9. There are some shoes .... the bed.
10. In Britain, people drive .... the left.

e live in an apartment building. Use the picture and complete the sentences with **on** / **etween** / **above** / **below**.

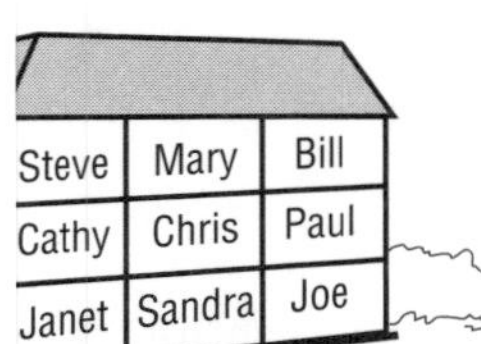

1. Chris lives *between* .... Cathy and Paul.
2. Joe lives .... the first floor.
3. Mary lives .... Steve and Bill.
4. Paul lives .... the second floor .... Chris.
5. Cathy lives .... Janet.
6. Chris lives .... Sandra and .... Mary.

the people in the big picture?

1. Dan is standing *on the left.* ....
2. Bob is sitting ....
3. Sue is sitting ....
4. Dan is standing .... Ron.
5. Bob is sitting .... Mark.
6. Mark is standing .... Jane.

UNIT 96

up over through, etc. (prepositions)

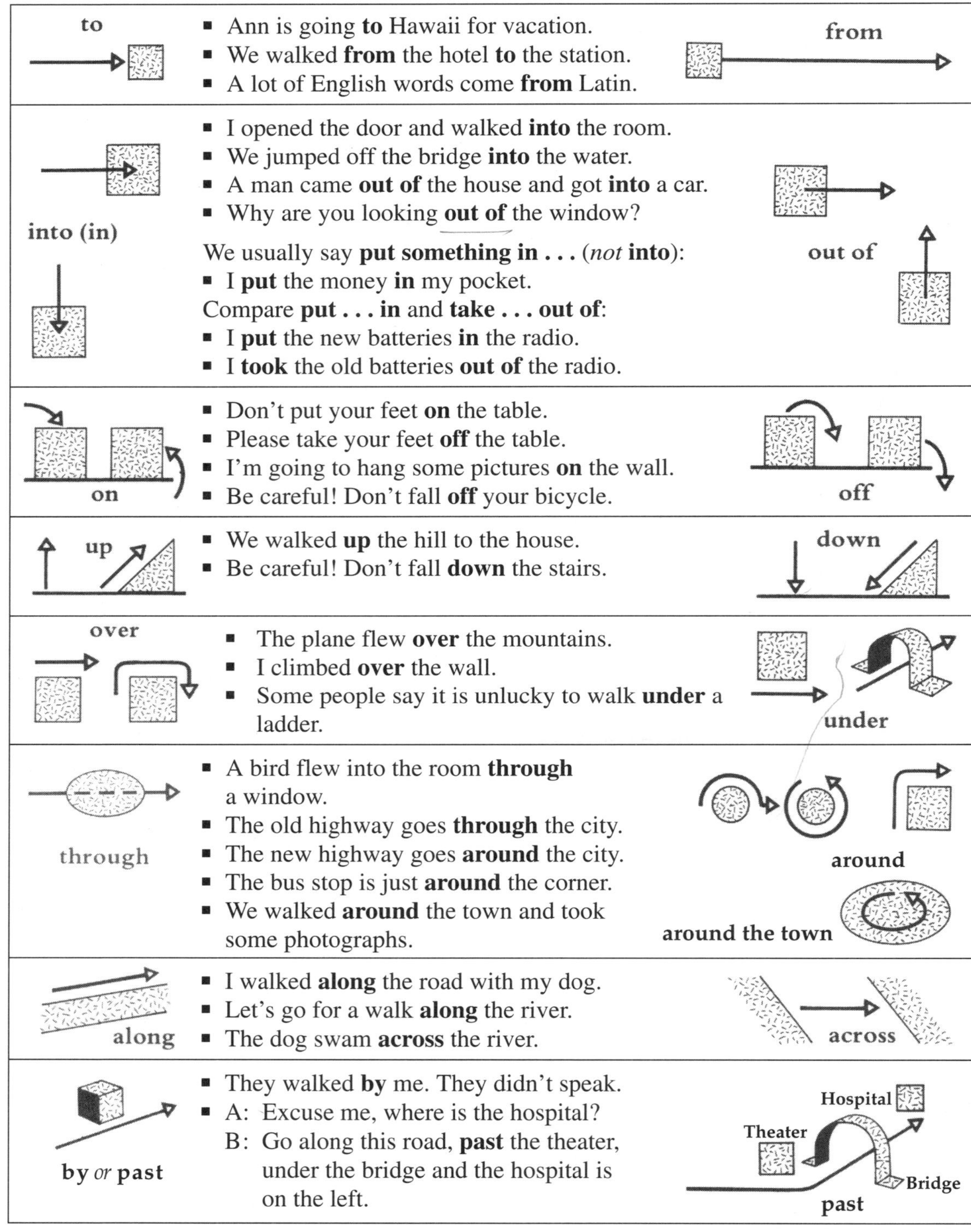

to / **from**

- Ann is going **to** Hawaii for vacation.
- We walked **from** the hotel **to** the station.
- A lot of English words come **from** Latin.

into (in) / **out of**

- I opened the door and walked **into** the room.
- We jumped off the bridge **into** the water.
- A man came **out of** the house and got **into** a car.
- Why are you looking **out of** the window?

We usually say **put something in . . .** (*not* **into**):

- I **put** the money **in** my pocket.

Compare **put . . . in** and **take . . . out of**:

- I **put** the new batteries **in** the radio.
- I **took** the old batteries **out of** the radio.

on / **off**

- Don't put your feet **on** the table.
- Please take your feet **off** the table.
- I'm going to hang some pictures **on** the wall.
- Be careful! Don't fall **off** your bicycle.

up / **down**

- We walked **up** the hill to the house.
- Be careful! Don't fall **down** the stairs.

over / **under**

- The plane flew **over** the mountains.
- I climbed **over** the wall.
- Some people say it is unlucky to walk **under** a ladder.

through / **around**

- A bird flew into the room **through** a window.
- The old highway goes **through** the city.
- The new highway goes **around** the city.
- The bus stop is just **around** the corner.
- We walked **around** the town and took some photographs.

along / **across**

- I walked **along** the road with my dog.
- Let's go for a walk **along** the river.
- The dog swam **across** the river.

by *or* **past**

- They walked **by** me. They didn't speak.
- A: Excuse me, where is the hospital?
  B: Go along this road, **past** the theater, under the bridge and the hospital is on the left.

:ises

y asks you the way to a place. Tell him or her which
. Look at the pictures and complete the sentences

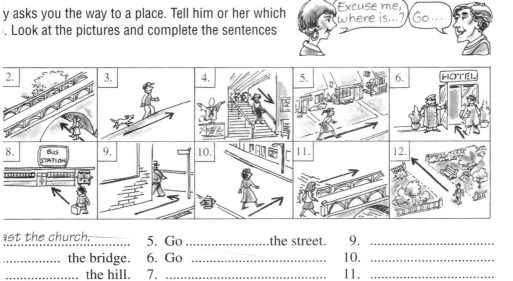

ast the church.

.... the bridge.

.... the hill.

.... the stairs.

5. Go ....the street.
6. Go ....
7. ....
8. ....
9. ....
10. ....
11. ....
12. ....

le pictures and complete the sentences with a preposition (**up**/**over**, etc.).

og swam across the river.

ook fell .... a shelf.

lane flew .... the town.

:ew the book .... the window.

5. They drove .... the village.
6. A woman got .... a car.
7. A man walked .... the store.
8. The moon travels .... the Earth.

reposition (**up**/**off**/**through**, etc.).

mped off the bridge into the water.

u know how to put film .... this camera?

an put your coat .... the back of the chair.

ok a key .... her bag and opened the door.

dn't have a key, so we climbed .... a window .... the house.

ed .... the window and watched the people on the street.

alked .... the museum and saw a lot of interesting things.

nis, you have to hit the ball .... the net.

forget to put a stamp .... the postcard before you mail it.

UNIT 97 at by with/without about (prepositions)

A

at

at (**the age of**) **20** / **at 90 kilometers an hour** / **at 100 degrees**

- Sue got her driver's license **at 16**. (*or* **. . . at the age of 16.**)
- He was driving **at 90 kilometers an hour**. (*or* He was **doing 90 kilometers an hour**.)
- Water boils **at 100 degrees Celsius**.

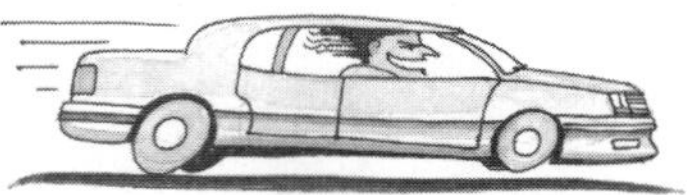

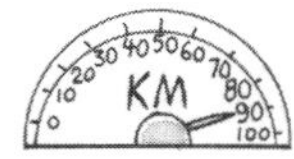

B

by

by = next to / beside:

- John is standing **by the window**.
- They have a house **by the sea**. (= next to the sea)

BY THE WINDOW

For **next to / beside**, see Unit 95.

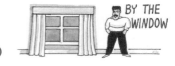

(go) **by car / by bus / by plane** (*or* **by air**) / **by bike**, etc.

- Do you like traveling **by train**?
- Jane usually goes to work **by bike**.

but **on foot**:

- She goes to work **on foot**. (= She **walks** to work.)

a book by . . . / a painting by . . . / a piece of music by . . ., etc.:

- Have you read any books **by Agatha Christie**?
- **Who** is that painting **by**? Picasso?

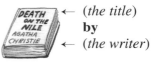

DEATH ON THE NILE AGATHA CHRISTIE ← (*the title*) **by** ← (*the writer*)

by after the passive:

- I was bitten **by a dog**.

See Unit 19.

C

with/without

- Did you stay at a hotel or **with friends**?
- Wait for me. Please don't go **without me**.
- Do you like your coffee **with** or **without milk**?

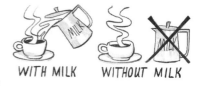

WITH MILK WITHOUT MILK

do something **with** something (= use something to do something):

- I **cut** the paper **with a pair of scissors**.
- She can't **read without glasses**. (= She needs glasses to read.)

a man with a beard / a woman with glasses / a house with a garden, etc.

- Who is **that man with the beard**?
- I'd like to have **a house with a garden**.

D

about

talk/speak/think/hear/know about . . ., etc.

- Some people **talk about their work** all the time.
- I don't **know** much **about cars**.

a book / a question / a program about . . ., etc.

- Did you see **the program about computers** on TV last night?

cises

ie pictures. Complete the sentences with a preposition (**at/by**, etc.).

he paper ..with.. a pair of scissors.
iitting .... the telephone.
is the woman .... short hair?
reading a book ....
ages .... Kim Lee.
isually goes to work .... car.

6. They are listening to music .... Mozart.
7. Who is the man .... the sunglasses?
8. They're talking .... the weather.
9. The plant is .... the piano.
10. The plane is flying .... 600 miles an hour.

the sentences with a preposition (**at/by/with**, etc.).

e people talk ..about.. their work all the time.
w did you get here? .... bus?" "No, ... foot."
orth America, children usually start school .... the age of five.
iot easy to live .... money.
nnis, you hit the ball .... a racket.
let, *Othello*, and *Macbeth* are plays .... William Shakespeare.
you know much .... economics?" "Yes, I studied it in college."
long does it take from New York to Los Angeles .... plane?
ich is your house?" "The one .... the red door."
e trains are very fast – they can travel .... very high speeds.
Sue tell you .... her new job in a bookstore?
Have you heard the new album .... the Cool Jazz Quartet?
Yes, It's great. I like their music a lot.
grandmother died .... the age of 98.
erday evening I went to a restaurant .... some friends of mine.
door is locked. You can't get into the room .... a key.
men were arrested .... the police and taken to the police station.
you give me some information .... hotels in this town?
e stories .... happy endings.
doesn't use her car very often – she goes everywhere .... bicycle.
ld you like something to drink .... your meal?
er freezes .... 0 degrees Celsius.
ome countries it's expensive to travel .... train.

UNIT 98 afraid of on vacation, etc. (word + preposition)

A

These words and prepositions (**at/in/of**, etc.) usually go together:

afraid of . . .	■ Are you **afraid** of dogs?
good at . . . / bad at . . .	■ Are you **good at** math? ■ She's very **bad at** writing letters.
interested in . . .	■ Bob isn't **interested in** sports.
different from /different than . . .	■ Ann is very **different from** her sister. (*or* Ann is very **different than** her sister.)
sorry about (something)	■ I'm **sorry about** the noise last night. We had a party.
sorry for (doing something)	■ I'm **sorry for** shouting at you. (*or* **I'm sorry I shouted . . .**)
married to . . .	■ She's **married to** a very nice man. (= Her husband is a very nice man.)
fed up with . . .	■ I'm **fed up with** my job. I want to do something different. (= I've had enough of my job – I want a change.)
nice of / kind of somebody to do something	■ It was very **kind of** you to help us. Thank you very much.
(be) **nice to / kind to** somebody	■ They were very **nice to** us. They helped us a lot.

B

on . . . Learn these expressions:

on vacation	Jane isn't at work. She's **on vacation**.
on television	We watched the news **on television**.
on the radio	We listened to the news **on the radio**.
on the (**tele**)**phone**	I spoke to Jack **on the phone** last night.
on fire	The house is **on fire**! Call the fire department.
on time (= not late)	"Was the train late?" "No, it was **on time**."

C

After a preposition, a verb ends in **-ing** (**at** do**ing** / **of** buy**ing** / **for** be**ing**, etc.):

Are you good **at**	repair**ing**	things?
I'm fed up **with**	do**ing**	the same thing every day.
She went away **without**	say**ing**	goodbye. (= she didn't say goodbye)
I'm thinking **of**	buy**ing**	a new car.
I'm sorry **for**	be**ing**	late.

Exercises

98.1 Look at the pictures and complete the sentences with a preposition (**at**/**of**, etc.).

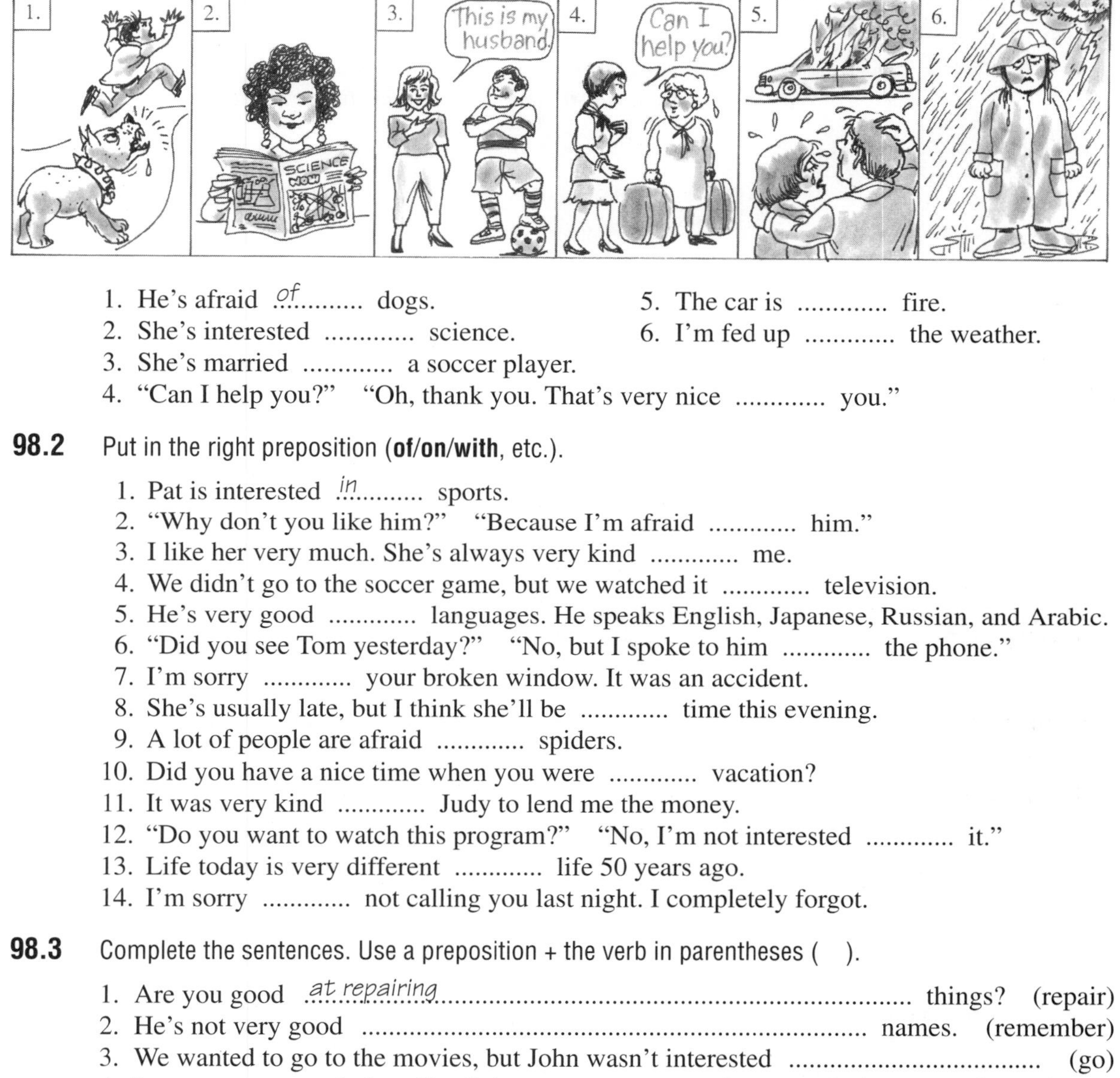

1. He's afraid *of*............ dogs.
2. She's interested .... science.
3. She's married .... a soccer player.
4. "Can I help you?" "Oh, thank you. That's very nice .... you."
5. The car is .... fire.
6. I'm fed up .... the weather.

98.2 Put in the right preposition (**of**/**on**/**with**, etc.).

1. Pat is interested *in*............ sports.
2. "Why don't you like him?" "Because I'm afraid .... him."
3. I like her very much. She's always very kind .... me.
4. We didn't go to the soccer game, but we watched it .... television.
5. He's very good .... languages. He speaks English, Japanese, Russian, and Arabic.
6. "Did you see Tom yesterday?" "No, but I spoke to him .... the phone."
7. I'm sorry .... your broken window. It was an accident.
8. She's usually late, but I think she'll be .... time this evening.
9. A lot of people are afraid .... spiders.
10. Did you have a nice time when you were .... vacation?
11. It was very kind .... Judy to lend me the money.
12. "Do you want to watch this program?" "No, I'm not interested .... it."
13. Life today is very different .... life 50 years ago.
14. I'm sorry .... not calling you last night. I completely forgot.

98.3 Complete the sentences. Use a preposition + the verb in parentheses ( ).

1. Are you good *at repairing*............ things? (repair)
2. He's not very good .... names. (remember)
3. We wanted to go to the movies, but John wasn't interested .... (go)
4. I want some new clothes. I'm fed up .... the same clothes every day. (wear)
5. I'm sorry .... angry with you yesterday. (get)

In these sentences, use **without -ing**.

6. She went away *without saying*............ goodbye. (say)
7. We ran ten kilometers .... (stop)
8. They walked past me on the street .... (speak)
9. Why did you take my camera .... me first? (ask)

UNIT 99

look at . . . listen to . . . , etc. (verb + preposition)

These verbs and prepositions (**to/of/at**, etc.) usually go together:

ask (somebody) **for . . .** (= ask somebody to give you . . .)
- A man stopped me and **asked me for** money.

belong to . . .
- Does this book **belong to** you? (= Is this your book?)

depend on . . .
- A: Do you like eating in restaurants?
  B: Sometimes, yes. It **depends on** the restaurant.

You can say **it depends what/where/how**, etc. *with or without* **on**:
- A: Do you want to go out with us?
  B: **It depends (on) where** you're going.

happen to . . .
- I put my pen on the table five minutes ago and now it isn't there. What **happened to** it?

listen to . . .
- **Listen to** this music. It's beautiful.

look at . . .
- She's **looking at** her watch.
- **Look at** those flowers. They're beautiful.
- Why are you **looking at** me like that?

look for . . . (= try to find)
- He lost his key. He's **looking for** it.
- I'm **looking for** Ann. Have you seen her?

take care of . . . (= keep safe)
- When Mr. and Mrs. Brown are at work, a friend of theirs **takes care of** their child.

talk/speak to somebody (**about** something)
- Did you **talk to** Jack **about** your problem.
- *(on the phone)* Can I **speak to** Ann, please?

thank somebody **for . . .**
- **Thank you** very much **for** your help.

think about/of . . .
- He never **thinks about** (*or* **of**) other people.
- I'm **thinking of** (*or* **about**) buying a new car.

wait for . . .
- Don't go yet. **Wait for** me.

write (a letter) (**to**) somebody
- I never get letters. Nobody **writes to** me. (*or* Nobody **writes** me.)

but **call** somebody (*not* call to . . .):
- Can you **call me** tomorrow? (not "call to me")

Exercises

99.1 Look at the pictures and complete the sentences with a preposition (**to**/**for**, etc.).

1. She's looking ...*at*... her watch.
2. He's listening .... the radio.
3. They're waiting .... a taxi.
4. Bill is talking .... Jane.
5. They're looking .... the picture.
6. She's looking .... Tom.

99.2 Complete the sentences with a preposition (**to**/**for**/**about**, etc.) if necessary. Sometimes no preposition is necessary.

1. Thank you very much ...*for*........ your help.
2. This isn't my bicycle. It belongs .... a friend of mine.
3. Goodbye! Have a nice vacation and take care .... yourself.
4. *(on the telephone)* Hello, can I speak .... Mr. Davis, please?
5. *(on the telephone)* Thank you .... calling. Goodbye!
6. What happened .... Mary last night? Why didn't she come to the party?
7. Excuse me, I'm looking .... Hill Street. Can you tell me where it is?
8. Jack's brother is thinking .... going to Hungary next year.
9. We asked the waiter .... coffee, but he brought us tea.
10. "Do you like going to museums?" "It depends .... the museum."
11. Please listen .... me. I have something very important to tell you.
12. When I take the photograph, look .... the camera and smile.
13. We waited .... John until 2 o'clock, but he didn't come.
14. "Are you writing a letter?" "Yes, I'm writing .... Maria."
15. Don't forget to call .... your mother this evening.
16. He's alone all day. He never talks .... anybody.
17. "Are you playing tennis this afternoon?" "It depends .... the weather."
18. Kathy is thinking .... changing her job.
19. I looked .... the newspaper, but I didn't read it carefully.
20. When you are sick, you need somebody to take care .... you.
21. Bob is looking .... a job. He wants to work in a hotel.

99.3 Complete the sentences. Use **It depends on . . .** + one of these:

what time I leave ~~where you're going~~
how much it is **how I feel**

1. Do you want to go out with us? — *It depends on where you're going.*
2. Are you going out this evening? — It depends on ....
3. What time will you arrive? — It ....
4. Are you going to buy the book? — ....

go in fall off run away, etc. (phrasal verbs 1)

A *phrasal verb* is a verb (**go/look/be**, etc.) + **in/out/on**, etc.

. . . in

go in

- I waited outside the house. I didn't **go in**. (= **into the house**)
- He opened the door and **walked in**.

. . . out

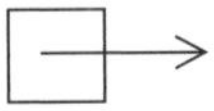

look out

- I went to the window and **looked out**.
- The car stopped and a woman **got out**. (= **got out of the car**)

. . . on

- The bus arrived and I **got on**.

. . . off

- Be careful! Don't **fall off**.

. . . up

stand up

- He **stood up** and left the room.
- Prices usually **go up**.
- I **looked up** at the stars.

. . . down

fall down

- The picture **fell down**.
- Would you like to **sit down**?
- **Lie down** on the floor.

. . . away *or* **. . . off**

run away

- The thief ran out of the store and **ran away**. (*or* . . . **ran off**.)
- The woman got into the car and **drove away**. (*or* . . . **drove off**.)

go away = go to another place:
- Ann **went away** last week. She's **coming back** next week.

. . . back

- After dinner at a restaurant, we **went back** to our hotel.
- **Go away** and don't **come back**!

. . . over

- The fence wasn't high, so I **climbed over**.
- I **fell over** because my shoes were too big for me.

fall over

. . . around

look around

- Somebody shouted, so I **looked around** to see who it was.
- We went for a long walk. After four miles we **turned around** and **went back**.

See Appendix 5 for other phrasal verbs.

Exercises

100.1 Look at the pictures and complete the sentences with **in**/**out**/**up**, etc.

1. I went to the window and looked *out*.
2. The door was open, so we went ....
3. He heard a plane, so he looked ....
4. She got on her bike and rode ....
5. I said hello and he turned ....
6. The bus stopped and he got ....
7. There was a free seat, so I sat ....
8. A car stopped and two men got ....

100.2 Complete the sentences. Use **out**/**away**/**back**, etc.

1. "Why is that picture on the floor?" "It fell *down*."
2. Please don't go .... ! Stay here with me.
3. She heard a noise behind her, so she turned ....
4. I'm going .... now to do some shopping. I'll be .... at 5 o'clock.
5. I'm tired. I'm going to lie .... on the sofa.
6. Ann is going on vacation next month. She's going .... on the 5th and coming .... on the 24th.
7. When babies try to walk, they often fall ....
8. Jim is from Canada. He lived in Asia for ten years, but last year he went .... to Canada.

100.3 Complete the sentences. Use one of the verbs in the box + **on**/**up**/**off**, etc. (These verbs are all in Appendix 5.)

breaks	**clean**	**gave**	**got**	**hold**	+	**up**	**down**
~~**hurry**~~	**kept**	**slowed**	**speak**	**takes**		**on**	**off**

1. *Hurry up*.................... ! We don't have much time.
2. I was very tired this morning. I .... very late.
3. This car isn't very good. It .... a lot.
4. It's difficult to hear you. Can you ...., please?
5. "It's time to go." ".................................. a minute. I'm not ready yet."
6. The train .... and finally stopped.
7. I like flying, but I'm always nervous when the plane ....
8. I told him to stop, but he .... talking. Maybe he didn't hear me.
9. I tried to find a job, but I .... It was impossible.
10. The house is very messy. I'm going to ....

put on your shoes **put** your shoes **on** (phrasal verbs 2)

Sometimes a phrasal verb (**turn off / put on**, etc.) has an *object*. For example:

verb	*object*	*verb*	*object*	*verb*	*object*
turn off	the light	**put on**	your shoes	**call up**	my friend
				(**call up** = telephone)	

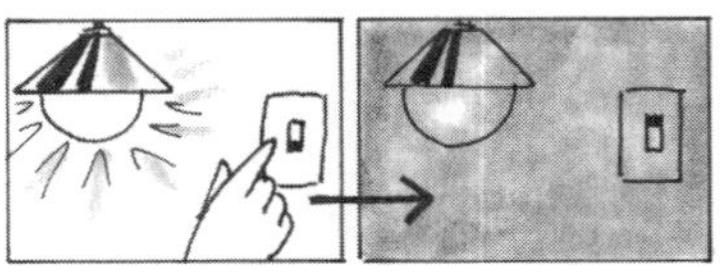

You can say:

turn off the light
or **turn** the light **off**

put on your shoes
or **put** your shoes **on**

call up my friend
or **call** my friend **up**
You can also say **call** *without* "up":
I **called** my friend.

but **it/them/me/us/you/him/her** *(pronouns)* always go *before* **off/on/up**, etc.:

turn **it off** (*not* "turn off it")
put **them on** (*not* "put on them")
call **her up** (*not* "call up her")

put on / take off

- It was cold, so I **put my coat on.** (*or* . . . I **put on my coat.**)
- Here's your coat. **Put it on.**
- **Take off that hat!** It looks stupid. (*or* **Take that hat off!**)

turn on / turn off

- It was dark, so I **turned on the light**. (*or* . . . I **turned the light on**.)
- I don't want to watch this program. You can **turn it off**.

pick up / put down

- That's my key on the floor. Can you **pick it up** for me, please?
- She stopped reading and **put her book down**. (*or* . . . **put down her book**.)

bring back / take back / give back / put back

- You can take my umbrella, but please **bring it back**.
- I **took my new shirt back** to the store. It was too small for me.
- John gave me his keys, but I **gave them back** to him.
- I read the letter and then **put it back** in the envelope.

For other phrasal verbs + object, see Appendix 6.

Exercises

101.1 You can write the same sentence in three different ways. Complete the table.

1.	I turned off the light.	*I turned the light off.*	*I turned it off.*
2.	He put on his shirt.	He	He ....
3.	She put on her glasses.	She	.... them ....
4.	Can you .... ?	Can you turn the TV on?	Can .... ?
5.	She called up her brother.	She	....
6.	....	We took our shoes off.	....
7.	They gave back the money.	....	....
8.	She put down her bags.	....	....
9.	....	I turned the engine on.	....
10.	....	She filled the form out.	....
11.	We put out the fire.	....	....

101.2 Complete the sentences. Use one of the objects in the box + **on/off/up**, etc.

object

my book	**my gloves**	**my jacket**	**them**	**it**	**it**
~~**the light**~~	**the radio**	**the photograph**	**them**	~~**it**~~	

\+ **on** **off** **back** **up** **down**

1. Don't forget to turn *the light off* .... before you go to bed.
2. That hat looks stupid! Take *it off.* ....
3. I wanted to hear the news, so I turned ....
4. Thanks for lending me your cassettes. I'll give .... to you tomorrow.
5. I was reading when the phone rang. So I put .... and went to answer it.
6. There was some money on the floor, so I picked ....
7. My hands were cold, so I put ....
8. It was warm, so I took ....
9. She borrowed my keys and she hasn't brought .... yet.
10. I picked ...., looked at it, and put .... on the table.

The verbs in 11–20 are in Appendix 6.

object

your cigarette	**a glass**	**it**	**it**
some shoes	**us**	**it**	
ten buildings	**it**	**them**	

\+ **on** **over** **around** **up** **down** **out** **away**

11. I knocked .... and broke it.
12. If you don't understand the word, look .... in a dictionary.
13. I want those magazines. Don't throw ....
14. They knocked .... when they built the new highway.
15. Please put .... You're not allowed to smoke here.
16. That music is very loud. Can you turn .... a little?
17. I tried .... in the store, but they were too big.
18. We visited the school. One of the teachers showed ....
19. I wrote the wrong name on the form, so I crossed ....
20. "Do you still play tennis?" "No, I gave .... two years ago."

UNIT 102

and but or so because

and	**but**	**or**	**so**	**because**

We use these words *(conjunctions)* to put two sentences together. They make one longer sentence from two shorter sentences:

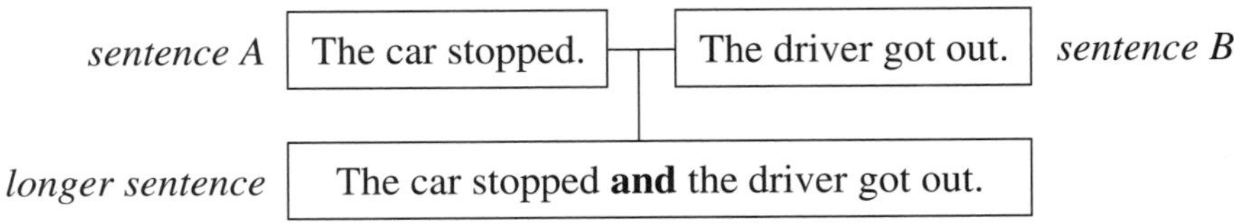

sentence A
The car stopped.
The driver got out.
sentence B
longer sentence
The car stopped **and** the driver got out.

A and/but/or . . .

sentence A	**and/but/or**	*sentence B*
We stayed home	**and**	(we)* watched television.
My sister is married	**and**	(she)* lives in Seoul.
He doesn't like her,	**and**	she doesn't like him.
I bought a newspaper,	**but**	I didn't read it.
It's a nice house,	**but**	it doesn't have a garage.
Do you want to play tennis,	**or**	are you too tired?

* The subjects in sentences A and B are the same. It is not necessary to say "we" and "she" in sentence B.

B so . . . *(the result of something)*:

sentence A	**so**	*sentence B*
It was too hot,	**so**	I opened the window.
The water was dirty,	**so**	we didn't go swimming.
They were hungry,	**so**	they got some food.

C because . . . *(the reason for something)*:

sentence A	**because**	*sentence B*
I opened the window	**because**	it was too hot.
We didn't go swimming	**because**	the water was polluted.
She's hungry	**because**	she didn't have breakfast.

Because + *sentence B* is also possible at the beginning:

- **Because the water wasn't clean**, we didn't go swimming.

D

You can use more than one conjunction to make a longer sentence:

- It was late **and** I was tired, **so** I went to bed.
- I always enjoy visiting New York, but I wouldn't like to live there **because** it's too big.

Exercises

102.1 Make longer sentences. Use **and**/**but**/**or** + the sentences in the box.

He didn't see me.	**Did you stay home?**	**I can't remember his name.**
Don't come back!	~~**We watched television.**~~	**She swam to the other side.**
She looked out.	**Do you want to get a taxi?**	**They took some photographs.**
~~**I didn't read it.**~~	**They don't use it very often.**	

1. We stayed home *and watched television.*
2. I bought a newspaper, *but I didn't read it.*
3. She went to the window ....
4. I saw Jack, ...
5. The girl jumped into the river ....
6. Did you go out last night, ... ?
7. They walked around the town ....
8. They have a car, ...
9. I can remember his face, ...
10. Go away ....
11. Do you want to walk to the hotel, ... ?

102.2 Make longer sentences. Use **so**/**because** + the sentences in the box.

She was sick.	**We didn't play tennis.**	~~**It was very hot in the room.**~~
Don't call me.	~~**We didn't go swimming.**~~	**She's friendly and interesting.**
I walked in.	**They don't have a key.**	**She does the same thing all the time.**
We walked home.	**I couldn't sleep.**	

1. I opened the window *because it was very hot in the room.*
2. The water wasn't very clean, *so we didn't go swimming.*
3. The door was open, ...
4. Ann didn't go to work ....
5. I like Carol ....
6. It was raining, ...
7. There were no buses, ...
8. I got up in the middle of the night ....
9. I won't be at home this evening, ...
10. They can't get into the house ....
11. She doesn't like her job ....

102.3 Write sentences about what *you* did yesterday.

1. (and) *In the evening I stayed home and studied.*
2. (because) *I went to bed very early because I was tired.*
3. (and) ....
4. (but) ....
5. (so) ....
6. (because) ....

UNIT 103

When . . .

A

When I went out, it was raining.

This sentence has two parts:

part A when I went out	+	*part B* it was raining

You can begin with part A *or* part B:

{ **When I went out**, it was raining.
{ **It was raining** when I went out.

We write a comma (,) if part A (**When . . .**) is before part B:

{ **When you're tired**, don't drive.
{ Don't drive **when you're tired**.

{ Ann was very happy **when she passed the exam**.
{ **When Ann passed the exam**, she was very happy.

We do the same in sentences with **before/while/after**:

{ Always look both ways **before you cross the street**.
{ **Before you cross the street**, always look both ways.

{ **While I was waiting for the bus**, it began to rain.
{ It began to rain **while I was waiting for the bus**.

{ He never played tennis again **after he broke his leg**.
{ **After he broke his leg**, he never played tennis again.

B

When I am . . . / When I go . . ., etc. for the *future*:

> I will be in Madrid **next week**.
> **When I'm** in Madrid, I'm going to visit the Prado Museum.

The time is *future* (**next week**) but we say:

When **I'm** in Madrid, . . . (*not* "When I **will be** in Madrid . . .")

We use the *present* (**I am / I go**, etc.) with a *future meaning* after **when**:

- **When** I **get** home this evening, I'm going to take a shower. (*not* "When I will get home")
- I can't talk to you now. I'll talk to you later **when** I **have** more time.

We do the same after **before/while/after/until**:

- Please close the window **before** you **go** out. (*not* "before you will go")
- Ann is going to stay in our house **while** we **are** away on vacation. (*not* "while we will be")
- I'll wait here **until** you **come** back.

For **before/while/after**, see Unit 92. For **until**, see Unit 91.

Exercises

103.1 Write sentences. Use **when** + a sentence from box A + a sentence from box B.

when +

A
~~I went out~~
I'm tired
I called them
she first met him
she goes to Toronto
the program ended
they arrived at the hotel

+

B
I turned off the TV
she always stays at the same hotel
she didn't like him very much
there were no rooms free
~~it was raining~~
there was no answer
I like to watch TV

1. *When I went out, it was raining.*
2. ...
3. ...
4. ...
5. ...
6. ...
7. ...

103.2 Complete the sentences. Choose an ending from the box.

while I was reading	**when you heard the news**	**before I go to sleep**
when I explained it to her	~~**before you cross the street**~~	**while I was out**
before he answered the question	**after they got married**	

1. Always look both ways *before you cross the street.*
2. Were you surprised ... ?
3. He thought carefully ...
4. She understood the problem ...
5. They went to live in New Zealand ...
6. Did anybody call ... ?
7. I fell asleep ...
8. I usually read in bed ...

103.3 Which is right? Choose the correct form.

1. ~~I wait~~ / I'll wait here until you come / ~~you'll come~~ back. (I'll wait and you come are *right*)
2. I'm going to bed when I finish / I'll finish my work.
3. We come / We'll come and see you when we're / we'll be in Washington again.
4. When I see / I'll see you tomorrow, I show / I'll show you the photographs.
5. Would you like something to drink before you go / you'll go to bed?
6. Don't go out yet. Wait until the rain stops / will stop.
7. She's going away soon. I'm / I'll be very sad when she leaves / she'll leave.
8. I'm going to Buenos Aires next month. While I'm / I'll be there, I hope to see lots of old friends.
9. A: Don't forget to give me your address.
   B: Okay, I give / I'll give it to you before I go / I'll go.

UNIT 104

If . . .

You want to travel from New York to Montreal. You are not sure which train you will travel on – the 7:30 or the 10:40.

If you leave at 7:30 a.m., you will arrive at 5:35 p.m.
If you leave at 10:40 a.m., you will arrive at 8:45 p.m.

New York to **Montreal**

DEPART	ARRIVE
7:30 a.m.	5:35 p.m.
10:40 a.m.	8:45 p.m.
12:00 p.m.	10:05 p.m.
3:30 a.m.	1:35 a.m.

A

If can be *at the beginning* of the sentence or *in the middle*:

If . . ., . . . (**if** *at the beginning*)

If you speak slowly,	I can understand you.
If we don't hurry,	we'll be late.
If you're hungry,	have something to eat.
If the phone rings,	can you answer it, please?

. . . **if** . . . (**if** *in the middle*)

I can understand you	**if**	you speak slowly.
We'll be late	**if**	we don't hurry.
I'm going to the concert	**if**	I can get a ticket.
Do you mind	**if**	I close the window? (= Is it okay to close the window?)

In conversation, we often use the **if**-part of the sentence alone:

- "Are you going to the concert?" "Yes, **if I can get a ticket**."

B

if you **see . . .** / **if** I **am . . .**, etc. for the *future*. For example:

- **If** you **see** Ann this evening, can you ask her to call me?

We say **if** you **see** (*not* "if you will see") / **if** I **am** (*not* "if I will be"). Use the present (*not* "will") after **if**:

- **If I'm** late this evening, don't wait for me. (*not* "If I will be late")
- What should we do **if** it **rains**? (*not* "if it will rain")
- **If** I **don't feel** well tomorrow, I'll stay at home.

C

if and **when**

if I go out = it is possible that I will go out, but I'm not sure:

- A: Are you going out later?
  B: Maybe. **If I go out**, I'll close the door.

when I go out = I'm going out (for sure):

- A: Are you going out later?
  B: Yes, I am. **When I go out**, I'll close the window.

- **When** I get home tonight, I'm going to take a shower.
- **If** I'm late tonight, don't wait up for me. (*not* "When I'm late")
- We're going to play tennis **if** it doesn't rain. (*not* "when it doesn't")

Exercises

104.1 Make sentences beginning with **If . . .** Choose from the boxes.

if +	~~we don't hurry~~ I can get a flight you come home late tonight I don't feel well tomorrow you have any problems	+	please come in quietly I'm not going to work ~~we'll be late~~ I'll try to help you I'll fly home on Sunday

1. *If we don't hurry, we'll be late.*
2. If ....
3. If ....
4. ....
5. ....

104.2 Make sentences with **if** in the middle (**. . . if . . .**).

~~I can understand you~~ It will be nice You'll be cold What are you going to do I'm sure they'll understand	+ if +	you don't wear a coat you don't pass your exams you explain the problem to them ~~you speak slowly~~ you can come to the party

1. *I can understand you if you speak slowly.*
2. It ....
3. ....
4. ....
5. ....

104.3 Choose the correct form of the verb.

1. If I don't feel / ~~won't feel~~ well tomorrow, ~~I stay~~ / I'll stay home. (don't feel and I'll stay are *right*)
2. If the weather is / will be nice tomorrow, we can go to the beach.
3. It will be hard to find a hotel if we arrive / we'll arrive late.
4. The alarm will ring if there is / will be a fire.
5. I'm / I'll be surprised if they get / they'll get married.
6. Do you go / Will you go to the party if they invite / they'll invite you?

104.4 Put in **if** or **when**.

1. *If* .... I'm late this evening, don't wait for me.
2. .... I don't see you tomorrow, I'll call you.
3. Do you mind .... I close the window?
4. .... I get up in the morning, I usually drink a cup of coffee.
5. Have something to eat. .... you don't eat now, you'll be hungry later.
6. John is still in high school. .... he graduates, he wants to go to college.
7. Be careful! .... you aren't careful, you'll fall.

a person who . . . a thing that/which . . . (relative clauses 1)

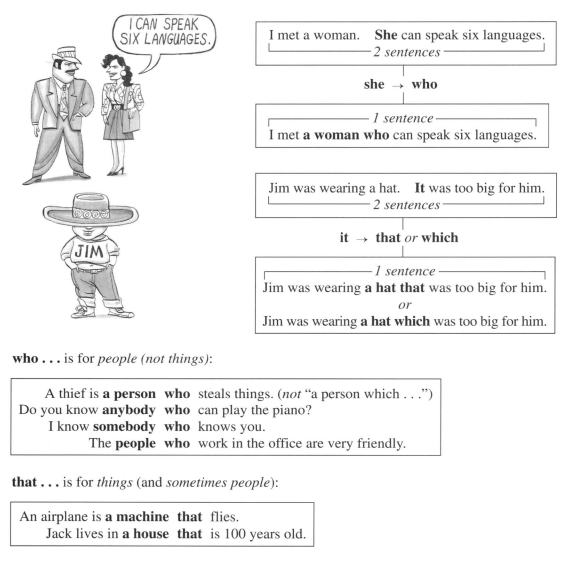

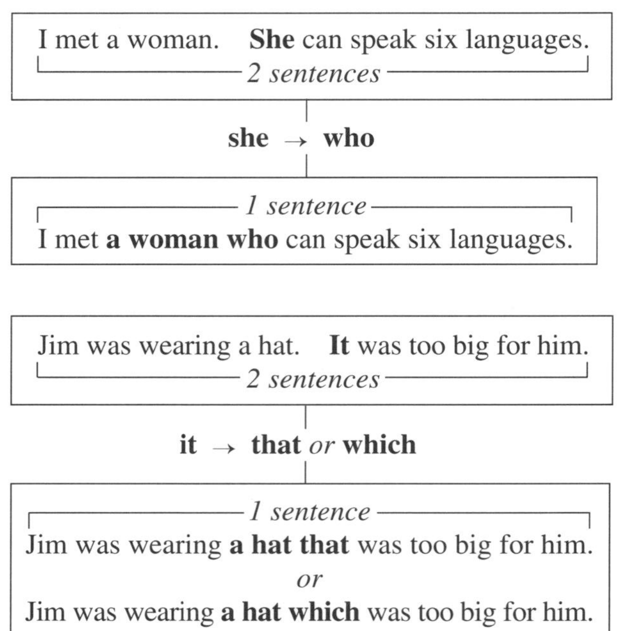

I met a woman. **She** can speak six languages.
2 sentences
she → **who**
1 sentence
I met **a woman who** can speak six languages.
Jim was wearing a hat. **It** was too big for him.
2 sentences
it → **that** *or* **which**
1 sentence
Jim was wearing **a hat that** was too big for him.
or
Jim was wearing **a hat which** was too big for him.

A

who . . . is for *people (not things)*:

A thief is **a person**	**who**	steals things. (*not* "a person which . . .")
Do you know **anybody**	**who**	can play the piano?
I know **somebody**	**who**	knows you.
The **people**	**who**	work in the office are very friendly.

B

that . . . is for *things* (and *sometimes people*):

An airplane is **a machine**	**that**	flies.
Jack lives in **a house**	**that**	is 100 years old.

That is also possible for people ("Do you know **anybody that** can play the piano?"), but it is usually better to say **who**.

C

which . . . is only for *things*:

An airplane is **a machine**	**which**	flies. (*not* "a machine who . . .")
Jack lives in **a house**	**which**	is 100 years old.

Do *not* use **which** for people:

- Do you know **the man who** was playing the piano at the party?
  (*not* "the man which . . . ")

Exercises

105.1 Write sentences about the people in box A: **. . . is a person who . . .** Choose an ending from box B to complete your sentence. Use a dictionary if necessary.

A	
~~a thief~~	a dentist
a butcher	a genius
a musician	a liar
a patient	a photographer

B	
takes photographs	is very intelligent
sells meat	plays a musical instrument
is sick in the hospital	doesn't tell the truth
~~steals things~~	takes care of your teeth

1. *A thief is a person who steals things.*
2. A butcher is a person who ....
3. A musician is a person ....
4. A patient is ....
5. ....
6. ....
7. ....
8. ....

105.2 Make one sentence from two sentences. Use **who**.

1. A man called. He didn't give his name.
   The man who called didn't give his name.
2. A woman opened the door. She was wearing a yellow dress.
   The woman .... a yellow dress.
3. Some people live next door to us. They are very nice.
   The people ....
4. A police officer stopped our car. He wasn't very friendly.
   The police officer ....
5. A boy broke the window. He ran away.
   The boy ....

105.3 Put in **who/that/which**.

1. I met a woman *who* can speak six languages.
2. What's the name of the man .... lives next door?
3. What's the name of the river .... flows through the town?
4. Everybody .... went to the party enjoyed it very much.
5. Do you know anybody .... wants to buy a car?
6. Where is the picture .... was on the wall?
7. She always asks me questions .... are difficult to answer.
8. I have a friend .... is very good at fixing cars.
9. A coffee maker is a machine .... makes coffee.
10. I don't like people .... never stop talking.
11. Have you seen the money .... was on the table?
12. Why does he always wear clothes .... are too small for him?

the people we met   the hotel you stayed at
(relative clauses 2)

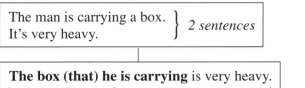

The man is carrying a box.
It's very heavy. } *2 sentences*

The box (that) he is carrying is very heavy.
1 sentence

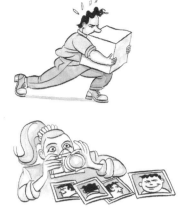

Ann took some photographs.
Have you seen them? } *2 sentences*

Have you seen **the photographs (that) Ann took**?
1 sentence

A

In these sentences, you do not need **that**. You do not need **that/who/which** when it is the *object*:

Subject	*Verb*	*Object*	
The man	was carrying	a box.	→ **the box** (that) **the man was carrying**
Ann	took	some photographs.	→ **the photographs** (that) **Ann took**
You	wanted	the book.	→ **the book** (that) **you wanted**
We	met	some people.	→ **the people** (who) **we met**

- Did you find **the book (that) you wanted**?
- **The people (who) we met** were very nice.
- **Everything (that) I told you** was true.

B

Sometimes there is a *preposition* (**to/in/at**, etc.) after the verb:

Sue is **talking to** a man. → Do you know **the man Sue is talking to**?
I **slept in** a bed. → **The bed that I slept in** was very hard.
You **stayed at** a hotel. → What's the name of **the hotel you stayed at**?

You can also say *(a place)* **where . . .** :

- What's the name of **the hotel where we stayed**? (= the hotel we stayed at)

Note that we say:

- Do you know the man Sue is **talking to** ~~him~~? (*not* "**. . . talking to him?**")
- The movie **we saw** ~~it~~ was very good. (*not* "The movie **we saw it** . . . ")

C

Remember that you need **who/that/which** when it is the *subject*:

	subject	*verb*	
I met a woman	**who**	can speak	six languages.
Jim was wearing a hat	**that**	was	too big for him.

See also Unit 105.

Exercises

106.1 Make one sentence from two.

1. (Ann took some photographs. Have you seen them?)
   Have you seen the photographs Ann took .... ?
2. (You lost a key. Did you find it?) Did you find the .... ?
3. (Sue is wearing a jacket. I like it.) I like the ....
4. (I gave you some money. Where is it?) Where is the .... ?
5. (She told us a story. I didn't believe it.)
   I .... the ....
6. (You bought some oranges. How much were they?)
   How .... ?

106.2 Complete the sentences. Use the information in parentheses ( ).

1. (we met some people) The *people we met* .... were very nice.
2. (I'm wearing shoes) The shoes .... are not very comfortable.
3. (you're reading a book) What's the name of the .... ?
4. (I wrote a letter to her) She didn't get the .... I ....
5. (you gave me an umbrella) I've lost ....
6. (they invited some people to dinner)
   The people .... didn't come.

106.3 Complete the sentences. Use this information:

you went to a party	**Linda is dancing with a man**	~~**you stayed at a hotel**~~
we looked at a map	**you were looking for a book**	**I was sitting on a chair**
they live in a house	**you spoke to a woman**	

1. What's the name of the hotel *you stayed at* .... ?
2. What's the name of the woman you .... ?
3. The house .... is too small for them.
4. Did you enjoy the party .... ?
5. The chair .... wasn't very comfortable.
6. The map .... wasn't very clear.
7. Did you find the book .... ?
8. Who is the man .... ?

106.4 Complete the sentences with **where . . .** Use this information:

we had dinner at a restaurant	**John works in a factory**
~~**we stayed at a hotel**~~	**they live in a town**

1. What's the name of the hotel *where we stayed* .... ?
2. What's the name of the restaurant .... ?
3. Have you ever been to the town .... ?
4. The factory .... is the biggest in the city .

APPENDIX 1

List of irregular verbs

Verb	*Simple past*	*Past participle*
be (am/is/are)	**was/were**	**been**
beat	**beat**	**beaten**
become	**became**	**become**
begin	**began**	**begun**
bite	**bit**	**bitten**
blow	**blew**	**blown**
break	**broke**	**broken**
bring	**brought**	**brought**
build	**built**	**built**
buy	**bought**	**bought**
catch	**caught**	**caught**
choose	**chose**	**chosen**
come	**came**	**come**
cost	**cost**	**cost**
cut	**cut**	**cut**
do	**did**	**done**
draw	**drew**	**drawn**
drink	**drank**	**drunk**
drive	**drove**	**driven**
eat	**ate**	**eaten**
fall	**fell**	**fallen**
feel	**felt**	**felt**
fight	**fought**	**fought**
find	**found**	**found**
fly	**flew**	**flown**
forget	**forgot**	**forgotten**
get	**got**	**gotten**
give	**gave**	**given**
go	**went**	**gone**
grow	**grew**	**grown**
hang	**hung**	**hung**
have	**had**	**had**
hear	**heard**	**heard**
hide	**hid**	**hidden**
hit	**hit**	**hit**
hold	**held**	**held**
hurt	**hurt**	**hurt**
keep	**kept**	**kept**
know	**knew**	**known**
leave	**left**	**left**
lend	**lent**	**lent**

Verb	*Simple past*	*Past participle*
let	**let**	**let**
lie	**lay**	**lain**
light	**lit**	**lit**
lose	**lost**	**lost**
make	**made**	**made**
mean	**meant**	**meant**
meet	**met**	**met**
pay	**paid**	**paid**
put	**put**	**put**
read /ri:d/	**read** /red/	**read** /red/
ride	**rode**	**ridden**
ring	**rang**	**rung**
rise	**rose**	**risen**
run	**ran**	**run**
say	**said**	**said**
see	**saw**	**seen**
sell	**sold**	**sold**
send	**sent**	**sent**
shine	**shone**	**shone**
shoot	**shot**	**shot**
show	**showed**	**shown**
shut	**shut**	**shut**
sing	**sang**	**sung**
sit	**sat**	**sat**
sleep	**slept**	**slept**
speak	**spoke**	**spoken**
spend	**spent**	**spent**
stand	**stood**	**stood**
steal	**stole**	**stolen**
swim	**swam**	**swum**
take	**took**	**taken**
teach	**taught**	**taught**
tear	**tore**	**torn**
tell	**told**	**told**
think	**thought**	**thought**
throw	**threw**	**thrown**
understand	**understood**	**understood**
wake	**woke**	**woken**
wear	**wore**	**worn**
win	**won**	**won**
write	**wrote**	**written**

See Unit 36.

APPENDIX 2

Irregular verbs in groups

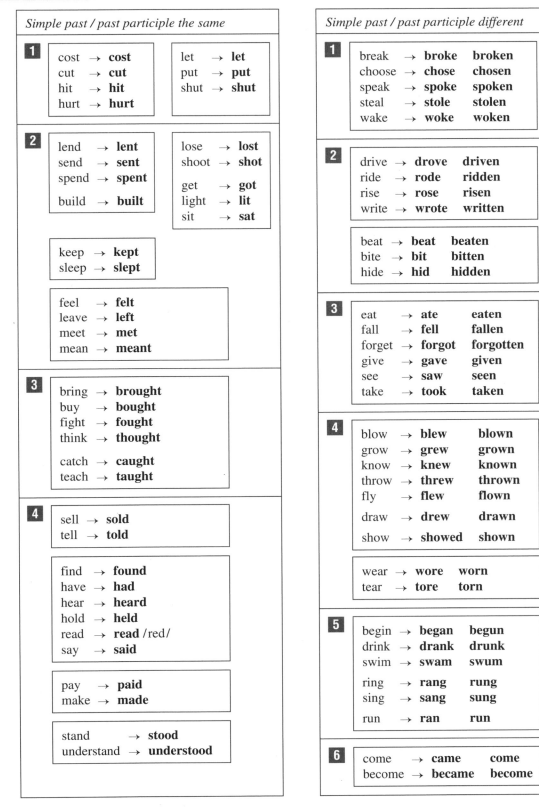

Simple past / past participle the same

1

cost	→	**cost**
cut	→	**cut**
hit	→	**hit**
hurt	→	**hurt**

let	→	**let**
put	→	**put**
shut	→	**shut**

2

lend	→	**lent**
send	→	**sent**
spend	→	**spent**
build	→	**built**

lose	→	**lost**
shoot	→	**shot**
get	→	**got**
light	→	**lit**
sit	→	**sat**

keep	→	**kept**
sleep	→	**slept**

feel	→	**felt**
leave	→	**left**
meet	→	**met**
mean	→	**meant**

3

bring	→	**brought**
buy	→	**bought**
fight	→	**fought**
think	→	**thought**
catch	→	**caught**
teach	→	**taught**

4

sell	→	**sold**
tell	→	**told**

find	→	**found**
have	→	**had**
hear	→	**heard**
hold	→	**held**
read	→	**read** /red/
say	→	**said**

pay	→	**paid**
make	→	**made**

stand	→	**stood**
understand	→	**understood**

Simple past / past participle different

1

break	→	**broke**	**broken**
choose	→	**chose**	**chosen**
speak	→	**spoke**	**spoken**
steal	→	**stole**	**stolen**
wake	→	**woke**	**woken**

2

drive	→	**drove**	**driven**
ride	→	**rode**	**ridden**
rise	→	**rose**	**risen**
write	→	**wrote**	**written**

beat	→	**beat**	**beaten**
bite	→	**bit**	**bitten**
hide	→	**hid**	**hidden**

3

eat	→	**ate**	**eaten**
fall	→	**fell**	**fallen**
forget	→	**forgot**	**forgotten**
give	→	**gave**	**given**
see	→	**saw**	**seen**
take	→	**took**	**taken**

4

blow	→	**blew**	**blown**
grow	→	**grew**	**grown**
know	→	**knew**	**known**
throw	→	**threw**	**thrown**
fly	→	**flew**	**flown**
draw	→	**drew**	**drawn**
show	→	**showed**	**shown**

wear	→	**wore**	**worn**
tear	→	**tore**	**torn**

5

begin	→	**began**	**begun**
drink	→	**drank**	**drunk**
swim	→	**swam**	**swum**
ring	→	**rang**	**rung**
sing	→	**sang**	**sung**
run	→	**ran**	**run**

6

come	→	**came**	**come**
become	→	**became**	**become**

APPENDIX 3

Contractions (**he's/I'd/don't**,etc.)

3.1 In spoken English, we usually pronounce **"I am"** as one word. The contraction (**I'm**) is a way of writing this:

I am → **I'm**		■ **I'm** feeling tired this morning.
it is → **it's**		■ "Do you like this jacket?" "Yes it**'s** very nice."
they have → **they've**		■ "Where are your friends?" "They**'ve** gone home."
etc.		

When we write contractions, we use ' (*an apostrophe*):

I ~~a~~**m** → **I'm**   he ~~i~~**s** → he**'s**   you ~~ha~~**ve** → you**'ve**   she ~~wi~~**ll** → she**'ll**

3.2 We use these contractions with **I/he/she**, etc.:

am → **'m**	**I'm**						
is → **'s**		**he's**	**she's**	**it's**			
are → **'re**					**we're**	**you're**	**they're**
have → **'ve**	**I've**				**we've**	**you've**	**they've**
has → **'s**		**he's**	**she's**	**it's**			
had → **'d**	**I'd**	**he'd**	**she'd**		**we'd**	**you'd**	**they'd**
will → **'ll**	**I'll**	**he'll**	**she'll**	**it'll**	**we'll**	**you'll**	**they'll**
would → **'d**	**I'd**	**he'd**	**she'd**		**we'd**	**you'd**	**they'd**

- **I've** got to go now.
- We**'ll** probably go out this evening.
- It**'s** 10 o'clock. You**'re** late again.

's = **is** *or* **has**:

- She**'s** going out this evening. (she**'s** going = she **is** going)
- She**'s** gone out. (she**'s** gone = she **has** gone)

'd = **would** *or* **had**:

- A: What would you like to eat?
  B: **I'd** like a salad, please. (**I'd** like = I **would** like)
- I told the police that **I'd** lost my passport. (**I'd** lost = I **had** lost)

Do *not* use contractions if the verb is at the end of the sentence:

- "Are you tired?" "Yes, I **am**." (*not* "Yes, I'm.")

3.3 We use contractions with **I/you/he/she/it**, etc. But we use contractions (especially **'s**) with other words too:

- **Who's** your favorite singer? (= who is)
- **What's** the time? (= what is)
- **There's** a big tree in the garden. (= there is)
- **My sister's** working in Tokyo. (my sister is working)
- **Jack's** gone out. (= Jack has gone out.)
- **What color's** your car? (= What color is your car?)

3.4 Negative contractions

not → **n't**:

isn't	(= is not)	**don't**	(= do not)	**can't**	(= cannot)
aren't	(= are not)	**doesn't**	(= does not)	**couldn't**	(= could not)
wasn't	(= was not)	**didn't**	(= did not)	**won't**	(= will not)
weren't	(= were not)			**wouldn't**	(= would not)
hasn't	(= has not)			**shouldn't**	(= should not)
haven't	(= have not)				
hadn't	(= had not)				

- We went to her house, but she **wasn't** home.
- "Where's John?" "I **don't** know. I **haven't** seen him."
- You work all the time. You **shouldn't** work so hard.
- I **won't** be here tomorrow. (= I will not)

3.5 -'s (*apostrophe* + s)

-'s can mean different things:

1. **'s** = **is** *or* **has** (See section 3.2 of this appendix.)
2. **let's** = **let us**
   - The weather is nice. **Let's** go out. (= **Let us** go out.)

   See Units 30 and 48.
3. Mary**'s** camera (= her camera) / my brother**'s** car (= his car) / the manager**'s** office (= his/her office), etc.
   See Unit 57.

Compare:

- **Mary's** camera was very expensive. (**Mary's** camera = **her** camera)
- **Mary's** a very good photographer. (Mary**'s** = Mary **is**)
- **Mary's** bought a new camera. (Mary**'s** = Mary **has**)

APPENDIX 4 Spelling

4.1 -s and -es (birds/watches, etc.)

noun + **s** (*plural*) (See Unit 59.):
bird → bird**s** place → place**s** question → question**s**

verb + **s** (**he/she/it -s**) (See Unit 5.):
think → think**s** live → live**s** remember → remember**s**

but

+ **es** after **-s**, **-sh**, **-ch**, *or* **-x**:

bu**s**	→ bus**es**		pa**ss**	→ pass**es**		addre**ss**	→ address**es**
di**sh**	→ dish**es**		wa**sh**	→ wash**es**		fini**sh**	→ finish**es**
wat**ch**	→ watch**es**		tea**ch**	→ teach**es**		sandwi**ch**	→ sandwich**es**
bo**x**	→ box**es**						

also
potato → potato**es** do → do**es**
tomato → tomato**es** go → go**es**

-f/-fe → **-ves**:
shel**f** → shel**ves** kni**fe** → kni**ves** *but* roof → roof**s**

4.2 -y → -i- (baby → bab**ies** / study → stud**ied**, etc.)

-y → **ies**:
study → stud**ies** (*not* "studys") family → famil**ies** (*not* "familys") baby → bab**ies**
story → stor**ies** city → cit**ies** fly → fl**ies**
try → tr**ies** marry → marr**ies**

-y → **ied** (See Unit 9.):
study → stud**ied** (*not* "studyed") marry → marr**ied**
try → tr**ied** copy → cop**ied**

-y → **ier/iest** (See Units 80 and 83.):
easy → eas**ier**/eas**iest** (*not* "easyer/easyest") lucky → luck**ier**/luck**iest**
happy → happ**ier**/happ**iest** funny → funn**ier**/funn**iest**
heavy → heav**ier**/heav**iest**

-y → **-ily** (See Unit 79.):
easy → eas**ily** (*not* "easyly") lucky → luck**ily**
happy → happ**ily** heavy → heav**ily**

y does *not* change to **i** if the ending is **-ay/-ey/-oy/-uy**:
holid**ay** → holid**ays** (*not* "holidaies") st**ay** → st**ays**/st**ayed** k**ey** → k**eys**
enj**oy** → enj**oys**/enj**oyed** b**uy** → b**uys**

but
say → **said** **pay** → **paid** (*irregular verbs*)

4.3 -ing

Verbs that end in **-e** (mak**e** /writ**e** /driv**e**, etc.): **-e** → ~~e~~**ing**
make → mak**ing** write → writ**ing** come → com**ing** dance → danc**ing**

Verbs that end in **-ie** (die/lie/tie): **-ie** → **-ying**
lie → l**ying** die → d**ying**

4.4 **stop** → **stopped** (**p** → **pp**) / **big** → **bigger** (**g** → **gg**), etc.

vowel letters (*V*): a e i o u
consonant letters (*C*): b c d f g k l m n p r s t

Sometimes a word ends in *a vowel* + *a consonant* (*V* + *C*) – for example, st**op**, b**ig**.
Before **-ing/-ed/-er/-est**, the consonant at the end (**-p/-g/-t**, etc.) is "doubled" (→ **-pp-/-gg-/-tt-**, etc.).
For example:

	V + C				
stop	S T **O** **P**	**p** → **pp**	sto**pp**ing	sto**pp**ed
run	R **U** **N**	**n** → **nn**	ru**nn**ing	
get	G **E** **T**	**t** → **tt**	ge**tt**ing	
swim	S W **I** **M**	**m** → **mm**	swi**mm**ing	
big	B **I** **G**	**g** → **gg**	bi**gg**er	bi**gg**est
hot	H **O** **T**	**t** → **tt**	ho**tt**er	ho**tt**est
thin	T H **I** **N**	**n** → **nn**	thi**nn**er	thi**nn**est

This does *not* happen:

1. if the word ends in *two consonant letters* (*C* + *C*):

	C + C		
help	H E **L** **P**	he**lp**ing	he**lp**ed
work	W O **R** **K**	wo**rk**ing	wo**rk**ed
fast	F A **S** **T**	fa**st**er	fa**st**est

2. if the word ends in *two vowel letters + a consonant letter* (*V* + *V* + *C*):

	V + V + C		
need	N **E** **E** **D**	nee**d**ing	nee**d**ed
wait	W **A** **I** **T**	wai**t**ing	wai**t**ed
cheap	C H **E** **A** **P**	chea**p**er	chea**p**est

3. in longer words (two syllables or more) if the last part of the word is not stressed:

			stress	
	happen	=	**H A P**-pen	→ happe**n**ing/happe**n**ed (*not* "happenned")
	visit	=	**V I S**-it	→ visi**t**ing/visi**t**ed
	remember	=	re-**M E M**-ber	→ remembe**r**ing/remembe**r**ed
but	prefer	=	pre-**F E R** (*stress at the end*)	→ prefe**rr**ing/prefe**rr**ed
	begin	=	be-**G I N** (*stress at the end*)	→ begi**nn**ing

4. if the word ends in **-y** or **-w**:
enjoy → enjo**y**ing/enjo**y**ed snow/sno**w**ing/sno**w**ed few/fe**w**er/fe**w**est

APPENDIX 5 Phrasal verbs (**look out / take off**, etc.)

This is a list of some important phrasal verbs:

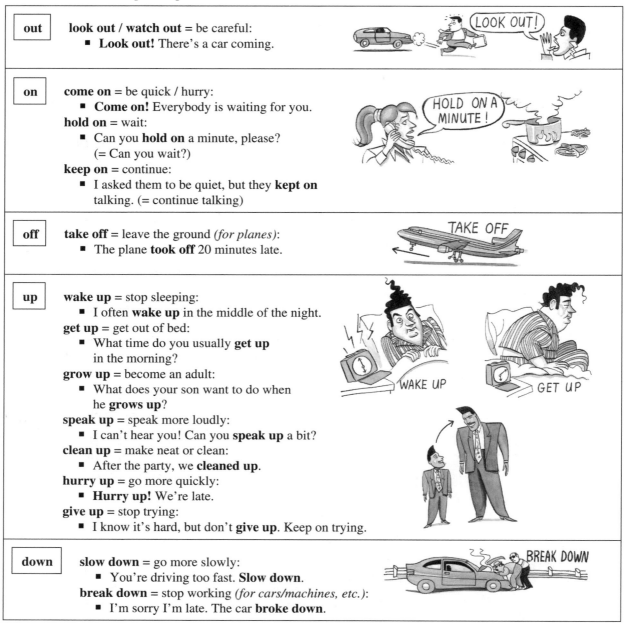

out

look out / watch out = be careful:
- **Look out!** There's a car coming.

on

come on = be quick / hurry:
- **Come on!** Everybody is waiting for you.

hold on = wait:
- Can you **hold on** a minute, please? (= Can you wait?)

keep on = continue:
- I asked them to be quiet, but they **kept on** talking. (= continue talking)

off

take off = leave the ground *(for planes)*:
- The plane **took off** 20 minutes late.

up

wake up = stop sleeping:
- I often **wake up** in the middle of the night.

get up = get out of bed:
- What time do you usually **get up** in the morning?

grow up = become an adult:
- What does your son want to do when he **grows up**?

speak up = speak more loudly:
- I can't hear you! Can you **speak up** a bit?

clean up = make neat or clean:
- After the party, we **cleaned up**.

hurry up = go more quickly:
- **Hurry up!** We're late.

give up = stop trying:
- I know it's hard, but don't **give up**. Keep on trying.

down

slow down = go more slowly:
- You're driving too fast. **Slow down**.

break down = stop working *(for cars/machines, etc.)*:
- I'm sorry I'm late. The car **broke down**.

See Unit 100.

APPENDIX 6

Phrasal verbs + object (**call up my friend / put out a fire**, etc.)

This is a list of some important phrasal verbs + object:

out

put out (a fire / a cigarette):
- The fire fighters arrived and quickly **put the fire out**.

cross out (a mistake / a word, etc.):
- If you make a mistake, **cross it out**.

knock out = make unconscious:
- A stone fell on my head and **knocked me out**.

fill out (a form) (= complete a form):
- Can you **fill out this form**, please?

on/off

turn on/off (a light, TV, etc.) = turn on/off:
- Don't forget to **turn off the light** when you leave.

on

try on (clothes) = put on clothes to see if they fit you:
- *(in a store)* I like that jacket. I'm going to **try it on**.

up

call up = telephone (*also* **call** *without* "up"):
- Can you **call me up** tomorrow? (*or* . . . **call me** tomorrow?)

give up = stop something that you do:
- Tom **gave up smoking** three years ago. (= he stopped smoking)
- I started learning Italian, but I **gave it up**.

look up (a word) *(in a dictionary)*:
- I didn't know the meaning of the word, so I **looked it up** in a dictionary.

turn up = make louder (TV, radio, music, etc.):
- Can you **turn the radio up**? I can't hear it.

down

knock down (a building) = demolish:
- They are going to build a new school and **knock down the old one**.

turn down = make more quiet (TV, radio, music, etc.):
- The radio is too loud. Can you **turn it down**, please?

over

knock over (a cup / a glass / a person, etc.):
- Be careful with your cup. Don't **knock it over**.

(be) **run over** (*by a car*, etc.):
- A lot of animals are **run over** on busy roads.

around

show (somebody) **around** = take somebody on a tour of a place:
- We visited a factory last week. The manager **showed us around**.

away

throw away (garbage, etc. things you don't want):
- These apples are rotten. **Throw them away.**
- Don't **throw away that picture**. I want it.

See Unit 101.

INDEX

The numbers are unit numbers, not page numbers.

Index

Index